Should Mom Be Left Alone?

Should Dad Be Driving?

Should Mom Be Left Alone?
Should Dad Be Driving?

Your Q & A Companion for Caregiving

Dr. Linda Rhodes

 NEW AMERICAN LIBRARY

New American Library
Published by New American Library, a division of
Penguin Group (USA) Inc., 375 Hudson Street,
New York, New York 10014, USA
Penguin Group (Canada), 10 Alcorn Avenue, Toronto,
Ontario M4V 3B2, Canada (a division of Pearson Penguin Canada Inc.)
Penguin Books Ltd., 80 Strand, London WC2R 0RL, England
Penguin Ireland, 25 St. Stephen's Green, Dublin 2,
Ireland (a division of Penguin Books Ltd.)
Penguin Group (Australia), 250 Camberwell Road, Camberwell, Victoria 3124,
Australia (a division of Pearson Australia Group Pty. Ltd.)
Penguin Books India Pvt. Ltd., 11 Community Centre, Panchsheel Park,
New Delhi - 110 017, India
Penguin Group (NZ), Cnr Airborne and Rosedale Roads, Albany,
Auckland 1310, New Zealand (a division of Pearson New Zealand Ltd.)
Penguin Books (South Africa) (Pty.) Ltd., 24 Sturdee Avenue,
Rosebank, Johannesburg 2196, South Africa

Penguin Books Ltd., Registered Offices:
80 Strand, London WC2R 0RL, England

First published by New American Library,
a division of Penguin Group (USA) Inc.

First Printing, April 2005
10 9 8 7 6 5 4 3 2 1

NEW AMERICAN LIBRARY and logo are trademarks of Penguin Group (USA) Inc.

LIBRARY OF CONGRESS CATALOGING-IN-PUBLICATION DATA:

Rhodes, Linda M. Colvin.
   Should mom be left alone? should dad be driving? : your q & a companion for caregiving /
Linda Rhodes.
      p.   cm.
   ISBN 0-451-21482-X (trade pbk.)
   1. Aging parents—Care—United States.   2. Older people—Health and hygiene—United
States.   3. Adult children of aging parents—United States—Family relationships.   4. Aging parents—United States—Family rela-
tionships.   I. Title.
   HQ1063.6.R48 2004
   306.874—dc22   2004024975

Set in Fairfield
Designed by Ginger Legato

Printed in the United States of America

PUBLISHER'S NOTE
Every effort has been made to ensure that the information contained in this book is complete and accurate. However, neither the publisher nor the author is engaged in rendering professional advice or services to the individual reader. The ideas, procedures, and suggestions contained in this book are not intended as a substitute for consulting with your physician. All matters regarding your health require medical supervision. Neither the author nor the publisher shall be liable or responsible for any loss or damage allegedly arising from any information or suggestion in this book. The opinions expressed in this book represent the personal views of the author and not of the publisher.
   While the author has made every effort to provide accurate telephone numbers and Internet addresses at the time of publication, neither the publisher nor the author assumes any responsibility for errors, or for changes that occur after publication.

To my husband, Eric,

the light at the end of many a tunnel

ACKNOWLEDGMENTS

It started at the watercooler. One of those Monday-morning conversations, not about football but about everyone they knew coping with some type of aging parent issue. If they—editors of a very large newspaper—were having a hard time, how were their readers navigating the rough waters of caregiving?

Within weeks of that conversation, John A. Kirkpatrick, editor and publisher of the *Patriot-News*, Pennsylvania's "capital newspaper," had me writing a weekly newspaper column, "Our Parents, Ourselves," and has featured it on the front page of the living section on Monday mornings ever since. Four years later, the columns have now become this book. I am extremely grateful to John for his foresight in "reading" the needs of his public and giving me the opportunity to give them a helping hand as they care for their aging parents. I'd also like to thank his team who've become my colleagues, providing ongoing inspiration and editing: Cate Barron, managing editor; Nance Woodward, editor of the living department; and copy editors of family life, Connie McNamara and Jen Shaheen. A special thanks to Dee Mills, chief librarian, for tracking down long-lost columns amid the world of e-files.

A few others have been instrumental in bringing this book to fruition: Barbara O'Shea, senior vice president of special markets at Penguin Group (USA) Inc., and Maryvel Bergen, director of custom product and special markets at Penguin, believed in this book early on and took the initiative to share it with others in the Penguin family. It found its home with Kara Welsh, vice president, publisher of New American Library, and was nurtured along the way by the fine editing eye of Tracy Bernstein, executive editor of New American Library. Thanks for taking me under your wing.

And a final thanks to my faithful readers of the *Patriot-News,* who keep me grounded and informed by sending me the questions they grapple with day in and day out.

CONTENTS

- Should my dad just sign all those hospital consent forms or actually question them?
- What is a hospital patient advocate?
- Hospital mistakes scare me. How do you prevent them?
- How do I find out about the track record of my dad's surgeon?
- The hospital says that Medicare will not pay the bill for my father's surgery. Now what?
- How can I stop the hospital from discharging my dad too quickly?
- How can my mom *not* get an infection during her hospital stay?
- Why won't the hospital give me any information about my mother's health status?
- What are clinical trials and how do you find them?
- What do "phases" mean in clinical trials? Are they the same as "stages" in cancer?
- Are all ambulance services alike?

3. Lifestyle │ 146

- How can my parents give away their "good stuff" to good causes?
- We are moving away. How can my parents make long-distance grandparenting work?
- How can we make the outside of my mother's house safer?

III   NAVIGATING LEGAL & MONEY MATTERS

1. Benefits & Resources | 181

- How does my mom apply for Social Security benefits?
- Are VA benefits automatic or do you have to enroll?
- What are some of the best Web sites dealing with aging parent issues?
- What is an Area Agency on Aging?
- Is there a one-stop shop to find out what benefits my parents can get?
- How can my mom apply for handicapped parking tags?
- Are there tax credits for caring for an elderly parent?
- My mom keeps confusing Medicaid with Medicare. Just what is the difference?
- A friend of my mother's rarely has any food in the house, and we know she's not eating well. Do you think she could get food stamps?
- What is the Family Caregiver Support Program?

2. Legal Issues | 195

- I suspect that the prizes my mom keeps winning are scams. How do I know and what do I do?
- What are the most common scams targeting the elderly?
- Is being an executor of my parent's will an honor or just a huge headache?
- How do I talk with my parents about their will?
- How do I use the Family Medical Leave Act to take care of my mom?
- What's the difference between living wills and durable health care powers of attorney?
- Does having a general power of attorney status allow me access to my parents' medical records?
- What is "HIPAA" all about?
- My dad was just fired. How does he file age discrimination charges?
- What paperwork should I have prepared in the event of a health crisis?

- How can I prevent my parents from becoming victims of identity theft?
- I think my friend's mother is a victim of domestic violence. Do I report it as elder abuse—and how?

Where do I turn? Who can help? Is this covered? What's the best treatment? Should Mom be left alone since Dad died? Should my dad be driving? The questions just keep coming. It's overwhelming trying to figure out where to turn when a parent starts needing *you* to find answers. If your parents are getting older, this book answers 150 questions that you're likely to ask. The questions have been appearing every week for the past four years in the *Patriot-News,* one of Pennsylvania's largest newspapers; so they are tried and true, with real people's stories and questions. The answers are to the point, easy to understand and chock-full of resources and how-to steps.

I was secretary of aging for the Commonwealth of Pennsylvania and had the honor of launching one of the first family caregiver support programs in the country. Talking with hundreds of families in this program—and caring for my husband's grandmother in our home—taught me to appreciate the quiet, heroic efforts so many people make every day caring for an aging spouse, parent, relative or friend. Being better informed makes the caregiving road easier to travel and can save you from detours and costly dead ends. So take this book and treat it like your own personal navigator.

While I was working on this book two people I dearly loved died. My mother-in-law, Bernice L. Schnurer, died of breast cancer, and my youngest brother, Paul Michael Colvin, died of malignant melanoma. Through their personal fights with cancer, they inspired my columns on cancer care, clinical trials, pain management, alternative medicine, telling children about death, end-of-life decisions and hospice care. I thank them for what they taught me, and what my readers teach me every day through their questions. It really is all about family, about each generation caring for the other. May the questions and answers in this book help each of you along life's journey to better care for you and yours.

—Linda M. Rhodes, Ed.D.
www.lindarhodes.com

NAVIGATING HEALTH CARE

I

Hospitals, Clinical Trials & Ambulance Service

Q: **Should my dad just sign all those hospital consent forms or actually question them?**

A: If your hospital stay is planned, the hospital will often send their blanket consent forms in advance so that you can go over them. If not, call and request them. If the hospital stay is un-expected, you could sign the form and simply write on the bottom, *"I am signing this on a tem-porary basis so that my parent can be admitted."* This gives you some added time to thoroughly review the consent form without holding up your parent's much-needed admittance. Depend-ing upon the type of procedure or surgery that your parent will have, your parent (or you, if they are not legally competent) will be asked to sign a consent form that identifies the specific risks related to that type of surgery.

Several years ago I had to have neck surgery. My eyes couldn't get past "paralyzed from the neck down" as just *one* of the risks listed on the consent form. But it is important and right that hospitals lay out the cold, hard facts on the risks that any surgery presents. You and your parents need to weigh the benefits against the risks. No matter how minor the procedure, it isn't risk-free!

Many people don't realize that you can make changes on the consent form. My surgery was performed at a very fine teaching hospital and I searched for the best neurosurgeon in the state. I wanted him to do the actual surgery and no one else. I didn't mind young doctors learn-ing from him by being alongside him during the surgery. But that's where I wanted them to be—at his side. So on the section of the consent form where it said I gave permission for the surgery to the "surgeon *or* those under his supervision" I crossed out *or those under his super-vision*. You can do the same, if this is a concern of yours.

Besides the surgeon, the other critical person to your dad's surgery is the anesthesiologist—the one who will put him to sleep during the surgery and monitor him throughout it. Anesthesiologists are physicians who administer anesthesia to relieve pain and manage vital life functions, including breathing, heart rhythm, blood pressure, and brain and kidney functions during surgery. They also manage and treat any medical problems that may be present before surgery or that may develop during or immediately after surgery. Anesthesia requires very sophisticated skills, especially when it's administered to elderly patients. Changes in their physiology and conditions like heart problems, multiple medications or diabetes can cause unexpected complications with geriatric patients. It's very appropriate for you to ask about this person's credentials. He or she should be Board Certified; this means that they passed a comprehensive test to receive certification providing you with an added measure of their qualifications. There are also Nurse Anesthetists; make sure they have CRNA after their name (meaning they are certified) and ask about the qualifications of the physician anesthesiologist who will be supervising them.

The anesthesiologist should have a face-to-face meeting with your dad before the surgery. Hopefully, you, your mom and/or a sibling is sitting alongside him. They'll be asking him questions that he's probably answered before. That's okay. They're doing this to double-check. Don't mind the repetition.

Q: What is a hospital patient advocate?

A: Every hospital is required by law to employ patient advocates, also known as patient representatives, to resolve patient concerns. Look in the hospital directory or ask the receptionist at the Information Desk to give you the name and number. Hospitals are also required by law to present each patient, upon admission, a copy of the Patient Bill of Rights, which frequently provides that contact information.

Patient representatives focus on the needs of the patient and the family. They will listen to your concerns, respond to a complaint, explain hospital policies and procedures, provide information on community services, provide information on insurance coverage and broker a dispute between you and the medical team. Their goal is to resolve conflicts so that the remainder of a patient's stay can be purely focused on getting well.

Hospitals, medical care and insurance have become very complex and it's easy to become overwhelmed by the hospital environment while, at the same time, responding to your parent's recovery. Add to the mix the nursing shortage that makes it difficult for nurses to find enough time to communicate with families and patients—you can see how misunderstandings quickly evolve. So the sooner you talk to a patient advocate, the better. Their goal is to resolve a patient's concern during the hospital stay so that the patient can concentrate on recovery.

Patient advocates can also help you if you think that your mom or dad is being discharged too quickly, or assist in identifying home health care and community services. And they can explain coverage issues regarding Medicare. If they can't resolve the issue within the hospital system, they will give you the contact information to make an appeal outside of it.

Communication is key, so be sure to stay informed on your parent's condition; make a list of questions when you talk to the doctor and nurse in charge of him or her, and share the answers with other family members. It's also helpful to the nursing staff to appoint one family member to become the spokesperson for the whole family. The family spokesperson, in turn, can then inform all of the other members of any new developments or information on your parent's condition. You don't want to bombard the nurses' station with questions and calls from every relative. They'll be very appreciative.

Q: Hospital mistakes scare me. How do you prevent them?

A: You might have heard about a report by the Institute of Medicine, a member of the non-profit National Academies studying health and medicine, in which they found that medical errors kill some 44,000 people a year in U.S. hospitals; however, another study said the number was closer to 98,000. Most of the medical errors are not the result of individual recklessness but of basic flaws in the way the health care system is organized. Deadly mistakes can derive from the illegible handwriting of doctors' orders, for example, or the practice of stocking medicines at toxic, full-strength levels, thereby increasing the risk that a hurried technician will administer them without diluting them first.

Even though most hospitals run tight ships and your parent's surgery could save his life, he's still at risk. So here's a crash course on how you can become your parent's personal patient advocate:

1. Read up on his condition and the surgical procedure. Familiarize yourself with the terms. Create a little "cheat sheet" so you can refer to it when you're talking with the nurses and doctors.
2. Get to know the nurses at the nurses' station and choose one or two members of your family to act as the liaison between the nurses and the rest of the family, to give updates on your mom or dad's condition. The staff will appreciate not being bombarded by five or six family members.
3. Don't be afraid to insist on speaking with the doctor. Many doctors make their rounds early in the morning, so ask the nurses when the doc is due and make it a point to be

there. If you can't, have the doctor paged as soon as you arrive so he or she can call or stop by your parent's room.

4. During the first few days following surgery, make sure that someone is with your parent at all times. If he complains of feeling dizzy, nauseated or in pain, you can immediately go to the nurse rather than expect him to hit the call bell and wait for someone to attend to him.

5. If you are concerned that something isn't "right" about your parent's recovery, ask to see the registered nurse on the shift and express your concerns to her. Don't assume that everyone wearing white is a registered nurse. With today's nursing shortages, many hospitals have hired nursing assistants to provide care. They are not trained to make sophisticated, diagnostic decisions that warrant calling in the doctor.

6. If your parent is allergic to certain medications, post a sign on his headboard listing his allergies. Yes, this data should be on his charts, but people die each year because they've been given the wrong drug. So be extra careful.

7. Don't be embarrassed to ask anyone caring for your parent—especially the technicians who take blood samples—to wash their hands in your parent's room. (This goes for you and all visitors, too.) If someone comes in with gloves on, tell him you'd feel more comfortable if he'd put a new pair on. Why? The Centers for Disease Control and Prevention reported that during one year alone, nearly 88,000 deaths were from hospital-borne infections. It's one of the biggest problems hospitals face.

If you have an issue with your parent being discharged too early or you are concerned about the care he is receiving, ask to see the patient advocate employed by the hospital. If that doesn't work to your satisfaction and your parent is on Medicare, call the Medicare Beneficiary Hotline at (800) 322-1914 and ask them to connect you with the agency contracted by them to handle a complaint against an early discharge.

The bottom line on being a patient advocate is to ask questions. Be as informed as a college student cramming for a test and as persistent as a four-year-old running around asking, "Why?"

Q: How do I find out about the track record of my dad's surgeon?

A: I've usually found that very good doctors don't mind you asking about their credentials, and they understand your need to be comfortable with their level of expertise. It's important for a physician to earn your trust, not to think that you'll just blindly hand it over to him or her. If you've never met the physician, and your dad is about to put his life in this stranger's hands, then asking questions is just plain common sense.

Our parents' generation is inclined to think that it's impolite to question a doctor. I know my own father gets nervous when I insist on getting a second opinion for any major procedure. He thinks his doctor will get angry. But most doctors, given today's malpractice environment, prefer patients who have done their homework and have realistic expectations. A second opinion, for example, by validating what the doctor has told your dad, will contribute to the trust between doctor and patient, rather than working against it. Let your dad know that, nowadays, good doctors expect questions from their patients.

So what do you do? The most important thing you want to know is how competent and skilled this physician is to perform your dad's surgery. Getting the answer requires some research and a candid, yet polite conversation with the physician.

First, the research: Thanks to the Internet and a few publications, you can gain access to basic background information about physicians and learn whether they've been cited for malpractice, civil and/or criminal violations. Here's how:

"Doctor Finder" (www.AMA-assn.org) is offered by the American Medical Association. Click on "Doctor Finder" and you can check out basic data on every licensed physician in the country. You can find out where they went to school, when they graduated, where they practiced their residency and whether they are board certified in their specialty.

Doctors who are board certified have at least three to five years of postmedical training in a specialty. They have passed a difficult exam and have been approved by a specialty board of highly accomplished physicians in that field. It's a good quality marker when searching for a doctor.

Your State's Doctor Disciplinary Board. You can find out if any disciplinary action has been taken by a state licensing board for health professions on any physician licensed to practice in your state. Most states have a Professional Licensure Board affiliated with their health department, which is responsible for taking and reporting disciplinary action on health professionals.

Questionable Doctors by Public Citizen (www.citizen.org). This group has been around for thirty years, and it publishes a book called *Questionable Doctors*. The book is published in regional editions and can be purchased for about $20. You also can go to its Web site and pay the same price for access to a regional database. For free, you can click on the map of any state in the country to find an overview of each state's record and a direct link to each state that posts disciplinary results on the Internet. So if your parent lives in another state, this is a nice feature.

Now that you've done your homework, you're ready for a conversation with the physician. You can start with something like "I know you'd want to do the best by your father. I'm trying to do the same for mine. So if you could help me out by just answering a few questions, I'd really be thankful."

Here's what I suggest asking:

- Are you board certified? Could you explain what that entailed?
- How many times a year (or month) do you perform the procedure you're recommending for my dad? (It's important that he or she perform this procedure frequently.)
- Where do you hold hospital privileges?
- Do you consult with other doctors on difficult cases?
- What are the risks for my dad if he has this surgery?
- What are the risks for my dad if he does not have this surgery?
- Have you ever been professionally disciplined or had your hospital privileges revoked?

That last question might be a little difficult to ask. But this is your dad's life at stake. If you ask it sincerely and in a friendly tone, no doctor should be offended.

Q: **The hospital says that Medicare will not pay the bill for my father's surgery. Now what?**

A: The hospital should have given him an Advance Beneficiary Notice form before his surgery, stating that Medicare would probably deny payment for the specific surgery, the reasons why, and that if you proceed with the service then your dad would be fully responsible for the payment if Medicare does, in fact, deny the payment.

Right away there are two things to note. First, there are a number of procedures that Medicare will cover only when performed in an outpatient facility rather than a hospital. Second, hospitals don't have to give you an Advance Beneficiary Notice for services that already are excluded from Medicare such as routine dental care, or vision and hearing services. So always ask first! Don't assume Medicare will cover whatever your doctor prescribes as treatment.

If your dad did not receive the ABN form, then he definitely should not pay this bill and should immediately call the Fiscal Intermediary for Medicare in his state. These are private companies that contract with Medicare to pay Medicare Part A bills (hospital and skilled nursing care). Call Medicare at (800) 638-6833 to find out your dad's Fiscal Intermediary. The number should also appear on the denial letter. Be sure to explain that no one told your father that Medicare might not cover his surgical procedure in a hospital, and that he never saw or signed an ABN form (CMS-R-131).

ABNs also are used for Medicare Part B services, which cover physician, lab, home health and outpatient services. If you have a question or complaint about a Medicare denial with Part B services, you'll need to talk to the Fiscal Intermediary that covers Part B.

Advance Beneficiary Notices are meant to protect consumers from unexpected financial liability in cases where Medicare will likely deny payment. It gives you the opportunity to decide whether you want to receive the service (this also applies to medical supplies and equipment).

If you receive an ABN from your doctor or a provider, absolutely take the time to read it. You can then decide, for example, whether to find another doctor who could safely perform the surgery on an outpatient basis, which would be covered by Medicare.

According to the Centers for Medicare and Medicaid Services, if a consumer receives an ABN, they should choose one of two options on the form:

- Option 1. If you check this option, then you indicate YES: You want to receive the service or item and your claim will be sent to Medicare. You might be billed while Medicare is making its decision. If Medicare pays, you will be refunded any payments you made that are due to you. *But,* if Medicare denies payment, you will be personally and fully responsible for payment. You will have the right to appeal Medicare's decision. Medicare will not decide whether to pay unless you receive the service or item and have a claim submitted.
- Option 2. If you check this option then you indicate NO: You will not receive the service or item, and your claim will not be sent to Medicare. You will not be able to appeal the supplier's, physician's or provider's opinion that Medicare won't pay.

Please note that the only way you can appeal the decision is to take your chances and say yes on the ABN form. Medicare needs an actual claim for services in order to deny it. If you don't want to take the risk, then seek second opinions from other physicians and providers to see whether they can meet your needs and the eligibility requirements of Medicare.

The bottom line: Always question a bill that you think should have been covered by your insurance and/or Medicare. Far too often, conscientious, bill-paying elderly don't question their doctor's office or hospital bills and simply pay. Some even fear that they might be refused further treatment if they appeal or question the bill. That just isn't so.

The Fiscal Intermediaries are paid by Medicare to resolve these issues—so make use of the service.

Q: How can I stop the hospital from discharging my dad too quickly?

A: Once the physician decides that your father's health is stable enough to no longer need acute hospital care, she'll authorize his discharge. This doesn't mean that your dad is completely recovered and can resume a normal life. He might need other forms of care before he can go directly home and be on his own. That's where the discharge planners come in: Their job is to make sure that arrangements have been made *before* your dad leaves the hospital to assure that his discharge is, according to Medicare, "safe and adequate."

The discharge planner may be a nurse, a social worker or other professional who will be your primary contact in making plans for your dad's transition from the hospital to his next level of care. Perhaps your dad will need short-term care in a nursing home, rehab center, or assisted living facility, or he'll need home health care nurses to provide care in his own home.

What's meant by "safe and adequate" is up to you, the doctor and the discharge planner to determine. You really need to be involved in deciding whether or not your dad can safely make a transition to another level of care outside of the hospital. The discharge planner will surely ask whether or not your dad lives alone. If he does live with your mother, but your mother is not well enough to take care of him, you need to speak up. Plans for discharge must be realistic.

The discharge plan is immediate and short-term. It's not a plan for the long run. It's to get your dad past his most immediate health issues and onto the road to recovery. These first steps, however, should lead to a sound, feasible long-range plan to keep your dad healthy. To best assess his needs, ask the doctor to tell you exactly what your dad will be capable of doing once he leaves the hospital and what type of health care he will need. For instance, if he is recovering from a stroke you'll want to ask questions like: What level are his thinking skills? Will he need assistance with bathing, eating, using the toilet, grooming, dressing, or taking medications? Will he need physical and occupational therapy (how much and how often)? Answers to these questions determine whether or not you can take him home using home health care, or whether or not he needs care in a facility.

You might disagree with the physician's decision to discharge your parent. Perhaps you believe he is not well enough or that releasing him without adequate care will jeopardize his already precarious condition. You can do something. Your father's rights are clearly worded in the "An Important Message from Medicare" statement that the hospital must provide to you. It tells you that your parent has the right to receive all of the hospital care he or she needs and necessary follow-up care after leaving the hospital. The hospital will also give you a written notice known as a "Hospital-Issued Notice of Noncoverage," also referred to as a HINN. On that form, check out the phone number of the Quality Improvement Organization (QIO). Call them and tell them you want to file an appeal to delay your father's discharge. Until the QIO makes a decision, the hospital cannot force your dad to leave or force you to pay for his continuing care in the hospital.

The best defense against scrambling to find alternative care when the hospital is asking your parent to leave is planning in advance. It's really worth your time to engage in what I call the "If" game with your parents. You play it while they're well. Start by telling them you want to do what's best for them in the event they can't take care of themselves. So . . . "If you had a stroke and needed to recuperate before they let you back home, where would you like to go? If you had a heart attack, what hospital would you like to go to? If you broke your hip and could go home only if you had home health care, who would we hire? If you had cancer, would you want to try alternative treatment or opt for chemotherapy and radiation, and would you want us to call hospice?" Frankly, most people will not have ready answers to these questions, so ask your parents to start visiting and researching potential facilities, so you'll know where to turn. The goal is to keep them in charge and to make smart, informed decisions when "heads are cooler" rather than in the heat of an emotional crisis.

Q: How can my mom *not* get an infection during her hospital stay?

A: Recently, the Institute of Medicine, the prestigious nonprofit advising the nation and government on matters of health, reported that up to 98,000 people die every year from infections they acquire in hospitals—most of which could have been prevented. Hospitals, of course, are places for very sick people, and very sick people have germs. Doctors, nurses and technicians who care for these very sick people come in contact with them in the most intimate of ways: via blood, urine and bodily contact. It doesn't take much for germs to travel from one person's hands to dozens of people every day. The problem for patients, however, is that their immune systems are weakened. If they've had surgery, the site of the wound is a prime destination port for germs.

In response to this infection crisis, the American Hospital Association (AHA), the American Medical Association (AMA), and the National Patient Safety Foundation (NPSF) have created an excellent patient-education brochure, "Preventing Infections in the Hospital—What You as a Patient Can Do." The following ten action steps are listed in their brochure as effective ways for patients to protect themselves from getting a hospital-acquired infection:

1. Wash your hands carefully after handling any type of soiled material—especially after you have gone to the bathroom.
2. Do not be afraid to remind doctors and nurses about washing their hands before working with you.
3. If you have an intravenous catheter, keep the skin around the dressing clean and dry. Immediately tell your nurse if the dressing becomes loose or wet.
4. Similarly, if you have a dressing on a wound, let your nurse know right away if the dressing becomes loose or wet.
5. If you have any type of catheter or drainage tube, let your nurse know if it becomes loose or dislodged.
6. If you have diabetes, be sure that you and your doctor discuss the best way to control your blood sugar before, during, and after your hospital stay. High blood sugar increases the risk of infection noticeably.
7. If you are overweight, losing weight will reduce the risk of infection following surgery.
8. If you are a smoker, you should consider a smoking cessation program. This will reduce the chance of developing a lung infection while in the hospital and may also improve your healing abilities following surgery.
9. Carefully follow your doctor's instructions regarding breathing treatments and getting out of bed.
10. Ask your friends and relatives *not* to visit if they feel ill. Make sure that all visitors wash their hands when they come to visit and after they use the bathroom.

You might also want to ask if the hospital participates in the Centers for Disease Control's voluntary infection monitoring program—the NNIS system. This stands for National Nosocomial Infection Surveillance; the term "nosocomial" means "hospital-acquired." Hospitals that participate in this program report significantly lower infection rates than those who don't participate.

If your parent does acquire an infection, ask the doctor for the exact name and spelling of the infection. Also ask to see someone from the Infection Control Unit (every hospital must have one). Ask for an explanation of the nature of the infection, and what best practices are being used to treat it. If this infection has caused a real hardship for your parent, report the incident to your local health department. You may prevent somebody else's parent from going through the same thing since the health department will be obligated to look into your report and, if the hospital's infection rate is above the norm, will demand corrective action.

Q: Why won't the hospital give me any information about my mother's health status?

A: It's a call that none of us want to get: "Your mom was just taken to the hospital. We think she's had a heart attack." It's the call I received from a neighbor regarding my mother not long ago. I couldn't just hop in the car and meet her in the emergency room. She lives over two thousand miles away in Phoenix, Arizona. So the next best thing is getting on the phone. I immediately called the hospital to find out about her condition. But because of new federal standards on protecting health information, the nurse—despite his many apologies—couldn't tell me anything until he could reach my mother and have her sign a form allowing the nurse to talk with me.

This process took about an hour. And though I finally did receive information about my mother's condition, it taught me to be prepared for the next potential emergency. I flew out to Phoenix the next morning and took several steps to avoid being left in the dark ever again.

First, a quick recap on the Health Insurance Portability and Accountability Act known as HIPAA: This law sets federal standards that protect the privacy of your medical records and personal health information. The standards, though well intended, have created obstacles to family members who need to know how their parent is doing in an emergency. Without written permission from your parent, the hospital will not give out information, even to their child.

This might not be that much of a problem when your parents are aware and able to sign a form quickly, but what happens if they are admitted due to a stroke or heart attack? What happens if they are unconscious, in surgery, or being treated for something that requires immediate attention and there's little time for filling out forms?

So, while I was out in Phoenix, I wrote the following letter that may be of benefit to you as a guide, in which my mother gives permission to any health care provider to share her medical information with me or my sister. I made ten copies of the letter; she gave them to all of her physicians and has kept several copies handy to take with her to the hospital should an emergency arise. Since she knows the particular hospital that she will be taken to, she has also given copies to the Medical Records department. Both my sister and I also have copies signed by my mother that we could fax to the health care provider, if necessary, verifying that we do have permission to receive information.

Here's what her letter says:

Dear Health Care Professional or Provider:
I hereby authorize you to release my medical reports, such as summaries of medical consults, radiology reports, blood work and urinalyses results, pathology reports, discharge reports, screening and diagnostic tests to [Enter Name of Person Authorized to Receive Medical Information] who is my [Enter Relationship]. This authorization further gives you permission to verbally apprise the above as to my medical condition.

Sincerely:

Signature

Name of your parent
Address
Date of Birth

Contact Information of Person(s) Authorized to Receive Information
Name
Address
Phone Numbers [Home, Office and Cell]

Hospitals will provide you with their own form to sign to authorize the release of medical information. However, this type of letter should certainly get you through an emergency. If you know which hospital your parent will likely be taken to, it would be smart to give them a call now and ask them what procedures they would like you to follow so that you can solve this problem ahead of time. If you come from a large family, it's also helpful to the medical staff if *one* of you is chosen among the family to become the spokesperson and contact.

You'll be glad you took this proactive step.

Q: What are clinical trials and how do you find them?

A: Clinical trials are research studies to determine whether vaccines, drugs, new therapies or new treatments are safe and effective. These trials are offered to humans after researchers have tested these various procedures in laboratories and on animals. All clinical trials must be approved by an Institutional Review Board (IRB) that consists of researchers, physicians and consumers, who must review the proposed study and assure that it is safe and ethical, and that the rights of those being studied are protected. Be aware, however, that the sponsoring institution of the study forms the IRB.

Besides receiving the go-ahead from an IRB, pharmaceutical companies must gain approval from the Food and Drug Administration (FDA) that their animal and laboratory studies were successful enough to warrant safe testing on humans.

There are basically four phases to clinical trials, with each phase expanding to test more people. For instance, a Phase I study will research a small group of twenty to eighty people, and by Phase III up to three thousand people may be involved. The "protocol," which is the plan of study for the research project, describes the types of people who will be tested, the schedule of tests, treatment, medications, dosages, and length of time in the study. Frequently, patients in clinical trials are assigned either to a study group that receives the new treatment or a "control" group that receives standard treatment or a placebo (an inactive pill, liquid or powder with no treatment value, such as a sugar pill). It is unethical, however, to give a sick patient a placebo when there is a known beneficial treatment available.

The major benefit of participating in a clinical trial is to gain access to the latest "discovery" and, hopefully, the most advanced form of treatment. For someone who is becoming blind, dying of cancer or in great pain, a clinical trial may sound very appealing and may greatly improve their quality of life.

But there are definite risks. So, do your own research to make sure that the benefits outweigh the risks. Your first step is to check out the National Institutes of Health (NIH) Web site at www.clinicaltrials.gov or give them a call, (800) 411-1222. At the Web site you can simply search by topic, and you'll immediately find clinical trials related to the disease being conducted throughout the country along with their contact information. You can also go to other links for further research on medical conditions and news on clinical trials from disease-related associations (e.g., American Cancer Society).

If you're wondering what you should be asking the doctors who run the clinical trial, NIH and other experts suggest you ask:

- Who is sponsoring this study and who is funding this trial? Do you or the director have a financial stake in this treatment or drug?
- What can you show me to verify the credibility of the group sponsoring this clinical trial?
- What is the purpose of the study?
- How will my safety be monitored?
- Who is going to be in the study?

- Why do researchers believe the new treatment being tested may be effective? Has it been tested before? On how many people?
- What kinds of tests and treatments are involved?
- How do the possible risks, side effects, and benefits in the study compare with my current treatment?
- How might this trial affect my daily life?
- How long will the trial last?
- Will hospitalization be required?
- Who will pay for the treatment?
- Will I be reimbursed for other expenses?
- What type of long-term follow-up care is part of this study?
- How will I know that the treatment is working? Will results of the trials be provided to me?
- Who will be in charge of my care? How can I reach them if I have complications?

Always take a family member or friend to the preliminary visit, bring a tape recorder and very carefully read the Informed Consent Form. This form should answer many of the questions listed above and clearly spell out the risks. Be sure to consult your care physician and specialist, as you will want them to work with the clinical trial team. Ask them their opinion on the risks and benefits as they relate to your or your loved one's particular diagnosis. Remember: You can stop participating in the clinical trial at any time. This is absolutely voluntary.

Medicare will pay for qualifying clinical trials, so be sure to ask whether or not Medicare will be covering all of these expenses.

Clinical trials can be literal lifesavers. Just make sure that whoever offers the clinical trial is credible, is part of a highly regarded medical and/or academic institution and is forthright about the risks and who is funding the research study.

Q: What do "phases" mean in clinical trials? Are they the same as "stages" in cancer?

A: The quick answer is no. Cancer *stages* and clinical trial *phases* are not the same thing. The numbering of phases and stages (even though both use Roman numerals) do not correspond. Now for the long answer.

Cancer is characterized by four stages; Stage I is the most curable while Stage IV is the least. Staging is determined by grading the tumor itself; how large it is, whether it's affecting surrounding tissue, whether and to what extent the lymph nodes are involved, and how much the cancer has spread (metastasized).

Clinical trials, which are research studies to determine whether vaccines, drugs, new therapies or new treatments are safe and effective, are divided into four phases.

Phase I Trials are the first tests of the new drug being researched on humans. Researchers investigate findings on dosage, timing, and safety of the new drug or therapy. In this phase of clinical research, the dosage of the drug is gradually increased to identify the safest dose to give humans. Researchers are also looking at how the drug is absorbed, processed, and distributed in the body. At this phase of the trial, clinicians are *not* trying to determine the effectiveness of the drug. These trials are very small—oftentimes no more than twenty patients are involved.

Phase II Trials focus on how the new treatment accomplishes its aim. For example, a cancer trial will look at whether or not the tumor is shrinking and if blood work results are improving. Trials during Phase II usually take two years to complete and again involve a small number of patients, usually not more than forty. In order to proceed to the next phase, researchers must prove that the response rate to treatment is equal to or higher than the conventional standards of practice.

Phase III Trials take this potential new treatment and compare it against the current standard of care. Now the study group greatly expands in numbers so researchers can better determine if the new treatment is more effective, can be prescribed for shorter periods of time, and/or avoids any negative side effects. Many times trials during this phase will also look at how the drug fares in combination with other therapies. Patients who participate in Phase III trials are randomized to receive either the new drug or treatment being studied or the conventional one.

If a drug has been proven successful in a Phase III trial, then the researchers apply for FDA approval to market their product to the general public.

Phase IV Trials are conducted as an added measure to make sure that the results of Phase III trials apply to the general patient population across age groups, race, and gender.

To learn how to find a clinical trial, see page 14 and for a list of questions on what to ask a doctor if you are considering participating in a clinical trial, see page 15.

Q: Are all ambulance services alike?

A: Not at all. There are basically three types of health-related transportation. The most basic is "wheelchair van" transport. These vans are equipped with lifts so that individuals can remain in their wheelchairs to be secured and transported. The second level is a "stretcher van," used when a physician determines the patient must remain lying down and be on a stretcher. The van is equipped to lock the stretcher in place and, at the very least, oxygen equipment is on board. The third level is the most sophisticated and it is the "ambulance service" you receive when you dial 911. You will see the initials BLS (Basic Life Support) associated with ambulance services; they have the equipment and trained personnel to keep you alive on transport to the emergency room.

You need to know the differences among the three transport services because they are directly related to your mother's health and safety, and who will pay for what.

Medicare covers very limited ambulance services: "Ambulance services are covered only if transportation in any other vehicle could endanger your health." It will cover transporting your mom in an emergency to a hospital emergency room and, if a hospital cannot meet a patient's needs, Medicare *may* cover the transport to the closest facility that can meet those medical needs. Medicare will not cover transport to doctors' offices.

If a hospital or nursing home offers to call an ambulance to take your parent home, check to see if a physician has ordered it, and if it will be covered by Medicare. Otherwise, you could be hit with a pretty hefty bill.

If a parent needs nonemergency transportation in a wheelchair van or stretcher van, here's what I recommend you ask before you hire them:

1. *What kind of training have your attendants received?* Dave Crossley, an Emergency Medical Services Chief in Pennsylvania, told me, "I'd only feel comfortable putting my loved one on a nonmedical transport if the attendants have at *least* a state certification as a First Responder. Your loved one obviously has health problems if he needs the service in the first place, so make sure he's protected." Chief Crossley also wants you to know that wheelchair and stretcher vans are *not* regulated or licensed by the Department of Health or Medicare. Virtually anyone can go into the business and start offering rides.
2. *What kind of background checks do you conduct on your employees?* For example, driving history, criminal records and employment references.

3. *Do you always have another attendant riding on the van besides the driver?* If it's only the driver, they won't be able to deal effectively with a passenger emergency.

4. *What type of equipment do you have on the van (e.g., oxygen, safety features)?*

5. *What is your communications system with the driver? Can the driver reach a dispatcher in case of an emergency?*

6. *What are your rates? Do you offer membership programs with discounts?* Be sure to ask around as prices can really vary.

7. *What are my financial responsibilities? Is any of this covered by my insurance?* Most likely it is not; however, some nursing homes cover it as part of their contract with residents. But make sure first!

8. *Are you a stand-alone company or are you part of a Basic Life Support ambulance company?* Chances are, if they are part of a BLS company, their higher training and standards will spill over to the nonemergency side of the company.

One of the most important questions you need to ask medical personnel is, "Has the mode of transportation been ordered by an attending physician?" Doug Wolfberg, a former paramedic turned lawyer and national expert in EMS and public safety, warns consumers to make sure that a physician has determined the safest mode of transport for their loved one. "Say your dad has just had surgery for a hip replacement. Placing him in a wheelchair van rather than a stretcher van during a transfer to a rehab facility could possibly jeopardize his recovery." Make sure a physician is involved in the decision.

Nursing Homes, Hospice & Home Health

Who does what in nursing homes?

A: Nursing homes are fast becoming quasi-hospitals as people need more sophisticated long-term care. If your parent is meeting up with more and more therapists, it's because she needs specialized care and specially trained people are being asked to give her the added care she needs. And that's a good thing. On the other hand, it can seem downright overwhelming.

There are five types of therapists you're likely to encounter. Here's a brief rundown on what they do:

- **Physical Therapists (PTs)** restore the mobility and strength of patients who are limited or disabled, oftentimes as a result of strokes. Through exercise, massage and equipment, PTs alleviate pain and restore functioning. They also teach families and patients how to transfer from chairs, beds and toilets. These therapists are licensed and have postgraduate education and training.
- **Occupational Therapists (OTs)** help your parent perform the activities of daily living (eating, bathing, using the toilet, cooking, dressing and doing basic household chores). They can assess the home and identify ways to make living at home easier and safer. In the nursing home, they can show your mom how to use adaptive equipment and devices and get her involved in creative activities to help her with daily functioning. OTs have received special training and are licensed.
- **Respiratory Therapists (RTs)** evaluate, treat and care for patients with breathing disorders. They operate sophisticated equipment to administer oxygen, manage mechanical ventilation for people who can't breathe on their own, administer medications

in aerosol form and manage overall therapy to help patients breathe better. There are two levels of respiratory therapists: the certified therapist and the registered therapist. All RTs are required to have either an associate's degree (two years of college) or a bachelor's degree in the sciences (four years of college). They can then take a national voluntary exam to become a Certified Respiratory Therapist (CRT) or they can take two more exams to become a Registered Respiratory Therapist (RRT).

• **Speech and Language Therapists, also referred to as speech pathologists,** help your parent restore his or her speech, often lost or disabled due to strokes, surgery or injury. These therapists can also help with breathing, swallowing and muscle control. They are licensed and have postgraduate training beyond college.

• **Nutrition Therapists** who are **Registered Dieticians (RDs)** assist your parent and professional staff in developing a nutritional plan for certain medical conditions. They, too, are licensed following postgraduate training.

The professional services provided by all of these therapists must be considered medically necessary and be prescribed by a physician in order to be eligible for Medicare coverage. In many cases, Medicare will cover some of the costs while Medigap policies will also pay a portion, depending on your parent's plan. Nutrition therapy is covered by Medicare for people with diabetes, kidney disease and for those who have had a transplant. If you have questions about coverage, be sure to ask the nursing facility's social worker or someone in the finance office.

In most instances, these therapies are also covered by Medicare on an outpatient basis, *but always make sure that your parent meets Medicare's criteria for coverage before you begin the service, and that the provider is Medicare-certified.*

It is always helpful to get to know the staff in the nursing facility, and learn how you can be supportive of your parent's care. They'll appreciate your interest—and don't forget that a thank-you will go a long way with dedicated, overworked staff.

Q: How can I compare quality of care among nursing homes?

A: Medicare has just made understanding how to look for quality care in a nursing home a bit easier. They've identified ten basic measures of quality and report them for every nursing home in the country—all seventeen thousand of them. They also compare the quality measures for each home to state and national averages. As a result, you'll have a better perspective on how each home measures up to its competitors.

The project is part of Medicare's Nursing Home Compare program. The nursing home quality measures are derived from data that nursing homes routinely collect on all residents at specified intervals during their stay at the facility. The quality measures are based upon the care that is provided to the total population of residents in a facility.

Here is a list of each measure and what it means:

1. **Help with Daily Activities.** Percentage of residents who need more help feeding, moving from one chair to another, going to the bathroom alone, or changing positions in bed than when they were last assessed.

2. **Infections.** Percentage of residents who have infections (e.g., pneumonia, bladder, urinary tract).

3. **Pain.** Percentage of residents with very bad pain or moderate pain over the last week.

4. **Bedsores.** Percentage of residents with skin wounds caused by constant pressure on one part of the skin (usually bony parts of body, e.g., tailbone, heel, hip).

5. **Lost Too Much Weight.** Percentage of residents who lost too much weight (can indicate malnutrition, not receiving enough help feeding).

6. **Physical Restraints.** Percentage of residents who are physically restrained daily with any device, equipment or material that prevents them from moving freely.

7. **Improved Walking.** Percentage of residents who were admitted for a short stay (e.g., stroke rehab) whose walking improved.

8. **Short-Stay Residents in Pain.** Percentage of residents who have had very bad pain at any time, or moderate pain over the last week.

9. **Short-Stay Residents with Delirium.** Percentage of residents who have problems focusing, or are confused and unaware of their surroundings. This condition can appear suddenly but can be reversible. Delirium is not senility or dementia—these are memory and learning impairments.

10. **Number of Nursing Staff per Resident per Day.** Nursing Home Compare also reports the number of hours that a registered nurse, licensed practical nurse and nurse aide spends daily with each resident.

Every home is compared against state and national averages. The more nursing time given a resident, the better.

To get a report, go to www.medicare.gov and click on "Nursing Home Compare." Or call Medicare at (800) MEDICARE and ask for a customer representative to read to you the ratings of a particular nursing home.

Another feature at the Nursing Home Compare Web site is a report on the number of nursing hours that are spent on each resident at a facility. This is very important to know: The more time that nursing staff spends directly with your parent, the more likely he or she is receiving quality care.

Of course, you don't want to just rely on this one report to decide whether or not a nursing home is good for your loved one. You must visit the facility—I suggest once during the day and once during a weekend or night when staffing is lighter. Please don't think that surprise visits are a good idea—privacy and security reasons prevent you from roaming through a facility. Set up an appointment. Be sure to ask what percentage of the nursing staff is from a "temp agency." It's better to have permanent, stable staff providing care since continuity of care is a good quality predictor. Having your parent exposed to new staff every day increases the chances that care plans or routines are being disrupted.

If you'd like a list of questions to ask in an interview and a checklist of what to look for on your tour of the facility, along with research tips, visit my Web site at www.lindarhodes.com and print out my free Nursing Home Navigator.

Q: What is the best way of researching nursing homes?

A: Choosing a nursing home is never easy. It's certainly emotionally trying, as you wouldn't be looking at a facility unless your parent is quite ill and requires twenty-four-hour care.

Many homes are excellent, but there are plenty of news stories that raise a great deal of concern over how well our elderly are treated. What would I look for? The Internet will offer you the most up-to-date information. If you don't have online access, it's worth a trip to your local library to get online.

First take a look at your state's health department Web site. Most post the results of survey reports on every nursing home in the state. If you do not have access to a computer, then contact your local health department listed in the government blue pages of your phone book and ask them for the number to call about nursing home reports.

Also look at the federal government's Medicare Web site. Medicare requires annual inspections of all nursing homes, and it posts the results on every nursing home in the country. You can find it by visiting "Nursing Home Compare" at www.medicare.gov. The site is excellent.

There are ten "red flags" I'd look for in these survey reports. If the nursing home has been cited for *causing actual harm* to residents and there has been a *pattern of neglect* in any of the following areas, I'd be very concerned:

- Care assessments: No patient should lack one.
- Physical restraints: Residents shouldn't be tied down.
- Pressure sores: These are also known as bedsores, causing open sores on the skin.
- Bladder treatment: Sign that incontinent patients aren't being changed enough.
- Catheter use: Improper care or too high usage of catheters.
- Unnecessary drugs: Residents being given drugs they don't need.
- Medication errors: Residents given wrong drugs, wrong combination of drugs, or wrong dose.
- Malnutrition incidence: Residents losing weight, malnourished.
- Hydration: Residents not getting enough fluids.
- Infection control: Residents exposed to infections, poor standards of infection control and sanitation.

Next use the series of questions I designed known as the Nursing Home Navigator to interview each nursing home. You can print out a free copy by going to my Web site, www .lindarhodes.com, or purchase my Caregiver Kit, which will provide you with four workbooks in addition to a range of tools to help you with your caregiving needs. (See page 21 for more on evaluating nursing homes.)

Finally, have a conversation with the ombudsman assigned to the nursing home (to find out who that is, call your local Area Agency on Aging). Ask if there has been any recent complaint activity about the facility and if it has an ongoing record of consistent deficiencies. Don't ask the ombudsman for a specific recommendation, as they can't give it. Call (800) 677-1116 for the name of the Area Agency on Aging nearest you.

These steps will provide quite a bit of information—on paper—to assess the quality of care at the nursing home. The next step requires going to the facility and conducting a site visit.

Q: When I make a site visit to a nursing home, what should I look for?

A: I suggest visiting the homes twice, once during a weekday and once in the evening or on a weekend. It's really *not* to your advantage to make a surprise visit. The residents have a right to privacy, and the home will not allow you to simply roam the halls. After you've done your research on the facility, it's time to trust your senses and instincts when you visit. Here's my list of what to look for:

- When you visit a resident's room, does it feel like home? Are there personal effects in the room?
- Is staff interacting in a friendly manner with one another and the residents?
- Is the home free of odors? Is it clean? Well lighted?
- Is the temperature comfortable? Stop by a few rooms to see.
- Are residents well groomed? Are they dressed appropriately for the time of day?
- Where are the residents? In halls? Involved in group activities, or staring at TV for great lengths of time? Or are they in their rooms appearing isolated?
- Is there a wandering alert system?
- Is there an activity calendar? Are there pictures on the bulletin boards showing recent activities? Are the activities interesting and varied?
- How many volunteers do they have? Is there an active volunteer corps?
- Are lavatories clean?
- Are food trays left sitting out? Do you see a lot of leftover food on the trays?
- Are call buttons left unanswered for long periods of time?
- Ask to see the menus. Does the food sound appetizing? Ask about the qualifications of the person who oversees the menus. Taste the food, if possible.
- Does the equipment look up-to-date and in good condition?
- Is the outdoor area secure so that no one can wander off into an unsafe area?
- Go to the dining room. Are residents enjoying themselves? Is it pleasant? Is staff interacting with the residents?
- Are bed linens and towels cleaned daily? Ask what the laundry department does to prevent bedsores. (Poorly cleaned, starchy sheets and certain detergents can cause skin breakdown.)
- Are soiled linens piled up in the hallways or in residents' rooms?
- Are showers clean? Look for safety devices to prevent falls.
- Is there fresh water on nightstands, easily accessible for residents?

You might want to make a copy of this list and check off each item as you go through the facility. Then combine this information with the research you've done on survey reports, fall and incident reports, and conversations with the local ombudsman.

You can also download my free Nursing Home Navigator at www.lindarhodes.com or receive four workbooks on researching nursing homes as part of my Caregiver Kit, which can also be purchased at my Web site.

Q: How do I stay on top of my mom's nursing home care?

A: Nursing homes are very busy places and the nursing staff is in high demand, so one way you can help your mom is to become her very own "patient advocate" by staying on top of her care.

You do not need to be a doctor or nurse to pick up telltale signs that something's amiss. What follows is my list of what to look for every time you visit. Share this with other family members, and if you live out of town, share it with your mother's friends or with a volunteer who will visit her regularly and stay in touch with you.

- Check for any redness or bruises on the skin, especially near bony areas such as the tailbone, heels and elbows. You're checking for bed- or pressure sores. You can do this while you give your mom a massage or place lotion on her skin.
- Check for weight loss, change in appetite, sores in the mouth, problems with dentures or chewing, or extreme thirst. You're checking for malnutrition and dehydration. Make sure there's always fresh water at her bedside.
- Check for any ingrown toenails, infections, bunions and uncut nails on the feet. You're checking for potentially serious infections and problems in walking, especially if your parent is diabetic. These could be signs of poor care.
- Check for poorly kept hair or beard, clothing not clean or pressed, body odor, wet adult briefs, unclean sheets. These are signs of poor care and can lead to pressure sores, infections and depression.
- Check out how long it takes for call bells to be answered. And note if aides frequently tell you, "We're short-staffed today." Are meal trays served late? Is there rarely fresh water in the room? These are signs of lack of staff, which can lead to poor care.
- Check to see if your mom's clothes or belongings are missing.
- Check for high staff turnover: Does it seem like every time you turn around there's a new director of nursing or head nurse, or your mom has a different nurse aide from one week to the next? Does staff morale seem pretty low? It won't take long for high staff turnover rates to spill over into poor care.

If you think there is a problem, you can report your concerns to the ombudsman. Their job is to help solve problems among residents, their families and staff in long-term-care facilities. Most ombudsmen are employed by Area Agencies on Aging; their name and phone number should be posted on a bulletin board in the lobby of the nursing home. You also can call the Eldercare Locator at (800) 677-1116 for a nationwide listing.

Research has shown that residents who are visited regularly by family and friends fare better in nursing homes. So always stop by and let a staff member know you were there, and give them an update on your mom. And take a minute to let them know how much you appreciate their help.

Q: Should we care about the activity director in the nursing home?

A: Most people don't realize that nursing homes must offer social and recreational programs to the residents. According to federal law, all residents are to be offered psychosocial activities that are appropriate for their level of functioning. In fact, when a resident is admitted to a facility he or she must be assessed by an interdisciplinary team (nurse, physician, social worker) and the activity or recreation director (you'll find these titles used interchangeably).

These professionals are to provide programs that meet the various choices, needs and levels of abilities of each resident (both physically and cognitively). Of course, much of this can be accomplished in group activities, but some individuals will need one-on-one activities such as sensory interventions that can help an Alzheimer's patient. Whatever the diagnosis, every resident must have an activities assessment and plan.

So how do you know a good activities program when you see one? Here are some of the things that families might want to look for:

- The range of activities that the facility offers, such as exercise programs, music therapy, word and physical games, spiritual programs; the greater the range, the better.
- Are the residents going out of the facility for meals, school plays, and local events?
- Are outside groups coming in, such as Boy Scouts, Girl Scouts, schoolchildren, church groups and the local humane society for pet therapy?
- Is the recreation assessment done by a qualified professional? Ask if the activity director is full-time and whether or not he is certified.
- Look at the bulletin board to see if there are recent pictures of residents, family and staff enjoying activities together.
- Ask to see your loved one's assessment, and meet with the activity director to ask how your parent's intellectual, emotional, social and physical needs will be met through planned activities.
- Look at the calendar of activities and ask how many of them have taken place.

Family members can also help the activity directors by providing them with a profile of their loved ones. Let them know if they like belonging to groups or prefer to be alone. Share with them your parents' hobbies, organizations they've belonged to, military experience, membership in a synagogue or church, educational background and career. Describe your parents' activities during the last year and whether or not they enjoy being around pets and children. Many activity directors make use of a "memory box" filled with artifacts and photos that trigger positive memories and are effective conversation starters.

Family members can also be a great help as volunteers, joining their family member in activities whenever they can. It's a good idea to stop by and see the activity director during a visit in order to find out what your mom or dad is participating in and how they are doing.

Q: What are good holiday gift ideas for residents in nursing homes?

A: It doesn't matter where you live or how old you are—there's nothing like a cheerfully wrapped present to brighten your spirits. Residents in nursing homes present some unique challenges in gift-giving, so I've created a list that's received the "seal of approval" from those who work in nursing homes. And my guess is these gifts would make any resident feel special during the holiday season.

As you go through this list, consider what it would be like if you and everyone who reads this decided to go out and buy just one extra gift, and drop it off (or mail it) to their nearest nursing home to be given to a resident without family or friends.

Gifts to Brighten Up Their Room: picture frames, plants (live or silk), paintings, a calendar marked with birthdays of family members, artificial goldfish bowl or waterfall, sun catchers for the window, framed pictures of the resident in earlier days, a collage of pictures of families and friends—these make great conversation pieces—or an all-season wreath or decorative knocker to hang on their door.

Gifts for Pampering: basket of lotions and talcum powder (be sure to check with the nursing staff on what's best), shaving lotion, favorite perfumes, luscious bath towel and/or robe, gift certificates to the in-house beauty parlor or barber for hair and manicures, grooming products.

Gifts for Having Fun: a very simple-to-use VCR and new movies every month and videos of family events, large-print books, a simple-to-use CD Discman or tape Walkman so they can listen to their favorite music without disturbing roommates, low-vision playing cards, large-print crossword puzzles or other games appropriate for their cognitive ability, a box of all-occasion greeting cards with a book of stamps, a talking picture frame, stuffed animals.

Gifts for Staying Warm: lap afghans or fleece throws are very popular, cheerful holiday sweaters, sweat suits, no-skid slippers, fun socks that depict the holidays or interest of the resident (e.g., golf, flowers).

Gifts That Touch the Heart: handmade gifts, a framed poem or artwork from grand-kids or from you, phone cards to stay in touch and handle long-distance calls.

The most cherished gift, however, is a visit from *you*. If the resident is able, you might offer to take him or her out for an evening ride to enjoy the holiday lights along with a hot cup of cocoa. And one last idea: Make it a New Year's resolution to volunteer at your local nursing home or assisted living facility. A friendly visit to a resident without family is a gift that will make *you* all the richer for it.

Q: Is assisted living different from a nursing home?

A: Yes, assisted living is different from a nursing home (also known as a skilled nursing facility or long-term-care facility). Assisted living means receiving *some* assistance with the tasks of daily living. Nursing home care, on the other hand, provides twenty-four-hour nursing care and supervision because the residents need assistance all of the time. Assisted living means just what the term implies: Your parent receives assistance in such daily tasks as bathing, grooming, taking pills on time, housekeeping, getting meals, managing the bills and/or using transportation. You'll often hear these referred to as ADLs, for activities of daily living.

Sometimes you'll run into other terms that refer to assisted living, such as catered living, personal care homes or boarding homes. Whether assisted living makes sense for your parent will depend on how well she does by herself performing the tasks of daily living. Assisted living facilities rarely take people with Alzheimer's disease, although some do have specialized floors with this service. If you are looking at such a facility, make sure it is qualified to care for some-one with dementia by asking to see any certification papers they have received from state regu-lating bodies, and ask them to describe the training their staff have received to care for people with dementia.

Nursing homes offer skilled nursing care, rehab, medical services, and protective supervi-sion as well as assistance with the activities of daily living. People with long-term mental or physical conditions that require a twenty-four-hour protective environment offering medical and health care services need nursing home care.

Unlike nursing homes, assisted living facilities are unregulated, so be sure to do your research. Some assisted living facilities have voluntarily gone through an accreditation process and are listed at the Web site of the Commission on Accreditation of Rehabilitation Facilities at www.carf.org. For a list of nonprofit facilities and tips on what to look for in an assisted living facility, go to the American Association of Homes and Services for the Aging Web site at www.aahsa.org.

Q: **Does Medicare really pay for the first hundred days of nursing home care?**

A: The answer is a bit more complicated than a simple yes or no. But it is certainly a myth that Medicare covers long-term care. Regretfully, it's a myth that many people believe: In a recent survey conducted by AARP, more than half of the respondents believed that Medicare will cover all of their nursing home costs. It just isn't so.

As of 2004, Medicare will pay for *up to* one hundred days of *skilled* nursing care in a facility that is certified by Medicare *if* the following conditions are met:

- Placement in a skilled nursing facility (SNF) is within thirty days of a hospital stay.
- The stay in the hospital was for at least three days—but that doesn't include the day of discharge—so it's really four days.
- The care is medically necessary, which is usually defined as skilled-nursing or skilled-rehab care.
- The skilled care is directly related to the medical condition that resulted in the hospitalization.

If all of these conditions are met, Medicare may cover up to a hundred days of skilled care. But remember, the care must be skilled, not chronic or custodial care. Skilled care must be medically necessary and prescribed by a physician. The skilled care must improve or maintain the patient's condition and prevent it from further deterioration. The care requires registered nurses, physicians and professional therapists who manage, observe and evaluate the patient's condition. Under this scenario, Medicare will pay 100 percent of your parent's first twenty days in a nursing home. On average, most people need no more than twenty days of *skilled* care. Where they run into trouble is needing additional days of "chronic care," which Medicare won't cover.

If your parent needs additional "skilled" care beyond twenty days, Medicare will cover all but $101.50 per day, which is your hefty copay, for days twenty-one through one hundred.

The good news is that most Medigap policies (supplemental insurance) will cover the copay. But after one hundred days there will be no Medicare payments or Medicare supplements.

A beneficiary can collect under this benefit several times over a lifetime. How? A benefit period is not based on an annual or lifetime basis. It begins when your mother enters a hospital and ends when there has been a break of at least sixty consecutive days since her inpatient hospital or skilled nursing care was provided.

The two most important things to remember are: Always carry a Medigap policy that will cover the gap between what's charged for the care and what Medicare will cover, and never assume that Medicare will cover nursing home care. If, during a hospital stay, your parent is told that she needs to be transferred to a nursing home, make sure you talk with her physician to find out if he or she is prescribing *skilled* care. If so, also make sure that she's being transferred to a facility that has been certified by Medicare so that she can receive the coverage that Medicare does provide.

If you have any questions, be sure to ask to speak to the hospital social worker prior to discharge. Medicare also has an excellent Web site that features their handbook on "Medicare Coverage of Skilled Nursing Facilities" at www.medicare.gov. Just enter "SNF coverage" in the search bar. You can also call them at (800) 633-4227.

Q: What exactly is senior care and how would I find it for my mom?

A: Senior care companies offer individualized assistance with day-to-day living to older people living at home. I call it "stitch in time" care; they do the little things that can help people stay independent, remain socially engaged and stay in their own homes. Companies offering senior care services make it very clear that they provide *nonmedical* services. In other words, they are not in the home health care business. Instead, they offer such services as companionship, meal preparation, medication reminders, light housework, incidental transportation, errands, grocery shopping, pharmacy pickups, arranging doctor appointments, mailing bills and letters, and providing a stable bathing environment—to name a few.

If you're worried that your mom isn't getting enough social interaction, they'll even match her up with someone that she enjoys spending time with and who can engage in your mom's favorite hobby, watch movies, or just enjoy good conversation.

There has been quite a growth in the senior care industry over the last five years. You'll usually find providers listed in the phone book under "Home Care." Some are franchises, such as Home Instead, Wisdom Keepers, Comfort Care, Visiting Angels and Comfort Keepers, while others are independently owned. Home Instead Senior Care is the only national franchise that offers advanced training in Alzheimer's for its caregivers. They can be reached at www.homeinstead.com or (888) 484-5759.

In most states these companies are not licensed by a state agency because they are offering *nonmedical* care. So that means, as a consumer, you need to do your homework. Here is a list of questions that can help you identify the best agency for your parent.

1. Do you conduct criminal background checks on your employees and are they bonded?
2. Are the caregivers your employees or are you a referral agency?
3. Who is responsible for paying taxes and Social Security of the caregivers?
4. What type of training do your employees go through to be hired?
5. Is your training ongoing? Please describe it.
6. Please describe for me the background of your average caregiver (e.g., part-time homemaker, certified nurse aide, high school graduate, retiree).
7. If you provide transportation, have you checked out their driving record?
8. How do you go about making sure that the caregiver will be compatible with my parent?
9. How long have most of your employees worked for you?
10. Are your services covered by long-term care insurance and will you process the paperwork?
11. How do you supervise and oversee the quality of care provided by your workers?
12. May I see a sample service agreement and a listing of your prices?

Also check to see if there are any complaints lodged against the company through the Better Business Bureau. You could also ask the local Area Agency on Aging's ombudsman if they know of any complaints against the company (call Eldercare Locator at [800] 677-1116 to find your local Area Agency on Aging). I'd also ask if they would allow you to speak with any customers who have used the service.

You'll find that prices range from $12 to $22 per hour and there usually is a minimum service requirement of at least two hours. Services can be arranged for as many as twenty-four hours a day for a short-term or long-term arrangement, including weekends and holidays. This can be especially helpful when families need respite from daily caregiving.

Some long-term-care insurance policies do cover nonmedical senior care, so be sure to look over your mother's policy if she has one.

You may also find volunteer senior care services being provided by faith-based organizations, so if you are financially strapped, give your local church or synagogue a call to see what they provide. Local senior centers may also be a good resource for finding nonprofit groups that offer volunteer senior care.

Q: Any pointers on hiring home health care workers?

A: First, methodically think through what your mom or dad's day is like and what kind of help he or she needs to get through it. Let's say that we're talking about your mother. Does she need help taking her medications, getting to and from the bathroom, preparing meals, taking a bath or shower, getting dressed, or doing physical exercises? Does she have any medical conditions that require special attention? Are there symptoms that the caregiver must be aware of so that she can alert your mother's physician?

This list will guide you in creating a job description for your mother's caregiver. I'd also advise you to ask your mom to share her expectations, what she would like the caregiver to do. Once she has shared her expectations, then you should also express yours. The goal is to have everyone in sync, so that you can create a job description that is realistic and will serve your mother's best interests. This will also make it much easier for the caregiver to assess whether or not she is suited for this job.

Here's a list of interview questions and tips:

1. Inform the caregiver of your mother's medical condition(s) and ask her to describe what she knows about this condition, how she'll respond and whether she has cared for anyone else with this condition.
2. Share the job description list with her and ask her to go over each item on the list, telling you how she'll respond to each of your mother's needs.
3. Ask the worker to tell you what training she has had for each of the tasks described.
4. Ask the caregiver to show you any certificates or educational degrees she has received.
5. Ask for a resume that identifies any schools or training programs she has attended, previous jobs and contact information of all previous employers.
6. If your mother suffers from dementia, find out what specialized training the caregiver has received to work with cognitively impaired adults.
7. Ask what training she has received in lifting people, and how does she go about giving a bath? What safety measures does she use? Ask her to identify any physical demands of caring for your mother and how she will address them.
8. Ask the caregiver to provide you with a copy of the results of a police background check.
9. Ask for a list of references—and *call* them. Make sure that at least two references are from families who have used the caregiver's services.

It is a good idea to interview prospective caregivers at a neutral place, like a local coffee shop. This way, especially if your mother lives alone, her vulnerability is not disclosed to a stranger. Once you've narrowed down your search and checked out their references, then you can invite them to the home and see how the caregiver interacts with your mother.

If you're hiring a certified nurse aide, check their references with your state's Certified Nurse Aide Registry, which is usually run by the state's department of health and/or human services.

Once you've hired the caregiver, ask for a daily phone call to update you on how your mother's doing. As time goes on and you feel very secure with her services, then an update every few days or even once a week may seem reasonable.

I'd also stop by to see how things are going and how well your mother and the caregiver interact. Caregiving is a dynamic and evolving process that must constantly adjust to changes in your mother's health and caregiving needs. Thus, it's important for you to stay involved and monitor the effectiveness of the caregiving services.

Q: My mom has Alzheimer's and refuses to move to assisted living. Now what?

A: Sounds like a very tough dilemma: You know it's not safe for your mom to be left alone and you feel irresponsible if you don't do something. On the other hand, you're trying to respect your mom's wishes, and you don't want to make her feel that she's been placed under house arrest or traumatically remove her physically from her home.

But because your mom has Alzheimer's, "reasoning" with her will be very difficult—you don't share the same reality. So, let's look at some steps you can take to get her into a safe and nurturing environment while respecting her self-determination.

I assume that she has had a comprehensive geriatric assessment to arrive at the diagnosis of Alzheimer's. If not, get one by a physician certified in geriatrics. If she's had this, arrange an appointment with her doctor and explain that it's no longer safe for her to be alone. Provide the doctor with a list of examples that show she can no longer perform the tasks of daily living. Also describe your family support system and let the doctor know that you can no longer provide supervision for her at home.

Ask the doctor if he could "prescribe" a week at a "center" for necessary treatment for her condition. If this is coming from the doctor in the form of a handwritten prescription rather than from her "overprotective" kids, she might listen.

By making it a temporary situation, you're not backing her into a corner. Also, if her sense of time has been affected, the "week" might easily transition into a permanent solution. Another way of easing her into the idea might be to ask those in charge of the facility if you could bring your mom over for lunch and eat there as you would in any other restaurant.

Dr. Roger Cadieux, clinical professor of psychiatry at Penn State University, Hershey Medical Center, who practices adult and geriatric psychiatry, had this to say when I asked him how he would handle this situation. Once he has the hard data from a geriatric assessment, "The approach that I use is to empathetically but firmly present the findings and then state definitely that there is now a need for a higher level of care. There is usually a great deal of distress but the anger, if any, is directed toward the physician and not the family. I make sure that the patient understands that I am their advocate even though I am imparting difficult information. The trick is for the family to find a physician who can and will take this approach."

Dr. Cadieux recommends giving the patient the opportunity to participate, if possible, in the process of finding a facility that provides a higher level of care. When warranted, he added, medication, especially low doses of antidepressants and/or antipsychotics, can make the difference between easy acceptance or abject refusal of this necessary move.

Q: What is hospice and how do I find a good one for my dad?

A: Hospice care brings together medical care, pain management and emotional and spiritual support for terminal patients and their families. This care is provided in the patient's home when possible, or in an inpatient hospice facility with a homelike setting. The mission of hospice staff and volunteers is to address the symptoms of a terminal illness with the intent of promoting comfort and dignity. They are experts at pain management.

Based upon my personal experience with hospice and my professional work training hospice volunteers, I can't emphasize enough how helpful hospice can be to you and your family. It can manage your father's pain, help you understand what he is going through, and help you and other family members cope with your emotions. Many of us are at a loss as to what we should do before and at the time of death. The hospice folks can get you through it at your own pace. They also stay in touch with you following your loved one's death.

Medicare does provide a hospice benefit that covers almost all of the costs of caring for a dying person during his or her last six months of life. To qualify for the Medicare hospice benefit:

- Your parent must have Medicare Part A.
- Your parent's doctor and the medical director of the hospice must confirm that your parent has a life expectancy of less than six months.
- Your parent must agree in writing that he or she will not pursue any treatments to cure his or her illness.

The Medicare hospice benefit covers: skilled nursing services, physician visits, skilled therapy (e.g., physical, speech or occupational), medical social services, nutrition counseling, bereavement counseling, 95 percent of the cost of prescription drugs for symptom control and pain relief, short-term inpatient respite care to relieve family members from caregiving, and home care. Medicare does *not* cover twenty-four-hour round-the-clock care in the home; however, in a medical crisis, continuous nursing and short-term inpatient services are available.

Your dad's physician should be able to refer you to a good hospice. You can also visit the National Hospice Organization's Web site at www.nhpco.org and click on a map that will identify the Medicare-certified hospices in your area, call Medicare directly at (800) 633-4227, or look in the Yellow Pages under Hospices. Here's a list of questions you should ask:

- Are you Medicare-certified? (If not, Medicare will not pay.)
- Are you a member of any professional organizations or are you accredited?
- Are there certain conditions that patients and families have to meet to enter the hospice program?
- Are you willing to come to the home and conduct an assessment to help us understand if this is the best option for my parent?
- What specialized services do you offer, such as rehab therapists, family counselors, pharmacists, used equipment?
- What are your polices regarding inpatient care? What hospital(s) do you have a contractual relationship with in the event my parent would need to go to the hospital?
- Do you require a primary family caregiver as a condition of admission?
- What are the caregiver's responsibilities as related to the hospice?
- What kind of emergency coverage do you offer? Who is on call? Will a nurse come quickly to the home, if needed?
- What out-of-pocket expenses can we expect?
- Will your staff handle all of the paperwork and billing?

- What are your policies on the use of antibiotics, ventilators, dialysis, and/or nutrients given intravenously?
- What treatments are outside of your hospice's purview?

Take the time to visit with their staff and tour their inpatient facility. The journey you are about to take will leave you with a lifetime of memories. Make sure you feel very comfortable and at peace with the hospice professionals who will guide you along this path of letting go.

Q: **When is the right time to call in hospice? My mom is resisting calling in hospice for my dying father.**

A: I've seen family members get into quite a debate as to whether or not to call in hospice care, even though everyone knows that their loved one is dying. Sometimes the answer lies within the heart and mind of the person who is dying. If your father is aware of his end-of-life condition, which I imagine he is, then perhaps a heart-to-heart conversation with him is in order.

Today, oncologists and family physicians are much more open about telling patients the status of their disease, including "how much time they may have left." This is so different from the 1950s when my grandfather died of cancer. Everyone walked around acting like Grandpa would get better—especially around Grandpa. Families and physicians believed it was best to spare the loved one from the agony of knowing. Your mom, being part of that generation, might still feel that she wants to spare your dad from the heart-wrenching reality of his impending death. So she holds off calling hospice because she feels it is a symbol of dying.

Yet, if your dad knows his illness is terminal, chances are there are two very strong needs he's internally wrestling with. He wants to be reassured that his dying will be as painless as possible, and that your mom will be spared becoming physically ill herself from the toll of caring for him. And I'm sure that your mom also wants to see your dad out of his pain.

So if you stay focused on these two needs and then reintroduce the concept of hospice, your mom may be more receptive. If she sees hospice as helping with your dad's pain management, and if your dad sees it as helping your mom by coordinating all of his care, they may both see hospice in a new light. You can also reassure your mom that if your father decides to pursue treatment to extend his life (e.g., chemotherapy or radiation) he can opt out of hospice and go back to the service later.

There is another advantage to hospice care, as Medicare will also cover respite care for your mother as long as your dad is receiving hospice care. Thus, if your dad needs to stay in a nursing home, inpatient hospice facility or hospital to provide him palliative care in order for your mother to get a break, Medicare will pay 95 percent of the Medicare-approved amount for inpatient respite care for up to five days.

See page 35 for information on finding and choosing a hospice.

Q: My dad is terminally ill. Can you tell me what dying people want?

A: It is terribly difficult to prepare for the death of a loved one. No matter how *full* a life anyone has had or how much forewarning you've been given, the shock and loss are never really lessened. When the time feels right, or perhaps when your dad brings it up, ask *him* how you can be helpful. Besides addressing the standard tasks of how your dad will distribute his property and assets, and the end-of-life decisions about his medical care, the most lasting memories will come from how you both travel the emotional journey you are about to take.

I'd like to share with you the results of a compassionate and comprehensive study by the Veterans Affairs Medical Center in Durham, North Carolina. They interviewed terminally ill patients, their doctors, social workers, hospice volunteers, chaplains and family members. They asked what makes for a positive end-of-life experience. This is what they learned:

- Preventing pain was the most important to patients. Many people fear dying in pain more than dying itself. Doctors can be very helpful in managing pain and reassuring both patients and their families that pain can be controlled.
- Patients want to be involved in making decisions regarding their treatment. Gone are the hush-hush days of "sparing" the patient from the truth. Letting the patient's desires direct decision-making relieves families of guilt and prevents conflicts and debates among family members. What your parent wants becomes the unifying rallying point, even if it isn't what you would have chosen for yourself.
- Patients and families need to know what to expect from the fatal condition and the treatment. This knowledge helps them better prepare for events, symptoms and treatment outcomes surrounding the impending death. It will also help your dad feel in control.
- Patients and families search for meaning to their lives and their relationship with each other. They'll seek the solace of faith, review their lives, resolve conflicts, spend time with family and friends and say good-bye. At your dad's direction, facilitate meeting and talking with loved ones and friends so that they can gain closure together.

- Patients find satisfaction in contributing to the well-being of others. They find peace in helping their loved ones come to terms with their dying and helping loved ones let go. They also find it satisfying to leave behind the means to care for their loved ones' physical and financial needs.
- Patients do not want to be seen as a "disease" or a "case" but as a unique, whole person.

I hope this advice from people who've walked in your shoes will be helpful to you. Also, be sure to contact your local hospice, which can provide wonderful physical and emotional support (see pages 35 and 37 for more on hospice care).

3

Prescriptions & Alternative Medicine

Q: How can my parents cut the costs of their prescriptions?

A: It's no wonder your parents feel the crunch. A recent study by the nonprofit consumer advocacy group Families USA uncovered that drug prices rose 30 percent in the last six years among drugs most frequently used by the elderly. It's not uncommon for older people to shell out an average of $3,000 each year on prescriptions.

Most Medigap insurers will offer a prescription benefit, but the premium is usually quite high. You'll need to calculate your parent's monthly cost of prescriptions and the deductibles they'll have to pay, even with the insurance, to determine if the policy is a good return on their investment.

But if an insurance policy doesn't make economic sense, here are several cost-cutting ideas to help control their prescription costs:

- Ask if there is a generic equivalent of the drug being prescribed. Generics are less expensive and by law are biochemically equivalent to the brand.
- If the physician prescribes a brand-new drug on the market—which is usually the most expensive and without a generic substitute—ask if an older version of that class of drug would be feasible to try first.
- If your parent is taking a new drug for the very first time, ask for a trial size rather than the thirty-day supply. That way, if your mom or dad has an adverse reaction from the new drug, they will not have wasted their money on a month's supply.
- Ask the doctor for drug samples as another means to try out a drug before investing in a thirty-day supply.

- If your parent is taking a maintenance drug—one they have to take for a long period of time to maintain their health—buy the drug in ninety-day supplies, which is cheaper.
- You can also buy maintenance drugs online for a good cost savings. Check out the National Association of Boards of Pharmacy's Web site at www.nabp.net/vipps to see if there is a legitimate pharmacy from which to buy on the Internet. (For a copy of my column on tips for buying prescriptions online just send me an e-mail.)
- Shop around. You'd be surprised at the difference in prices among pharmacies. It's worth the call, and many pharmacies will deliver to homebound elderly.
- If your parent is in a nursing home and takes medications, take a look at the monthly bill. You might find that you are paying a higher rate for your parent's prescription because you're going through the nursing home's pharmacy. It might be less expensive to purchase their medications directly yourself and have them delivered to the facility.
- Some drug companies offer free or reduced medications in certain cases. Visit www.phrma.org/patients to see if the manufacturer of your parent's drug participates. In most cases, only your parent's physician can apply for the drug or a substantial discount. Print out the results of your search and share it with your parent's physician.
- Sign up for a Medicare Drug Discount Card—a topic of another column in this chapter.

Hopefully, this will help cut down some of the costs your parents are facing when it comes to taking pills.

Q: How does my dad get a Medicare Drug Discount Card?

A: If you thought your life just got easier, think again. There are over seventy plans approved by Medicare to offer drug discount cards, each of them offering different discounts on different drugs among different pharmacies with different enrollment fees. So what's the same? You will be able to get some drugs cheaper than before the program came into effect. And all of the plans must be approved by Medicare, and to prove it, they must display the Medicare seal of approval.

Here's the Least You Need to Know: First, if your father is a member of a Medicare-HMO or managed care plan, then call them and find out if they offer a drug discount plan approved by Medicare. If they do, stop right there—that is the discount plan your dad *must* join. So life just got easier for you, after all. Ask them how your dad should enroll.

If your dad belongs to traditional Medicare and pays Part A and Part B, he is eligible to enroll. If he is receiving Medical Assistance, he *cannot*. The enrollment process is very simple and you will save money, so it is worth the effort to apply.

To find out who offers a drug discount card, your best bet is getting online and going to www.medicare.gov and clicking on "Find a Medicare-Approved Drug Discount Card." At this site, you can find out who offers what and you can compare the drug discount lists against each other. They even allow you to list the prescriptions you take, so that you can identify which companies actually discount *your* pills. If you can't get online, then give Medicare a call at (800) 633-4227. I'm sure your dad is getting plenty of mail advertising different programs, so you can also call the companies directly.

Now for a few rules. Your dad can only enroll in *one* program. It's not like all those nifty little key chain cards you get with every grocery store you go to. Once he's enrolled, he has to stay with that program for the calendar year. He must pay an annual enrollment fee but no company is allowed to charge him more than $30 for the entire year. If any company charges monthly fees, it's a scam, so stay clear. The discounts are offered by drug, and the company will provide you with a discount drug list so that you'll know the exact amount they are discounting for each drug. In other words, you do not get a flat percentage discount on all drugs.

What should you look for? Every new program is fertile ground for scam artists, so make sure that any program you are looking at has the Medicare seal of approval and, if you have doubts, check with Medicare to make sure you're dealing with a participating company. Make a list of the drugs that your dad takes and check that list against the company's discount drug list. Go with the company that will provide him the most savings for the drugs that he takes. Also, make sure that the local pharmacies that your dad frequents are on the list. If they are not, then the card will not be accepted by them. Compare enrollment fees, as they range from $10 to $30 per year. Don't always go for the cheapest enrollment as it might be worth paying a higher fee if your dad will save more money every month on the discounts they offer on his refills.

Once you do enroll, make a copy of the discount drug list so that your dad can take it to every physician office visit; that way the doctor will know to prescribe your dad pills offered under his plan.

Q: Will my mom qualify for a $600 Medicare credit for prescriptions?

A: To find out if she qualifies, your mother's first step is to apply for a Medicare Drug Discount Card offered by private companies that have been contracted by Medicare to offer card members discounts on their prescriptions. You can then receive a $600 credit toward your prescription costs if you meet these criteria:

1. You have Medicare Part A and/or Part B.
2. You have no other health insurance that covers outpatient prescription drugs. (If you have drug coverage in a Medicare + Choice plan or under your Medigap policy, it's okay. You can still qualify for the credit.)
3. Your annual income during 2004 is no more than $12,569 if you are single or $16,862 as a married couple.

What counts as income? Everything that you would normally report as income on your tax return generally counts as income. This includes retirement benefits from Social Security, Railroad Retirement, Veterans Administration, disability benefits and any income that you receive from the federal government.

Do not bother applying for the $600 credit if you are a Medicaid beneficiary, receive military health insurance through TRICARE or get federal retiree health benefits through FEHBP. If you belong to a Medicare managed care plan that offers its own drug discount card, you can't go after the $600 credit, nor can you apply if you are covered under an employer group health plan or receive other health insurance coverage.

So, if you've still survived all of the eligibility hoops, here is what you do: When you apply for your drug discount card there will be a section on the enrollment form that will ask you questions related to your income and other benefits that you receive. Once you fill this out, and send it to the company offering the drug discount card, they'll send the information on to Medicare.

If Medicare decides that you qualify, they'll pay your enrollment fee for the drug discount card. If you already paid it, don't worry, they'll give you a refund. And, of course, you'll receive your $600 credit toward prescriptions but you'll still need to pay a percentage of the cost of each drug through a 5 percent or 10 percent co-pay, which is based upon your income. The $600 credit can be used for most prescriptions, even drugs that are not listed on the company's discount drug list for which you enrolled.

If Medicare considers you eligible for the credit in 2004 you don't have to bother reapplying in 2005. You'll simply get another $600 credit for 2005. When you use your discount card, the statement you get with your prescription will show you how much of the $600 credit you have left. Every company has a toll-free number for their enrollees to call.

If you have questions about the drug discount plan, give Medicare a call at (800) 633-4227 or visit their Web site, www.medicare.gov.

Q: **Are online pharmacies a good idea?**

A: Cyber pills. You knew it had to come. Instead of getting your pills at the friendly corner drugstore, you're a click away from online buying. There are certainly some advantages to getting drugs online:

- Easy access if your parents are homebound.
- Easy comparative shopping for the best price.
- Access to a great variety of products.
- Ability to consult with a pharmacist and order products in the privacy of your own home.

The FDA, however, warns that there are a growing number of rogue sites that are downright dangerous. They'll send you pills without a prescription, which is never, never a good idea. Or they'll have you fill out a questionnaire, then tell you that a doctor has looked over your dad's symptoms and recommends the following medication—when no such doctor ever looked it over.

In a famous national case, a man ordered Viagra online. He also had a history of chest pains and a family history of heart disease. All he did was fill out an online questionnaire. He died of a heart attack as soon as he started taking the drug. Though there is no direct proof that the man's death was linked to the drug, FDA officials contend that a traditional doctor-patient relationship with a good physical might have prevented the death.

In the meantime, Congress is scrambling to keep up with online drug buying and come up with legislation to regulate it for the public's safety, as they do any pharmacy. So what if you want this convenience and to be assured that you are purchasing drugs online from a credible source?

Here are some smart Internet buying tips from the FDA:

1. Check with the National Association of Boards of Pharmacy to make sure that the site is a licensed pharmacy in good standing. Visit their Web site at www.nabp .net/vipps to find out or call (847) 698-6227. The association, in response to public concern about the safety of pharmacy practices on the Internet, created the Verified Internet Pharmacy Practice Sites (VIPPS) program in the spring of 1999. A coalition of state and federal regulatory associations, professional associations and consumer advocacy groups provided their expertise in developing the criteria that all VIPPS-certified pharmacies must follow.

2. Stay clear of sites that offer to provide a prescription for a drug the first time without a physical exam.

3. Don't buy from sites that sell a prescription drug without a prescription or that sell drugs not approved by the FDA.

4. Beware of sites that advertise a "new cure" for a serious disorder or a quick cure-all for lots of ailments. It's cyber snake oil!

5. Don't do business with sites that don't provide you access to a registered pharmacist.

6. For any first-time drug, always go through your physician.

Help out the FDA: If you think you've come across an illegal pharmacy Web site, let them know by e-mailing them at webcomplaints@ora.fda.gov. In general, legitimate online pharmacies will ask you to open an account with them, and then submit credit and insurance information. They'll ask you to submit a valid prescription that your mom's doctor can call in, fax or mail. The online pharmacy can ship it to you, or you can pick it up at a local drugstore.

Most sites have an online registered pharmacist you can e-mail questions to or call at a toll-free number. If you do go online, make sure you keep in touch with your mom's physician.

But there's nothing quite like your neighborhood pharmacist—the one who knows you and your family, readily answers your questions and looks out for you when you might be about to take a drug that, instead of making you well, could very well make you sick. Technology does have its costs. Only you can weigh the "trade-off."

Q: Are there any programs that offer free prescriptions?

A: There actually are a number of programs offered by drug companies for older people who do not qualify for any other state or Medicaid programs yet are of modest means. Here's a thumbnail sketch of what's out there.

Pfizer Share Card. To qualify for the Pfizer Share Card an individual's income cannot exceed $18,000 a year, and for married couples it cannot exceed $24,000. An applicant must be sixty-five years of age or older, or a Medicare enrollee, and have no other drug insurance coverage. Call (800) 717-6005 to find out more on how to enroll or go to their Web site at www.pfizerforliving.com/sharecard.

Together Rx. This is a discount drug program offered by seven companies including Bristol-Myers Squibb, Johnson & Johnson, GlaxoSmithKline and Novartis. Among them, more than 150 drugs are covered. The card yields between 20 and 40 percent from the usual price paid at the pharmacy. Medicare beneficiaries with incomes less than $28,000 for individuals and $38,000 for couples qualify. Call (800) 865-7211 to apply or go to www.together-rx.com.

Lilly Answers. This program offers a $12 flat rate for each thirty-day supply prescription of a Lilly medicine. Medicare beneficiaries (and people with disabilities) with incomes below $18,000 for individuals or $24,000 for a household of more than one and who have no other prescription coverage can qualify. Call (877) 795-4559 to enroll or go to www.lillyanswers.com.

www.needymeds.com. For an excellent Web site that provides you with all kinds of tips on discount programs for prescription drugs, visit this address. They provide a chart that compares all of the discount programs and cites all contact information. They offer all kinds of tips on how to get affordable drugs. A similar site that also identifies all state programs is www.rxassist.org sponsored by the Robert Wood Johnson Foundation.

PHRMA. The Pharmaceutical Research and Manufacturers of America, the trade association of the drug makers, will provide you with a directory of all the companies that give away free prescription drugs to consumers who cannot afford them. Most of the time your parent's physician will need to make the application. But at least you can become aware of the process and bring it to the attention of the physician, or even download applications at their Web site. You can call for a copy of the directory at (800) 762-4636 or go to www.phrma.org and click on "Patient Assistance Programs."

Q: What does it mean when my doctor prescribes a drug off-label?

A: Prescription drugs must undergo a rigorous process to prove the safety, reliability and validity of a drug before it is approved by the Food and Drug Administration for public consumption. Part of the approval process requires that drug manufacturers provide evidence gathered through clinical trials of what *specific* conditions are treatable by the drug, including dosage regimen, duration and what age ranges are appropriate for its usage. The FDA grants its approval based upon this evidence. So, if you are taking a drug that was proven to treat a heart condition and the FDA approved it as such, then the drug company can't also recommend that you use it for stomach ulcers.

The drug company must publish in their drug package inserts the approved uses of the drug, potential complications and a lot of scientific data that consumers rarely understand. These indicated uses of the drug are considered "labeled." In contrast, when a physician prescribes the drug for a use not specifically indicated on the label approved by the FDA then the physician is prescribing for an "off-label" use. The FDA approves the label, also known as the language of the drug package insert.

You might wonder, why would a doctor prescribe a drug off-label? Once a drug has been on the market and is used by large numbers of people, doctors begin to gather clinical experience on a wide range of drugs. They may find that a drug they've prescribed for one indication had an added benefit to their patients for another condition. They may share their clinical experience in medical journals or with other physicians at conferences, and the word spreads. It is not uncommon, for instance, for chemotherapy drugs to be prescribed for off-label indications as physicians try to find a life-saving formula for cancer patients.

Sometimes this practice can be life-saving and sometimes it can be life-taking. A six-month study of off-label practices by Knight-Ridder Newspapers found that in 2002 over 100 million prescriptions were written for off-label uses, such as epilepsy drugs given for depression, powerful antipsychotics given for insomnia, and high-blood-pressure pills given for anxiety. The study cited the case of the drug Risperdal, a drug approved by the FDA to treat schizophrenia, being widely used by family practice physicians to treat dementia. But in April of last year, after alarming reports of elderly patients suffering strokes after using the drug for dementia, the drug maker Johnson & Johnson was forced to send letters to doctors throughout the country warning them of the increased risk of strokes among the elderly when using the drug off-label.

So what can you do? You really need to take the time to educate yourself every time you or your parent is given a new prescription drug. It starts with the physician prescribing the medication, so ask your doctor:

- Is this drug approved for what you are treating me for by the FDA or is this an off-label prescription?
- What is your reason for prescribing this off-label treatment? What studies or evidence are you basing this on?
- What are the risks and benefits to this treatment? Is there an alternative?
- What is the lowest dose I can take and are you prescribing it?
- How long should I be on this medication as approved by the FDA?
- What side effects should I be aware of that could indicate I'm having an adverse reaction?

Be sure to take the time to read the drug package insert—that tiny-printed tissue paper found in the box packaged with your medicine. You'll know whether or not the drug is being prescribed off-label by reading the section titled "Indications and usage," which will tell you what the drug is approved to treat. It is also wise to read about the contraindications that explain when a drug should not be used, and the "Warnings and precautions" section. Don't assume that a pamphlet provided by your pharmacy gives you the same complete information on the drug as what is on the label. Go to the original source! If it doesn't come with your medicine, ask the pharmacist for a copy. And feel free to ask your pharmacist the same list of questions you've asked your doctor.

Check out the FDA Web site at www.fda.gov and click on the "Drugs" sidebar. You can search for every FDA-approved drug in the United States and read the actual approved label (drug package insert) for the drug, an FDA description of the drug and a copy of any Letters to Health Professionals that the FDA forced the drug makers to send, advising of problems associated with the drug.

Q: What should my mom *ask* her doctor when he gives her a prescription?

A: One of the most dangerous problems that older adults face when taking drugs is how multiple drugs interact with each other. One quarter of the elderly take at least three drugs a day. The older they are, the more drugs they take. The more drugs they take, the greater the risk for an adverse reaction that could land them right in the hospital. That is why it's critical that your mom learns to ask questions rather than blindly take every drug given her.

A recent study in the *Journal of the American Medical Association* reported that drug reactions kill an estimated 100,000 people a year in U.S. hospitals. The researchers also claim that another 2.1 million are injured by adverse reactions. The elderly are especially vulnerable because of the number of drugs they take.

Chances are your mom has more than one chronic condition, so she gets to meet a number of specialists. As she visits one doctor after the next, she might walk away from each visit with a prescription in hand. If she forgets to tell a doctor about what she's taking, she's placed herself in danger of an adverse drug reaction.

Besides taking drugs that may negatively interact with each other, your mom might also be taking the same drug twice—and not know it. I've seen this happen when one doctor gives a drug in the *generic* name and another in the *brand* name. Because the names are different and the pills don't look alike, your mom may think she's taking two different medications. If the pharmacist or doctor doesn't pick this up, the double whammy could set off some pretty significant health problems.

Not all combinations of drugs are bad. For instance, a physician might prescribe an antiulcer medication with an anti-inflammatory medication. The doctor is doing this because the anti-inflammatory drug can cause severe irritation to the lining of the stomach. So, as a precautionary measure, he or she will prescribe the antiulcer drug.

So back to your original question: Here's my list of questions that I suggest your mom ask every doctor who gives her a prescription. It's also a list that you can copy and encourage your mom to ask any time she's given a new medication.

- What is the name of the medication (brand name *and* generic name)?
- What is the medication supposed to do?
- Why are you recommending that I take this?
- How often should I take the drug?
- How long should I take the drug?
- When should I take it? (Whenever I need to? Before, during, or after meals? At bedtime?)
- Should I avoid certain foods or alcohol when taking this drug? Should I stay out of the sun?
- Should this medicine be refrigerated?
- If I forget to take it, what should I do?
- What side effects might I expect? Under what circumstances should I call you?
- Is there any written material on this drug in lay terms?
- Is there something else I could try first, such as a change in diet, exercise or therapy?
- How much does this drug cost? (Let the doctor know if you cannot afford it. Ask if there is a generic substitute, which costs less.)

If you want to get understandable information on the drugs your mom is taking, the latest news on new drugs, clinical trials and health warnings, check out the National Library of Medicine's Web site at www.nlm.nih.gov/medlineplus/. It offers a guide to nine thousand prescription and over-the-counter medications. Just click on "Drug Information." This is one site I have bookmarked; it's excellent.

Q: What should my mom *tell* her doctor about all the pills she takes?

A: If your mom doesn't have one general practitioner quarterbacking all of the prescriptions she's taking, then you need to create your own playbook.

Make a chart that identifies her name, Social Security number and allergies, placing this information on the top of the chart. Then add four columns with the following headings: Name of the Drug, Dosage Level (e.g., 15 mg), Number of Pills a Day, and Time of Day. Simply list each medication she is taking and fill out the information for each under the headings.

This chart should be continuously updated and must be taken by your mom to each visit. It's smart to keep extra copies, so that if your mom becomes hospitalized, you can quickly grab a copy and give it to the physicians at the hospital or, in the case of an emergency, hand it to the paramedics.

Now it's your parent's turn to give information to the doctor. Here's what Mom or Dad should be telling her:

- The name of all prescription drugs they are taking, including how long and how frequently they've taken the drugs.
- Any over-the-counter drugs they're taking, such as cough medicine, aspirin or ibuprofen.
- Any vitamins they are taking.
- All allergies to medications and food.
- Any serious side effect they've had to a particular medication.
- If Mom or Dad has stopped taking a medication, your parent can't keep it a secret. They might not tell because they think it will upset the doctor; however, the physician needs to know since some medications work in combination with other drugs.
- Any concern about not being able to afford the medication. (Studies show that one in four elderly don't take the drugs they are prescribed because they can't afford them.)
- If they consume alcohol frequently (every few days or more).

The reason for all of this information sharing is to prevent serious medical problems for your mom. Research from the federal General Accounting Office reports that more than 5 million Americans use medications that are either inappropriate or could cause adverse interactions serious enough to warrant hospitalization.

You'll find that your mom's local pharmacist can be an excellent resource—if you just ask. You and your parents will find it helpful to ask the pharmacist the same list of questions that you asked the doctor. Hearing it twice and double-checking doesn't hurt. The pharmacist also can advise your mom about over-the-counter drugs, as to how they might interfere with your mom's medicines or might not be suitable for the geriatric population. Many pharmacies have additional consumer-friendly information on the drugs that they dispense, so ask for a copy.

Thanks to the computer age, almost all pharmacies keep a profile on what drugs customers take and all of their allergies. So when your mom is given a new medication, be sure to ask the pharmacist to run a scan on her profile to make sure that she won't have a problem with the new drug. The pharmacist is also the most up-to-date person on whether there is a generic available for the drug your mom has been prescribed. (You usually don't have to check with your doctor to substitute a generic.)

And when it comes to keeping track of multiple medications, ask your pharmacist about devices that can help your mom. (The pharmacist calls them "compliance aids.") To name a few, there are check-off calendars, containers for daily doses and bottle caps that beep when it's time to take a dose. They are definitely worth looking into, as taking the wrong dose can send your mom on an unexpected trip to the hospital. You can also check out my Caregiver Kit, which includes several tools to help your parents keep track of medications, at www.lindarhodes.com.

An excellent Web site with up-to-date consumer information on both prescription and over-the-counter medications can be found at www.nlm.nih.gov/medlineplus.

Q: I need to organize my dad's pill taking. What would you do?

A: First of all, it's a good idea to take your father to his primary physician or a physician certified in geriatrics to review all of his medications and give him a thorough physical to see what is going on. I recommend taking all of his prescription bottles to the doctor, so that the physician can see who has prescribed what medication and when it was prescribed. All too often, with our parents seeing so many specialists, one physician may not know what the other has prescribed. I've seen some older people taking the same medication twice because it was prescribed by two different doctors—one prescribing it in the generic form and the other in the brand name.

So your first stop is a review of all medications with his primary physician or a geriatrician. Local hospitals can give you names of physicians certified in geriatrics.

If your father lives alone, you need to set up a system so he will not mix up his medications. Here are some suggestions, some of which I've used for my mother as she cannot see very well and is on six different medications:

1. Purchase a "pill organizer" at the pharmacy. These plastic containers are found in a number of sizes: some are for one day, some for each day of the week and some for the entire week. Choose the one that your father will find easiest to use. The one that I prefer, if your dad needs to take medicines at different times of the day, is organized for seven days of the week with each day marked on top. Along the side are four rows marked for morning, noon, dinner and bedtime. You simply place the pills for each time of day in its space and he'll open it at the right time and take those pills. Every Saturday he should fill the organizer for the following week. If he has difficulty seeing,

perhaps either you or a friend can assist. Many of the full week pill organizers are designed so that a day's supply can pop out. That way if he is out for the day, he has a day's supply with him.

2. Buy round plain white stickers at least one inch in size and, in large print, write what each pill is for on one and stick it on top of the pill bottle. For example, if he is taking Lasix (diuretic) write WATER on the sticker; if he is taking a blood thinner like Plavix, write THINNER, or BP for a blood pressure medicine. By doing this, he'll be less likely to confuse the medications, especially given the hard-to-pronounce names of many generics. If color coding works, like a blue sticker for a water pill, then create a color coding system.

3. There are more sophisticated systems for dispensing pills, but you'll want to make sure that it is easy for him. Sharper Image, for example, sells an electronic pill organizer with alarms to remind him when to take each pill. You can also purchase a "talking prescription bottle." If your parent is visually impaired this is a terrific device that offers a digital audio recording on a label placed on the prescription bottle. Ask your local pharmacist if they would recommend a particular brand, or you can perform a search on the Internet by simply using the keywords "talking prescription bottle," and you'll find a number of companies that sell them.

4. Create a list of what medications your father is taking. List the drug, what it is for, who prescribed it, when they prescribed it, the dose and when it is to be taken each day. Your dad should take this list to every doctor appointment.

5. Keep track of any adverse reactions your father has on any drug (e.g., dizzy, confused, nauseated), so that when he is hospitalized or sees a new physician, he'll be able to alert them to problems he has had in the past with that particular drug. This list is in addition to any known allergic drug reactions.

6. Always talk with your dad's pharmacist. He or she can be an excellent resource on possible side effects, contraindications, and when to take each medication and under what conditions. This information is very important when your father starts taking more than three medications. Read and study those inserts that the pharmacist includes with each prescription. If you don't understand any of the directions or information, then give them a call.

7. Always let the doctor and pharmacist know of any over-the-counter drugs and vitamins your dad is taking, as these do interact with prescriptions.

My Caregiver Kit includes a number of tools to help your father keep track of his medications, store them and label them. You can check it out at www.lindarhodes.com.

Q: Just what is alternative medicine, anyway?

A: Complementary and alternative medicine (CAM) offers a wide array of health care practices such as homeopathic, naturopathic and Chinese medicine, biologically based therapies found in nature (herbs, foods, and vitamins), chiropractic or osteopathic manipulation, and energy therapies.

Getting the mind and body to work effectively with their *own* natural healing process is the mantra of the alternative medicine crowd. Once you delve into this field, you'll learn about detoxifying the body so that the immune system can resume its job, to fight the growth of cancer cells. Any parent pursuing this route of care will require a good dose of personal responsibility and initiative. Furthermore, alternative medicine is most successful when it is pursued as a partnership with your parent's physician. The bottom line is to keep everyone involved in your parent's care on the same page!

So who's who in the CAM lineup? The National Center for Complementary and Alternative Medicine (NCCAM) classifies CAM therapies into five categories. This is a brief recap of what they describe:

1. **Alternative Medical Systems.** These systems have evolved separately from the conventional medical approaches used in our country. Some of these systems include: homeopathic, naturopathic, chiropractic and, to some extent, osteopathic medicine. *Naturopathic* doctors (N.D.) are similar to a general practitioner as they are trained to use and prescribe a wide range of approaches in CAM that may include dietary, massage, exercise, acupuncture, minor surgery and various other interventions to assist their patients. *Homeopathic* doctors believe that "like cures like," meaning that small, very diluted quantities of medicinal substances are given to cure symptoms. If, however, these substances were given at greater or more concentrated doses, they would actually cause the very symptoms being treated. *Chiropractic* focuses on the relationship between bodily structure (especially the spine) and function, and how that relationship affects and restores health. Chiropractors use manipulative therapy as their integral treatment tool. *Osteopathic* medicine is also seen as a form of conventional medicine. These doctors (D.O.) believe that, in part, disease arises as a result of dysfunction in the musculoskeletal system, and that all of the body's systems work together. Disturbances in one system may affect function elsewhere in the body.

2. **Mind-Body Interventions.** The focus here is to enhance the mind's capacity to affect bodily function and symptoms by using techniques such as meditation, visualization,

prayer, mental healing, and therapies that use creative outlets such as art, music, yoga or dance.

3. **Biologically Based Therapies.** These therapies use substances found in nature, such as herbs, foods and vitamins. There are basically two schools of herbalists: Western and Chinese. Both camps believe that herbs can nurture and protect the immune system, especially during chemotherapy treatments.

4. **Manipulative and Body-based Methods.** These therapies use manipulation and/or movement of one or more parts of the body. Some examples include chiropractic or osteopathic manipulation, and a wide range of massage therapies.

5. **Energy Therapies.** There are two types. First is *biofield therapies* that are intended to affect energy fields that surround and penetrate the human body, by applying pressure and/or manipulating the body by placing the hands in, or through, these fields (e.g., qi gong, Reiki, and therapeutic touch massage). The second is *bioelectromagnetic-based therapies* involving the use of electromagnetic fields, such as pulsed fields, magnetic fields, or alternating current or direct current fields.

Within each of these systems there is a wide array of treatments—far too many to detail in this book.

Q: How do you find a reputable practitioner in alternative medicine?

A: With complementary and alternative medicine (CAM) offering such a wide array of health care practices, it can become very confusing to know who can best meet your needs. Here are some generic guidelines to follow in finding a qualified CAM practitioner:

1. **Find Good Referrals.** The first place to start is among family, friends and coworkers whom you respect. Ask if any of them have had a positive experience with a practitioner who has treated your health problem. Call local professional associations, as many offer lists of practitioners who are affiliated with them. Go to local support groups. For instance, your mother might call or go to a breast cancer support group and ask other women if they have had any positive outcomes with alternative medicine and by whom. Local health food stores often become an informal hub for people involved in alternative medicine. They know most of the practitioners in town and they can tell you if there is a formal alternative medicine network or newsletter. Once you start hearing the same name(s) of highly regarded practitioners among all of these sources, you know you have a good lead.

2. **Ask the Right Questions among Your Referrals.** In an excellent book, *Five Steps to Selecting the Best Alternative Medicine* by Mary and Michael Morton, they recommend that you ask your referral sources the following questions: *Why did you seek out this particular provider? What were your expectations and were they met? What is the provider's specialty? Did they listen to you and do they communicate well? Are they experts in a particular treatment or health condition? How many treatments did you have? Was it successful? Was their fee reasonable? What is their educational and clinical background?*

3. **Ask about Their Education and Clinical Training, and if They Are Licensed.** The first thing to know is the difference between someone telling you they are registered, certified or licensed. Registered simply means that they have submitted their name with some entity to have it listed—it is by no means a benchmark that they are qualified. If they are "certified" it usually means that a professional body reviewed their qualifications, set standards that the practitioner had to meet (e.g., graduating from an accredited school, spending a set amount of hours in clinical training) and then required the individual to take an exam to prove their knowledge. This is usually a solid marker of competency; however, you must also research the certifying body—if they are not credible, then neither is the certificate. "Licensed" means that the individual had to take a rigorous exam administered by state law and a state licensing body that also oversees any complaints and investigations over any licensed professional in the state. A license provides you with extra protection in finding a practitioner but it is not a gold seal.

Not all states license naturopathic doctors (N.D.). However, all states do license chiropractors (D.C.) and osteopaths (D.O.), which both fall under the alternative medicine system. You can call a state's State Department, which most likely runs the professional and occupational licensing board, to find out if they license any of the CAM professions. Without a licensing guidepost, it is very important for you to ask the provider to tell you where they received their education, if the school is accredited, and how many clinical hours they spent in training. There are several accredited naturopathic colleges, one of which is the well-known Bastyr University of Natural Sciences in Seattle, Washington. Be extremely leery of anyone who received their degree through a correspondence program. This holds true for a conventional doctor with M.D. behind their name. Just because they are a licensed medical doctor does not mean that they know how to practice holistic, integrative alternative medicine.

4. **Interview the Practitioner.** Now that you have done your research, you are in a position to meet with your potential CAM practitioner. Again, Mary and Michael Morton offer some very good sample questions for you: *After you have described your condition ask them what tests, treatment and techniques they would propose doing for you. Then ask:*

How will I know these treatments are working? How often and how many people have you treated with my condition? How do you keep informed on the latest research and treatments for my condition? What are the side effects? How long will it take for me to see results? Do you have patients that would be willing to talk to me about their experience with your practice?

Q: What are good consumer resources on alternative medicine?

A: The field of complementary and alternative medicine is exploding and it may seem overwhelming to you, so here are some national resources that can guide you through the world of alternative medicine:

1. **Contact the American Holistic Medical Association (AHMA).** This is the oldest association in the United States representing physicians (MDs and DOs) who practice alternative medicine—in fact, the internationally known integrative medicine physician Dr. Andrew Weil is a member. You may contact them to find members who practice in your area and those who have become board certified in CAM by requesting a printed directory. Write to them at American Holistic Medical Association, 12101 Menaul Blvd. NE, Suite C, Albuquerque, NM 87112, or visit their Web site at www.holisticmedicine.org. The American College for Advancement in Medicine also provides referrals to alternative MDs in the United States, and they can be reached at (800) 532-3688 or www.acam.org. If you'd like to find a referral of a Chinese medicine practitioner then contact the American Association of Oriental Medicine (AAOM) at www.aaom.org or call (866) 455-7999.

2. **Check Out Programs at Your Local Hospital.** More hospitals are adding CAM or "integrative" medicine to their list of health care services. Call them to find out if they have any special programs in CAM, or any physicians who have trained in the field. A growing number of hospitals are now offering programs in Reiki, shiatsu, acupuncture, massage, nutrition consultations, meditation, imagery and hypnosis.

3. **The Moss Reports.** Internationally recognized, Ralph Moss, Ph.D., has authored eleven books on cancer and alternative medicine, and is a founding member of the National Institutes of Health Alternative Medicine Advisory Council. If you want an extensive, in-depth and comprehensive report on your particular cancer, detailing conventional and alternative therapies available to you with Moss's top recommendations on the most

effective therapies, with contact information, then consider ordering a Moss Report. Visit his Web site www.cancerdecisions.com or call (800) 980-1234.

4. **Web Sites and Books.** Many CAM practitioners may recommend supplements and other nutrition products. As a way of sorting through what claims are valid about these products and which are exaggerations, consumers can visit www.consumerlab.com. This group provides, and posts online, independent test results and information to help consumers and healthcare professionals evaluate health, wellness and nutrition products. The National Foundation for Alternative Medicine (www.NFAM.org) investigates, validates and reports on clinics throughout the world that demonstrate promising treatment options for degenerative diseases. For a solid, commercial Web site go to www.alternativemedicine.com, connecting you to many of the developments in the field. This group has also published a book, *Cancer Diagnosis: What to Do Next* by W. John Diamond, M.D., and Lee Cowden, M.D. And finally, another top notch resource is *Healing Outside the Margins: The Survivor's Guide to Integrative Cancer Care* by Carole O'Toole and Carolyn Hendricks, M.D.

4

Living with Chronic Illness

Q: **What are the top ten signs that your parent needs help?**

A: Many older relatives won't ask for help because they fear that they'll be a burden to their families. Or they think that if their children see any sign of dependence, they'll jump to the conclusion that it's not safe for them to live on their own. A dear friend of mine fell in her bathroom and was unconscious for a short period of time. She kept the incident from her daughter because, as she put it, "They'll make me move in with them, but I don't want to move to another city even though they'll be wonderful to me." Yet my friend was frightened by the incident, so we explored new housing options. She's now thriving in her apartment, surrounded by a new set of friends along with assisted living support when and if she needs it.

Rather than expecting loved ones to tell you they could use some help, there are things that you can look for whenever you visit. Recently, the Home Instead Senior Care Advisory Board (www.homeinstead.com) released its take on ten telltale signs that your older relative may need assistance or additional companionship. Here is their list:

1. **Household Bills Piling Up.** The simple task of opening and responding to daily mail, as well as balancing a checkbook, may become overwhelming, particularly if eyesight is deteriorating. Look for overdue bills, utilities being turned off due to lack of payment and other creditor issues.

2. **Reluctance to Leave the House.** Seniors who are having trouble walking, remembering directions, seeing or hearing will slowly pull away from their community and isolate themselves, which can lead to loneliness, depression and malnutrition.

3. **Losing Interest in Preparing/Eating Meals.** Are excessive amounts of junk and convenience food around the house? Is outdated food in the refrigerator or are there signs of excessive weight loss? Poor diet can increase the risk of dementia in seniors and weaken the immune system.

4. **Declining Personal Hygiene.** Take note of unkempt hair, body odor, unshaven faces and wearing clothing that is unclean, unchanged for days or inappropriate for the weather. Doing the laundry or getting in and out of the tub may be too physically challenging. Many who live alone also fear slipping and falling in a shower or bathtub.

5. **Decline in Driving Skills.** Look for evidence of parking or speeding tickets, fender benders, dents or scratches on the car as signs that driving skills may be deteriorating. Decreased ability to see, poor sense of direction, inability to merge into traffic and slow reaction time are a recipe for disaster.

6. **Signs of Scorched Pots and Pans.** This may be a sign of short-term memory loss or even the onset of Alzheimer's, as pots used in cooking are left on the open flame of the stove and burn. Fire is one of the greatest safety concerns that families of older relatives face.

7. **Symptoms of Depression.** Depression causes marked changes in behavior and one's daily routine over time. Be on guard for increased listlessness, not wanting to get dressed, decreased visits with family and friends, change in sleeping patterns (sleeping long periods or not sleeping at all), and lack of interest in usual hobbies and activities.

8. **Missed Doctors' Appointments and Social Engagements.** While this can be a symptom of increased forgetfulness, it is often simply a result of not having transportation and not knowing how to access transportation options.

9. **Unkempt House.** Changes in housekeeping may occur simply because it is too difficult or tiring. From dirty laundry to dirty dishes, these everyday tasks become too much to handle on their own.

10. **Losing Track of Medications.** Missed doses and medication mistakes (overdosing and running out of pills before the next prescription can be refilled) can lead to very serious medical complications.

Q: **Does seeing a geriatrician make a difference?**

A: The short answer? Yes. A RAND-UCLA study published in the *Annals of Internal Medicine* found that two out of three older patients with health problems threatening their independence do *not* receive the health care they need for geriatric or age-related conditions like malnutrition, pressure sores, dementia, incontinence, osteoarthritis, falls and mobility disorders. One out of two do not receive adequate care for ischemic heart disease and pneumonia.

Those numbers are downright alarming. Imagine any other business where two out of three customers didn't receive the services they paid for. It certainly wouldn't be around very long. The researchers contend that the health care system must take major steps to improve primary care physicians' diagnosis and treatment of diseases of aging, such as dementia, mobility disorders, urinary incontinence and osteoarthritis.

But while they're calling for reforms within the health care system, what should your parents do? They would do well to have a geriatric assessment by a team of physicians, nurses, therapists and social workers who are all specially trained in geriatrics. This would provide them with a comprehensive workup on their health status by a team of professionals who will view them as a whole person. All too often, older people see different kinds of physicians for each bodily system or part: cardiologists for their heart, podiatrists for their feet, ophthalmologists for their eyes, urologists for their kidneys and the list goes on. If these doctors aren't on the same page, they won't be aware of how the treatment and prescriptions each of them prescribes interacts with the others.

To find a geriatric assessment center near your parents, call your local hospitals and ask if they offer such a service or could provide you with a list of geriatric specialists. Most university-based hospitals have a geriatric specialty and perform such assessments. You can also call the American Geriatrics Society at (212) 308-1414 or visit their Web site at www.americangeriatrics.org. They can send you a list of physicians certified in geriatrics or e-mail the information to you. If you can't find a center, then look for physicians who have received certification in geriatrics by taking special courses and passing an exam. Ask the physician if he or she had a fellowship or received certification in geriatrics. The benefit of having a physician who has specialized in geriatrics is his or her ability to "piece things together." This type of doctor understands the physiological changes of aging and knows what's normal and what's not. He or she will also have a better appreciation of how medications interact with your parent's physiological changes. This is especially helpful since many drugs prescribed to the elderly were never tested on older subjects.

You can also find local internists who've received certification in geriatrics by writing to the American Board of Internal Medicine, 510 Walnut Street, Suite 1700, Philadelphia, PA 19106 and asking them for a list of local certified physicians. They only take letter requests in writing. You can send them a request by fax at (215) 446-3590.

One of the lead researchers of the RAND-UCLA study, Dr. Paul Shekelle, says, "Family members and patients need to make sure that everything is being done for age-related ailments, just as they would speak up if their chest pain wasn't being attended to."

Q: What is a geriatric care manager?

A: If you've been trying to juggle long-distance caregiving or you need professional advice on how to organize your parent's care, a geriatric care manager can be a godsend. These are members of a relatively new field of social workers, counselors and nurses who will assess, organize, monitor and manage your parent's caregiving needs. For example, they'll meet with your parent, conduct an assessment to identify his needs, determine his eligibility for a host of services, make arrangements for those services, interview home health care and senior care workers, monitor them, arrange for transportation to and from doctors' appointments, analyze financial, legal or medical information—they'll even oversee a move from your father's home to assisted living, a nursing home or retirement community.

Fees range from $50 to $150 per hour, depending upon the care manager's credentials and experience. Some charge by the hour while others charge set fees for a package of services. The initial assessment may cost from $150 to $350 and then, based upon your parent's needs, you and the geriatric care manager agree on a monthly fee. Make sure all of this is in writing and that you have clear expectations of what services will be performed.

When you interview a geriatric care manager, there are a number of questions you should ask:

- What services do you provide and who provides them?
- What are your credentials? Are you licensed in your profession?
- How long have you been providing care management services? How long have you been practicing in this community?
- Do you have any affiliations and memberships in community organizations?
- Are you available for emergencies? Who do you have on backup if you are not available?
- What can I expect to learn from your initial assessment? What does it include (e.g., physical and mental status, financial resources)? Who conducts the medical component, and what are their qualifications?
- How do you perform quality checks on the service providers and referrals you recommend?
- How do you communicate information to me about my parent and how often?

- How often will you have face-to-face contact with my parent?
- How many cases do you handle at one time?
- What are your fees and can you provide me with references?

It is very important for you to do your homework by checking out their references and asking them these questions because this is essentially an unregulated industry. Anyone can put up a shingle and call themselves a geriatric care manager. So ask if they have received any type of certification, where it is from and if they are a member of the National Association of Professional Geriatric Care Managers (a nonprofit association, not a credentialing institution).

To track down a geriatric care manager, call the National Association of Professional Geriatric Care Managers at (520) 881-8008 or visit their Web site at www.caremanager.org. On their site go to "Find a Care Manager," where you can search by state and ZIP code for a local manager, with a description of what services they offer and which degrees they hold. You will also find them listed in the Yellow Pages, usually under Social Workers, Eldercare and/or Home Health Care.

If your parent is low or moderate income, he or she may qualify for geriatric care management through their local Area Agency on Aging. You can find it by calling the Eldercare Locator at (800) 677-1116.

Q: Could my dad be showing signs of diabetes?

A: Three of the major symptoms of diabetes are extreme thirst or hunger, fatigue and itchy skin. Other common symptoms are weight loss, blurred vision, sores that don't heal and increased urination, especially at night. So, if your dad is showing any of these signs, get him to a doctor.

Most people think of diabetes as a childhood disease. But nearly one in twelve people over sixty-five comes down with what is known as adult-onset, or Type 2, diabetes. If your dad is over eighty-five, he is much more at risk of being affected by diabetes. One in four people in their mid-eighties and older becomes diabetic.

If your dad is also overweight and inactive, he's dramatically increasing his odds of becoming diabetic. Diabetes is the seventh-highest cause of death among the elderly and the leading cause of blindness for those who are middle-aged and over.

And it doesn't end there. With diabetes your dad's body can't regulate the level of glucose in his system. Without a regulator in charge, too little glucose reaches the body's cells. This badly affects the cells' performance, as they don't function or reproduce. At the same time, too much glucose hangs out in the bloodstream, running amok throughout the body, leaving in its wake hardened arteries, damage to the retinas, skin disorders and a deteriorated nervous system.

Make sure your father has a blood sugar level test (prick on the finger) as part of his annual cholesterol exam. The American Diabetes Association warns that of the sixteen million adults with diabetes, about five million aren't even aware of it, and only one in four people diagnosed with the disease is receiving proper treatment. Why? Many of the symptoms appear to be age-related, so older people think it is just part of the "aging package" and many people remain symptom-free until real damage has been done. Women actually get diabetes more often than men. African-Americans, people with high blood pressure and those who have parents or siblings with diabetes are at greater risk of acquiring diabetes. So if your dad *is* diagnosed with diabetes, you'll need to monitor your own health.

The doctor will probably recommend some lifestyle changes to your father, such as losing weight, exercising and following a diabetic diet. Insulin therapy, which will stimulate insulin secretion to get fuel levels regulated, might also be in order. Medicare covers some diabetic supplies, so be sure to check with your doctor's office as to what is covered.

Few patients take to this new routine like fish to water. Old habits, especially when they involve food, are hard to change. Become your dad's trainer and help with food preparation, exercising and medications. If you're worried he is not eating properly, hire someone (or take it upon yourself) to prepare meals for the week that are diabetic-friendly and freeze them in microwavable containers. Meals on Wheels programs also provide diabetic meals. Call your local senior center to find the program that's closest to your dad.

An excellent Web site with links to plenty of other top-notch sites is by the National Institute of Diabetes & Digestive & Kidney Diseases at www.niddk.nih.gov. Be sure to check out their "Am I at Risk for Type 2 Diabetes" online publication. The American Diabetes Association is another great resource. Call them at (800) 342-2383 or visit them on the Web at www.diabetes.org. Your father's blood sugar will need to be monitored every day with a blood-testing meter. Also watch out for his foot care; since he is vulnerable to nerve damage, he might not notice injuries to his feet. Infections can easily set in, placing him at risk for amputation.

And if *you're* over forty-five, the American Diabetes Association recommends that you add to your annual physical—or at least every three years—a blood glucose check, even if you don't have symptoms.

Q: How do I warn my diabetic mother about taking care of her feet?

A: In response to a column I wrote on Type 2 diabetes, a reader was inspired to send me the following letter. It is so compelling that I asked her if I could share it.

"Your column relating to diabetes was particularly noteworthy to me. My mom is one of those older people that developed Type 2 Diabetes about 15 years ago. Her condition has been exacerbated due to her failure to fully appreciate the devastating health effects that this disease may precipitate. She continued to smoke, did not lose her excess weight, and did not fully curb her sugar intake.

Recently, the effects of the disease (along with her associated high blood pressure) have reared their ugly head, and she's been hospitalized for about 3 weeks now, having undergone an artery bypass surgery in her leg to restore better blood circulation to her foot and ankle. Unfortunately, however, due to a foot ulcer that could not heal, she has had one toe amputated. She continued to struggle with an infection in her foot, and just underwent a transmetatarsal amputation. She's become bedridden due to the need for her foot to heal properly, and must undergo extensive physical therapy to restore her mobility. I am sharing these details with you because, obviously, the subject of your column hit very close to home and I think two simple points should be further emphasized. First, people diagnosed with Type 2 Diabetes need to take the diagnosis seriously from the minute they receive it. Weight management, sugar control and exercise can go far to limit the devastating effects that this disease can cause. By reducing your weight, it's easier on all bodily systems to manage glucose intolerance. Exercising increases blood flow and mitigates small and large blood vessel disease (plaque buildup) as well as high blood pressure.

Second, proper foot care is essential. Never walk barefooted. Make sure any cuts or sores to your feet receive immediate medical attention. If you are not able to wash your feet properly, don't be proud—ask for help."

D. K.

As D. K. says, diabetes can cause nerve damage (peripheral neuropathy) that reduces sensation in the foot. Small injuries can occur and your parent won't even notice it, which may lead to an infection. Since diabetes often affects blood flow in legs and feet, cuts or sores are very difficult to heal.

Life Clinic offers an excellent checklist on foot care for anyone with diabetes (www .lifeclinic.com):

DAILY FOOT CARE FOR DIABETICS:

- Look for cuts or sores
- Check for warning signs: redness, swelling, warmth, pain, slow healing, dry cracks, bleeding corns or calluses, tenderness, loss of sensation
- Wash your feet daily and dry them carefully, especially between the toes
- Use talcum powder
- Put your feet up when sitting
- Wiggle your toes and move your ankles up and down for five minutes, two or three times a day
- Don't cross your legs for long periods of time
- Do not cut corns or calluses—see a foot care specialist if needed
- Keep toenails trimmed and smooth
- Promptly treat dry skin or athlete's foot
- Keep blood glucose under control
- Wear shoes and socks at all times
- Keep a pair of slippers next to the bed
- Don't wear shoes or socks that are too tight
- Wear well-cushioned shoes
- Wear shoes that are roomy and "breathe"

Medicare covers annual foot exams by foot specialists (podiatrists) for anyone with diabetes. People diagnosed with neuropathy are covered twice a year. In fact, diabetics should make it a habit to take off their shoes and socks at every physician visit for a preventive foot exam. Medicare also covers therapeutic shoes if a physician certifies that your parent has diabetes and has one or more complicating conditions in one or both feet.

For an excellent booklet, "Prevent Diabetes Problems: Keep Your Feet and Skin Healthy (DM-205)," call the National Diabetes Information Clearinghouse at (800) 860-8747 and ask for a free copy or visit their Web site at www.niddk.nih.gov. Also call (800) DIABETES for a sample "Survival Kit" by the American Diabetes Association.

Q: Why do my parents get so depressed during the holidays?

A: For older adults, the holidays are often bittersweet: Your mom and dad may become more aware of the passing of time, the absence of their parents, the loss of their siblings and friends who have died, and the distance of loved ones who can no longer celebrate the season with them. Many family traditions that they once looked forward to are now gone. It's easy to see how the picture-perfect images of the holidays—when seen through the lens of real life—never come into focus.

Dr. Roger Cadieux, Clinical Professor of Psychiatry, Pennsylvania State University College of Medicine in Hershey, sheds further light on holiday blues: "The holidays are potentially both joyous and stressful, especially for the elderly. It is a time of high expectations and anticipation. If the expectations are not realized, then the individual may feel very disappointed and even guilty. The elderly, whose physical and emotional stamina is not at a level of their children, grandchildren and other relatives, are all the more vulnerable to depression.

"And widows or widowers," Dr. Cadieux warns, "may experience an *anniversary reaction* around the holidays. They are reminded of what they had and, unfortunately, what they have lost, and may become very depressed at this time of year."

So what do you do? Dr. Cadieux and the American Geriatric Psychiatry Association suggest that you do *not* ignore it. Instead, try to anticipate those who may become depressed at holiday time, or be sensitive to the signs and symptoms of depression and attempt to make an early intervention. A candid discussion about how they are doing *emotionally* may be both revealing and useful.

Here's what the American Geriatric Psychiatry Association recommends:

• Acknowledge that the holidays can be difficult, and that you have mixed feelings, too. Many people don't want to admit that life is not always as cheerful as portrayed in the media or in advertisements.
• If the older individual is not eating or has lost weight, you might start by gently asking about their appetite, or why they do not seem interested in food or preparing for the holidays as they have in the past.
• Once you have gotten past the initial awkwardness, you may be surprised to learn that your loved one will talk to you. At that point, it is up to you to listen and offer support.

• Too often, younger friends or family members do not want to hear some of the less than pleasant aspects—emotional and physical—of growing older. But one of the most important things you can do is listen.

If you notice a dramatic change in your parents' behavior surrounding the holidays—no decorations adorn the house, cards aren't sent like always or they don't care about sharing gifts—then gently ask what's going on. Perhaps they'd be open to creating a new tradition, such as doing something spiritual to honor the memory of a deceased loved one, or planning an event that you ask them to be in charge of. Some older adults miss their old role of *hosting* family events as they are now relegated to being a *guest*.

I'd also suggest acknowledging lost loved ones with a toast in their honor at dinner or another family event. Take time out to celebrate their life and show how their spirit lives on through the family. Some people think that by "not bringing it up," they'll make the survivor feel better. But on the contrary, the survivor often feels sad that everyone is acting like nothing has changed—as if the loved one didn't matter anymore. Sure, it might bring a tear or two, but those tears will heal the heart much more than silence. Being open to their sadness may be a gift in itself.

Q: My mother is very depressed. How do I talk to her?

A: It's so hard to see people we love suffering and it's not uncommon for us to be at a loss for words when it comes to consoling them when they are experiencing mental pain. It seems easier to cheer someone on following a broken hip, a short illness or even a heart attack. These will mend and the older person can look forward to resuming their life pretty much as they knew it. But depression affects the very way we look at life: our mood, how we think, how we see things, how we act; it even changes our biochemistry.

Getting older requires coping with quite a few losses. Chances are your mom has lost some of her independence from diminished sight, hearing or the ability to physically get around. Driving becomes more difficult, so parents stop going anywhere at night, while many figure it's not worth fighting traffic to visit friends or go to events they used to enjoy. Death steals away old friends and beloved spouses. Many older people begin to feel like a burden to those around them, so they'd rather not ask for help. Soon they become isolated. What a ripe environment for depression to take hold!

Most of us at one time or another will feel the "blues." It's usually short-lived and in reaction to an event in our lives that has us feeling down. But depression can lead to what psychiatrists term a "mood disorder," an illness that often requires both therapy and medications to treat.

According to the Diagnostic and Statistical Manual of Mental Disorders (DSM), there are nine symptoms of major depression: *changes in mood* (especially feeling consistently sad), *lack of pleasure, changes in eating patterns* (eats too little or too much), *changes in sleeping patterns* (can't sleep or sleeps much more), *changes in activity level* (reacts slowly, as in a haze, or is easily agitated and restless), *lack of energy, changes in perception of self* (feels worthless), *lack of focus* (can't make decisions), *lack of future* (life isn't worth living, hopeless). If your mother has been exhibiting these behaviors, it's best for her to see a professional as it is unlikely that she is going to just "snap out of it" on her own. Depression is an illness and should be treated as such; you'd be taking Mom or Dad to the doctor if either of them had the flu—so too with depression.

And what do you say to your mom? I recommend *Talking to Depression: Simple Ways to Connect When Someone in Your Life Is Depressed* by Claudia J. Strauss. This terrific book makes depression easier to understand and walks you through the day-to-day interaction of relating to a loved one who is depressed. Here are some of Strauss's do's and don'ts of approaching someone with depression:

- Don't say, "It's not that bad." Do say, "It sounds really bad. I'm sorry."
- Don't say, "Things could be worse." Do say, "I wish I knew how to help."
- Don't say, "There's light at the end of the tunnel." Do say, "We're going to get you through this. I'll help in any way I can."
- Don't say, "Buck up." Do say, "It's okay; this is going to take time—a lot of time."
- Don't say, "It's God's will." Do say, "You're right, this will never make sense."
- Don't say, "Put it behind you and move on." Do say, "I wish it didn't have to be this way."

If someone you love is depressed, reach out to her and quietly listen, learn about the disorder and get her professional assistance.

Q: What can my mother do about her incontinence?

A: When June Lockhart of *Lassie* fame starred in an adult briefs commercial, incontinence officially came out of the closet. That's the good news. The bad news is that it gave everyone the impression that incontinence is a normal part of aging and the only thing you can do is to get yourself some adult briefs: wrong on both counts.

Incontinence (now also termed "overactive bladder") affects at least eighteen million Americans, but it is not normal. About 25 percent of men over sixty-five face some degree of incontinence, along with 40 percent of women in that age range. Before your mom resigns herself to adult briefs, she needs to be seen by an internist or urologist to determine the cause of the disorder. Medications, an acute illness, a urinary tract infection or endocrine problems can all cause incontinence. It also could be the symptom of an underlying disease, and that's why she needs to see a physician.

A common sign and consequence of incontinence is isolation. All too often, people affected with the condition stop going on trips, to the movies and on outings with their friends because they live in constant fear of having an accident.

Chances are your mom won't be inclined to talk about her incontinence. So you might want to gently explore the topic by mentioning you read an article on overactive bladder and that you were surprised to learn that it's not a normal part of aging, that it can be the sign of something else, it may be reversible and it's something that some of her friends may be going through too. There are three major types of incontinence:

Stress Incontinence. The muscles of the pelvic floor, which have been dutifully supporting the bladder for all these years, become weakened—mostly due to the wear and tear of childbirth. The bladder slips down without that muscle support and now the abdominal muscles can squeeze the bladder to leak out urine, as when she coughs.

Overflow Incontinence. Urine in the bladder builds up to a point where the muscle that controls the flow (urinary sphincter) can't hold it. Urine leaks out throughout the day. Men who have an enlarged prostate are especially vulnerable as the prostate blocks the normal flow of urine, causing it to hold up in the bladder until it overflows.

Urge Incontinence. In this case, there's hardly any time between feeling the need to void and actually urinating. This might be caused by an infection or medications, which would make it reversible. If your mom has had a stroke or suffers from dementia or another neurological disorder, it can mean that the brain is no longer capable of sending "hold off" signals to the bladder.

Here are some basic tips to share with your mother:

• Schedule bathroom trips before the urge to urinate.
• Shut down drinking liquids three hours before going to bed.

- Eliminate drinks that irritate the bladder, such as coffee, tea, and sodas with caffeine. Alcoholic drinks also make this hit list.
- Stay clear of foods that are not bladder-friendly, such as sugar, chocolate, spicy foods and grapefruit.
- Inhaled cigarette smoke irritates the bladder. No smoking in the house.
- Take medications, especially diuretics, on a schedule that won't result in getting up in the middle of the night to urinate or waking up to soaked sheets. This also can save a nasty fall while groping to find the way to the toilet.
- When out at an event, know where the restrooms are before they are needed. Try to find seating closest to the rest rooms.
- Try bladder training by scheduling bathroom trips and slowly extending the time between them to train the bladder to "hold it."
- In extreme cases, surgery might be needed to remove a blockage, repair the urethra or reposition the bladder. Medications, pelvic devices, collagen injections and catheters are other possibilities, as well as wearing adult briefs.

Two great resources for more information are: Simon Foundation for Continence ([800] 237-4666; www.simonfoundation.org) and the National Association for Continence ([800] 252-3337; www.nafc.org).

Q: **We were told that my mom had a ministroke. Are there different kinds of strokes?**

A: It sounds like your mom had a TIA, which stands for a *transient ischemic attack,* a temporary deficiency in the brain's blood supply. These usually come on suddenly and last from two to thirty minutes. The symptoms are similar to a stroke but they are temporary and reversible. So your mom probably got dizzy, might not have been able to see and experienced slurred speech for a few minutes before returning to normal. This is a warning sign. About one-third of all strokes are preceded by a TIA, and half of those will strike within a year.

I am sure her doctor has given her a list of things that she can do to prevent a stroke, such as keep her blood pressure down, maintain a healthy weight, exercise and eat a well-balanced diet. If she smokes she should absolutely stop, and if she has diabetes or heart disease, she needs to manage these conditions so they don't contribute to a stroke.

There are two kinds of strokes—now often referred to as "brain attacks." With an *ischemic* stroke, an artery carrying blood to the brain is blocked, usually by fatty material. The lack of blood and oxygen damages the part of the brain that didn't receive them. In a *hemorrhagic* stroke, the blood and oxygen make it to the brain, but the vessel carrying them bursts and leaks blood into the brain, destroying brain cells in its wake. A stroke caused by hemorrhaging inside of the brain is considered more dangerous and is involved in about 17 percent of stroke cases. Both of these types of strokes may be referred to as a cerebrovascular accident.

Strokes are America's number three killer, right after heart attacks and cancer. You and your mom should be aware of the symptoms. The American Heart Association lists the following stroke signals:

- Sudden weakness or numbness of the face, arm, and leg on one side of the body.
- Sudden confusion, trouble speaking or understanding.
- Dimness or loss of vision, particularly in one eye.
- Sudden trouble walking, dizziness, loss of balance or coordination.
- Sudden severe headache with no known cause.

These symptoms definitely warrant calling 911. You should also be aware that a study of 38,000 Medicare patients—all of whom had strokes—revealed that patients who were seen by a neurologist within seventy-two hours had a much better recovery and survival rate than those who were not. The researchers contended that these specialists of the nervous system were better prepared to diagnose and treat a stroke quickly.

The only FDA-approved treatment for stroke is an intravenous clot-breaking drug known as TPA. Because the drug must be given within three critical hours from the onset of stroke symptoms, there is no time to waste in making a correct diagnosis. (It is not a drug to be given to a patient suffering a hemorrhagic stroke since it may cause bleeding, which would make matters worse.) Tragically, only 2–4 percent of stroke patients ever receive TPA—experts believe it is because patients coming into emergency rooms are not being treated quickly enough by stroke experts.

The message for you? Call your local hospitals and ask for the patient advocate. Ask if their hospital has a written plan on how they treat acute stroke patients. Is there a neurologist available at all times? Do they have a special stroke program? You might want to consider using the hospital that has this expertise. If your mom has a stroke, once you get to the emergency room request that she be seen by a neurologist quickly.

The National Institute of Neurological Disorders and Stroke has a top-notch Web site describing brain attacks and prevention strategies. Visit them at www.ninds.nih.gov. Also go to the National Stroke Association's site at www.stroke.org. You can also call them for information about family support groups and their services at (800) STROKES.

Q: **What is glaucoma and does Medicare cover its treatment?**

A: Yes, Medicare covers screenings every twelve months for people at high risk of glaucoma. According to Medicare, nearly three million people have glaucoma, which is a leading cause of blindness in the United States. Although anyone can get glaucoma, some people are at higher risk. They include:

• African-Americans over the age of forty
• Anyone over the age of sixty
• People with a family history of glaucoma
• People with diabetes

Note that Medicare won't automatically cover everyone over sixty. An eye-care professional, certified by Medicare to conduct the screening, has to state that the individual is at risk and should be tested. Be sure to ask the eye-care provider if he or she is Medicare certified so that the test will be covered. Your parents will pay 20 percent of the Medicare-approved amount after they pay their yearly Part B deductible. If they have a Medigap policy, that will cover the 20 percent.

The most common form of glaucoma is open-angled glaucoma. At the front of the eye, there is a small space known as the anterior chamber, in which clear fluid flows in and out to bathe and nourish nearby tissues. In glaucoma, the fluid drains too slowly out of the eye, causing the fluid to build up. This, in turn, creates pressure inside the eye. Unless this pressure is controlled, it may cause damage to the optic nerve and other parts of the eye. The end result can be partial or total blindness.

Glaucoma is downright sneaky. Chances are your parent won't complain of any symptoms. There's rarely any pain or loss of vision in the early stages. But as the disease progresses, a person with glaucoma may notice a decrease in their peripheral vision—the ability to see things off to the side. If this isn't treated, the disease worsens, narrowing the field of vision and finally leading to blindness.

Your parent might be given an "air puff" test or other tests used to measure eye pressure in an eye examination. But experts warn that this test alone cannot detect glaucoma. Glaucoma is found most often during an eye examination when the pupils are dilated, allowing an eye-care professional to see more of the inside of the eye.

Open-angle glaucoma cannot be cured but it usually can be controlled. The most common treatments are eyedrops, pills, laser surgery or surgery to help fluid escape from the eye and thereby reduce the pressure. The goal is to stop the disease from getting worse.

There are a number of organizations that can help you better understand glaucoma. Be sure to check out:

The Glaucoma Foundation (www.glaucomafoundation.org). The Glaucoma Foundation Web site contains excellent information on the causes, detection, treatment and new developments in combating glaucoma. The Glaucoma Foundation can also be contacted by calling (800) GLAUCOMA, (800) 452-8266.

National Eye Institute (NEI) (www.nei.nih.gov). The NEI Web site contains eye health information on the most common eye disorders and their treatments. It also identifies available consumer eye-care resources. There is no toll-free number.

Prevent Blindness America (www.preventblindness.org). The Prevent Blindness America Web site offers many programs and services to help fight blindness and save sight. You can find many consumer resources, basic eye tests and information on all eye services. You can reach them by calling (800) 331-2020.

Q: My mom says women rarely get heart attacks. Is she right?

A: I know mothers are hardly ever wrong (at least that is what mine has told me) but your mom is dead wrong on this one. Heart disease is the number one killer of women in the United States today, affecting one in nine over the age of forty-five. But the statistic that should really get your mom's attention is that heart disease affects one in three women by age sixty-five. Women who are overweight, smoke or have diabetes are at even more risk. Heart disease tends to strike women ten years later than men—after menopause—when female heart vessels are more prone to develop plaque.

So the bottom line is to get your mother a thorough physical, including a heart exam. Heart attacks in many women often go unrecognized until it is too late. This is due partly to the public's misconception that heart attacks are a "guy thing," and because women may experience less classic signs of a heart attack (such as chest pains).

The American Heart Association lists the following less obvious symptoms that women may experience as warning signs of a heart attack:

- Shortness of breath
- Pain in the abdomen, back, jaw or throat
- A general sensation of uneasiness, just feeling sick
- Unexplained anxiety
- Weakness or fatigue
- Palpitations, cold sweat or paleness
- Chest discomfort lasting more than a few minutes, or recurring chest discomfort, with light-headedness, fainting, sweating, nausea or shortness of breath

These symptoms are definitely worth paying attention to as almost a half million women annually die of heart disease, and half of that number die from a fatal heart attack. Within six years, one-third of the women who had a heart attack will have a second attack—twice the number experienced by men. The death rate from heart disease in African-American women is 70 percent higher than that of men. Heart disease is the number one killer of African-American women over the age of twenty-five.

Heart disease can take a number of forms:

Atherosclerosis is a thickening and hardening of the inner walls of the arteries. The walls become narrower due to plaque buildup from deposits of fat, cholesterol and other substances. This creates an environment for blood clots to form that block blood flow, resulting in heart attacks and strokes.

Coronary Artery Disease affects the blood vessels (or coronary arteries) of the heart. It causes angina (chest pain) as a result of some part of the heart not receiving enough blood. This eventually leads to a heart attack. The most common trigger for angina is physical exertion.

High Blood Pressure (or Hypertension) affects the force of blood being pumped from the heart against the walls of your blood vessels. More than half of all women over age fifty-five suffer from this potentially serious condition. It is more common and more severe in African-American women.

Heart Failure essentially means that the heart is not able to pump blood through the body as well as it should. This condition usually evolves slowly over time, and though the term "failure" implies that the heart literally stops, it does *not*. It simply means the heart is failing to do its job at its expected level.

Lifestyle changes such as losing weight, exercising, eating heart-healthy diets and quitting smoking are often in order. The Jewish Healthcare Foundation recently launched an excellent "Working Hearts" campaign focusing on women, called "Take Ten." Women are urged to take ten minutes every day to do something healthy for their hearts—such as taking a short walk, using steps rather than an elevator, parking a little farther from the mall, or getting up to answer the phone instead of keeping it right beside them—and another ten minutes to relax and lower blood pressure, by reading, meditating, trying yoga, praying, petting a dog or cat, or watching a sunset. Taking ten minutes here and there every day is great medicine for both body and soul.

For more information on heart disease and other conditions affecting women, visit www.4woman.gov or call their toll-free number at (800) 994-WOMAN (9662). And, of course, check out the American Heart Association's Web site at www.americanheart.org.

Q: How do I stop my dad from getting bedsores?

A: As you may know, your father's skin becomes more fragile with age. Lying in one position for long periods of time can irritate his sensitive skin, especially in weight-bearing, bony areas such as the heels, elbows, and tailbone, where *pressure* decreases the blood flow. Sometimes you'll hear the term "pressure sores" rather than bedsores for this reason. Other terms for bedsores are decubitus ulcers, ischemic ulcers or pressure ulcers. If your dad isn't being routinely repositioned or "turned" while he is bedridden, his skin will begin to get red and tender from the constant pressure. If not treated immediately, an open wound will develop, which becomes a prime source for infections.

According to the National Pressure Ulcer Advisory Panel there are four stages of decubitus ulcers.

Stage I. The surface of the skin is reddened yet is unbroken, and appears like a light sunburn. You need to determine the cause of the pressure and alleviate it. This is an early warning sign to turn the patient and reduce the pressure by covering, protecting, and/or cushioning the reddened area. An increase in vitamin C, proteins and fluids is recommended.

Stage II. A blister (broken or unbroken) appears, injuring a partial layer of the skin. The goal of care is to cover, protect and clean the area. The dressing you use should cover, insulate, absorb and protect the wound. Skin lotions or emollients should be used to hydrate surrounding tissues and prevent the wound from getting worse. It is also advisable to use additional padding to decrease the pressure on the injured area. If quick, preventive attention is given to a Stage II wound, it will heal very rapidly.

Stage III. The wound extends through all of the layers of the skin, becoming a likely site for a serious infection. Besides alleviating pressure on the wound and covering and protecting it, an increased emphasis should be placed on nutrition and hydration. Medical care is necessary at this stage to promote healing and prevent infection. This type of wound progresses very rapidly if left unchecked.

Stage IV. The wound protrudes through the skin and involves underlying muscle, tendons and even bone. The depth of the wound is more critical than the size, since the infection can become life threatening, especially if it gets into the bone or spreads throughout the bloodstream. Stage IV wounds require medical care by someone skilled in treating decubitus ulcers. Surgical removal of the decayed (necrotic) tissue is often necessary and amputation may be required. In extreme cases, death can occur from sepsis (infection throughout the body) or osteomyelitis (infection in the bone).

So now that you know the stages of pressure sores, how do you prevent them? Here is a list of action steps recommended by a wide range of experts:

1. Get your father to move his body regularly throughout the day—at least once every two hours. Assist him in moving his legs and arms.
2. Place pillows and foam pads under and around the "pressure points" of his body to reduce his full body weight upon them (e.g., elbows, tailbone, hips, buttocks, heels).
3. Be careful not to restrict blood flow with pillows and cushions. For example, if your father is lying on his back, place a pillow under his legs between midcalf and ankle. Don't place the pillow under the knees or use doughnut-shaped pillows.
4. Eggshell foam that you can place on top of the mattress is very helpful; so is a sheepskin pad underneath tender spots of the body.
5. Keep your father hydrated. Water is the best medicine to keep skin healthy. If he's using a bedpan, he might hesitate to drink eight glasses of water a day, but the hassle of using a bedpan is far less than the health problems he'll induce by refusing fluids.

6. Change his clothes whenever they are wet. Be sure to change adult briefs and pads frequently.

7. Keep a disposable, absorbent pad underneath him to soak up any bowel or bladder "accidents," and then be sure to wash and dry his skin immediately.

8. When helping your dad move in and out of bed, be careful not to pull or drag him so that the friction between his skin and the sheets causes an abrasion.

9. Be very careful using soaps as they can break down the skin. Use emollient or superfatted soaps as opposed to alkaline bars.

10. Provide your father with very gentle massages (don't rub the reddened skin), using lotions with vitamin E and/or aloe.

If a Stage II pressure sore isn't healing, ask a home health nurse or your father's physician to take a look at it and see if more aggressive measures need to be taken. Don't wait for it to become worse.

Q: My mom is ignoring signs of breast cancer. What can I do?

A: Your mom, like a good number of people in her generation, may have views of cancer and cancer treatment that are locked in the 1950s, when their parents may have been diagnosed with cancer. When I visit senior centers, I am often surprised at the number of older women who will tell me that they don't get mammograms because, as they put it, "what you don't know won't hurt you." I usually respond, "I guess you're right. You don't hurt when you're dead." Kind of harsh, but with Medicare covering the cost of the test, and the high incidence of breast cancer among older women, there's really no excuse to walk away from life.

Finding out if you have cancer can be frightening, and being told you have it feels like a verdict—only there's no trial. I know. I had a biopsy on a mole, and two days later I answered the phone and the nurse said, "The doctor wants to talk to you." Alarms went off. I was expecting that nifty little postcard that says, "You've tested negative." The doctor proceeded with one of those good news/bad news routines. Bad news: "You have malignant melanoma, one of the fastest-growing cancers." Good news: "It's not too deep. You're at stage II." Surgery, a battery of tests, and nine years later, I'm in the clear. I'm fortunate to have a happy ending, but I'll never forget lying on a cold table while they scanned my body to see if the cancer had spread. Would I be given a death sentence?

I share this with you because it's estimated that 40 percent of the adults diagnosed with cancer do survive. Every year, as a result of aggressive cancer research, new methods to stave off the progression of cancer are being discovered. Your mom, however, is from a generation when cancer wasn't discussed. Families felt ashamed if their parents had it, so they didn't tell their friends. It was common back then not to even tell the person who had cancer! In addition, your mom might have seen or known friends who became very ill from chemotherapy or radiation, but nowadays some people go for treatment in the morning and return to work the same day.

So how do you approach your mom?

- Acknowledge her possible fear. Let her tell you what she's thinking, explore what she's afraid of and then try to address each fear separately. For example, did she have a friend die of cancer? What was the friend's treatment like? Does she think the cancer is throughout her whole body? Not until you know what she fears can you change her behavior and get her to go see a doctor.
- Provide her with matter-of-fact information on cancer testing and treatment; show her how far treatment therapies have advanced.
- Share with her how early diagnosis highly increases survival rates.
- Make cancer screening a family affair. Perhaps both of you can go get a mammogram, and your dad should be screened for prostate and colon cancer.
- Enlist the support of her family physician and close friends to encourage her to be examined.
- Let her know how much she's needed. If there are grandchildren in the picture, encourage her to take care of herself for *them*. (Don't start with the "Grandma card." Deal with her fears first, but if all else fails then use it.)

Hopefully, this will get your mom to her doctor. She should also know that chances are that the lump could merely be a cyst or benign. Why live under a dark cloud when you don't have to? Two great resources dedicated to cancer education and treatment are: the American Cancer Society at 1-800-ACS-2345 or www.cancer.org and the National Cancer Institute at 1-800-4-CANCER or www.cancer.gov.

Q: What are the signs of dementia and Alzheimer's disease?

A: Dementia is an umbrella term (literally meaning *without mind*) for the progressive loss of thinking, judgment, and ability to focus and learn. More than half of dementia cases are caused by Alzheimer's, a disease named after the physician who discovered it back in 1906. No one is exactly sure what causes Alzheimer's but genetic factors are definitely in the mix.

The second leading cause of dementia is the death of brain cells due to ministrokes that block blood supply. These small, successive strokes oftentimes go unnoticed as they chip away at the brain. People with high blood pressure and diabetes are at considerable risk for this type of dementia.

We all become distracted, forget names and misplace our keys. So how do you know when forgetfulness slides into the world of dementia?

The Alzheimer's Association has developed a list of warning signs of Alzheimer's. If your parent experiences any of these symptoms, it's time to get him to a doctor.

TOP TEN WARNING SIGNS OF ALZHEIMER'S DISEASE

1. Memory loss affecting job skills: frequently forgets assignments, colleagues' names, appears confused for no reason.
2. Difficulty performing familiar tasks: easily distracted, forgetful of task at hand.
3. Problems with language: forgets simple words or substitutes inappropriate words, doesn't make sense.
4. Disorientation to time and place: may become lost on their own street, don't know where they are, how they got there or how to get back home.
5. Poor or decreased judgment: usually exhibited through inappropriate clothing, poor grooming, forgets to wear a coat when it's cold, or wears a bathrobe to the store.
6. Problems with abstract thinking: exhibits trouble with numbers, can no longer make simple calculations.
7. Misplaces things: not only loses things but places things in inappropriate places, like placing a purse in the freezer, a wristwatch in a sugar bowl, has no idea how they got there.
8. Mood and behavior changes: exhibits more rapid mood swings for no apparent reason.
9. Changes in personality: dramatic change in personality, someone who was easy-going now appears extremely uptight, can become suspicious and fearful.
10. Loss of initiative: becomes extremely uninterested and uninvolved in things that they used to enjoy.

Your parent's primary physician ought to be able to rule out any reversible causes, such as a drug reaction. After that, he or she needs to be seen by a geriatrician or a neurologist (an M.D.

who specializes in the nervous system). A full workup takes about two to three hours. The physician should listen to you and other family members describe changes in your parent.

Use the Top Ten Warning Signs list and note the behaviors you've seen under each one of them. We're looking for changes here, so do *not* count typical, lifelong habits of absent-mindedness. (My kids, for instance, certainly won't be using losing keys as a sign for me!)

Since there is no definite, proof-positive test to diagnose Alzheimer's, doctors rely on a battery of tests to rule everything else out. Between 5 percent and 10 percent of cases of apparent dementia are caused by a condition that can be reversed. This might be a good point to use to convince your mom or dad to be evaluated. They may be trying to hide their symptoms for fear of Alzheimer's, and refuse to see a doctor. Letting them know that there are a number of possible causes might alleviate their fears and encourage them to find out what's really wrong. Either way it turns out, your parent and you will be better off for knowing the truth.

Q: My dad has Alzheimer's disease and is very resistant to taking a bath. What do we do?

A: Many people who care for someone with Alzheimer's know exactly what you're going through. I know that when I took care of my children's great-grandmother a bath was always an ordeal. Searching for answers, I read an excellent book on caring for someone with Alzheimer's called *The 36-Hour Day* by Nancy Mace and Peter Rabins. You'll find it an extremely helpful resource.

Your dad's behavior is, for the most part, due to the disease. He may find taking a bath too confusing, or complicated. It may cause him great anxiety, and make him feel very vulnerable. The thought of having someone remind him to take a bath or shower may feel like a direct attack on his independence. Whatever his perception, you are still faced with the reality of him not taking a bath.

Here are some tips from Mace and Rabins that I found helpful, and hopefully you will too:

- Make sure you follow your dad's past routines. Did he usually shower or bathe? How often? What time of day? Certain days of the week? He does not need a bath every day.
- Showers, for most Alzheimer patients, seem to cause more anxiety than baths, but if getting in and out of a tub is also difficult, try getting a shower chair and use a handheld

shower hose. I actually think this is the best option. This way you are able to control the flow of water and just do one body part at a time. You can even place a towel around your dad's shoulder, or private parts, so he feels less vulnerable.

- Avoid getting into a debate about taking a shower or bath. For example, don't announce, "After breakfast, you'll need to take your bath," or give an ultimatum.
- Tell your dad—one step at a time—what to do in preparation for bathing and act as if it's just a normal part of his routine or that he's already agreed to it. For example, "Dad, your bathwater is ready." If he responds, "I don't need a bath," just hand him a towel and calmly state, "Now unbutton your shirt." Hopefully, he'll focus on the buttons. Continue, "It's time to stand up. Undo your trousers, Dad," and so forth. Just stay focused on the steps in taking a bath.
- Some families have found that their loved one responds better to a home health aide. Perhaps your dad might cooperate better with a male home health aide presenting the bath as part of an exercise routine.
- Focus on a possible skin rash or spot that might look like a sore and use that as an opportunity to slowly move into a sponge bath.

The authors also share the story of one daughter who drew her father's bath and would then wait until he'd go near the bathroom. She'd show him the filled bathtub and nonchalantly say something like, "Gosh, that bathwater looks so inviting. As long as it's here, why not take a bath?" He was the type of person who would never waste anything, including a tubful of water, so he'd take the bath. Another strategy is to connect it with a reward: "As soon as you're done with the bath, let's have some of your favorite cherry pie." Try to identify your dad's old habits and see if you can find a creative way to link it to bathing.

Whatever you do, please don't interpret his behavior as an act of defiance against you and other family members. Otherwise, you'll be caught up in a no-win, angry spiral of emotions.

Q: Does Medicare cover any treatment for Alzheimer's disease?

A: Yes, there is some coverage, fortunately. Nearly four million Americans have Alzheimer's disease and the number is expected to explode with the aging of the population. In the past, many claims for physical or mental therapy were automatically denied based on the premise that Alzheimer's patients could not benefit or improve. But recent studies contradicted this assumption and proved that people with Alzheimer's can, indeed, make improvements resulting from psychotherapy, physical therapy and/or occupational therapy, among other treatments. In addition, doctors and psychologists are now able to diagnose Alzheimer's disease in earlier stages, when timely interventions can slow the progression of the disease.

These services will keep people out of nursing homes. If Medicare pays for physical and occupational therapy, medications and mental health services, families will be able to care for them at home longer. For example, occupational therapists have found that training patients with certain behavioral cues enables them to remember how to put on a coat or dress, groom themselves or go to the bathroom.

The bottom line is that caring for someone with Alzheimer's is not hopeless. You can do things to help your parent manage the disease. Since most people live nearly a full decade after they have been diagnosed, it is important to have a positive outlook and get involved in their care rather than acting as a helpless bystander.

Beneficiaries, however, go through restrictive eligibility requirements to receive home health care. Long-term custodial care still isn't covered, nor is assisted living or nursing home care past the usual (but not guaranteed) first hundred days (see page 30 for more on nursing home coverage).

Your parent cannot be prevented from receiving Medicare-reimbursed services because he or she has Alzheimer's. If your parent is diagnosed with this disease and has been turned down for various therapies or couldn't afford a prescription to treat the disease, go back to his or her physician. Make sure they get a green light from the Medicare carrier that Medicare will, in fact, cover the treatment or service being prescribed.

For more information on what Medicare provides, go to www.medicare.gov or call the Medicare toll-free information line at (800) 633-4227. If you want to dispute nonpayment, you'll find the name and phone number of the carrier on the back of the "Explanation of Benefits" statement that your parent receives after a provider has billed Medicare for payment. Your local Alzheimer's chapter is also a good source of information, and they are listed in the blue pages of your phone book, or go to www.alz.org to find a chapter near you.

Q: How do we cope with my dad's constant need to wander?

A: Wandering is a common behavior among people with dementia. In fact, it is so common that many nursing homes have created "wandering tracks" in their facilities so that their roaming residents can safely wander in a secure area to fulfill their need to keep moving.

There are two things you do *not* want to do. The first is locking your dad in a room or restraining him to a chair or bed. The second is giving him over-the-counter sleeping aids, thinking that this will calm him down and induce him to sleep through the night. Some people have taken these actions because they think there is no other way to "protect" their parent from themselves. Sleeping aids, however, can have the opposite effect with a brain-injured person, so check with his doctor first. And despite the dementia, he'll realize that he is being tied down and/or locked in a room, making him extremely agitated and fearful. It's a strategy that will prove to be psychologically and physically abusive.

So what *can* you do? Here are a few tips that should prove helpful.

IN CASE HE BECOMES LOST:

- Get an ID bracelet with his name, your phone number, and "memory impaired" engraved on it. You can purchase these through MedicAlert. Visit their Web site at www.medicalert.com or call (800) 432-5378.
- Give your dad a card with your phone number on it, so he can call you if he is lost.
- Alert the local police and give them a photo of your dad, and contact any local store that he would likely go to if he found a way out of your home.
- Install alarms that will go off if he is leaving the house, or use childproof devices to prevent him from opening the outside door.

ADDRESSING THE NEED TO WANDER:

- While you are with him, constantly reassure him where he is and that everything is fine.
- Find ways to get him to exercise; go for walks together or enlist a schedule of friends for walks. If the weather is bad, there's always the mall. He can even exercise while sitting in a chair, so put on some of his favorite music and exercise with him.
- Give your dad simple tasks to do during the day. If he likes sorting through his toolbox, or folding grocery bags or clothes, ask him to "help you out" by doing these tasks.
- Reduce his water intake several hours before bedtime, so he won't need to get up to urinate in the middle of the night, risking a fall or inducing wandering.
- Get him involved in adult day services to keep him active during the day. Many families report a great improvement in their loved ones once they've started attending an adult day services program. They are less agitated during the day and are more likely to sleep at night, reducing the need to wander.
- Observe what he does just before he begins to wander and see if you can identify a pattern. Look for the cause or behavior that triggers his wandering and try to avoid it.

To find an adult day living center near you go to the National Adult Day Services Association's Web site at www.nadsa.org or give them a call at (800) 558-5301.

Q: **How can we keep my dad's bedroom from looking like a gloomy sickroom?**

A: When someone is chronically ill, it's very easy for the bedroom to become a victim of "sickroom" decor. Chances are there are pill bottles on the nightstand, lots of medical supplies lying around, the drapes are usually closed and the chronically ill person stays in bed much more than he should because getting in and out of bed is too much of a hassle.

More than getting the place to look like the cover of *Better Homes and Gardens*, however, your father needs to get out of bed. It can be dangerous for his health if he spends too much time in bed because the systems of the body become lazy and start to shut down. Muscles waste away; kidneys malfunction; blood pressure goes up; insulin production stops; fluid starts collecting in the lungs, leading to pneumonia; and blood clots start forming, increasing the possibility of an attack on the heart and brain. So even before we add a designer touch to the bedroom, whenever possible get your dad out of bed and walking around.

If he is bedroom-bound, here are some tips for making it a *living* room:

- If your dad does not take medicines on his own, place the medicine bottles out of view. Create a shelf in a closet, or perhaps keep them in a drawer. The pill bottles are a constant reminder that he's sick. Of course, if he needs to reach the pills, then they must be next to him. Even so, use daily pill dispensers, so he doesn't confuse when to take what.
- If it's difficult for your dad to get in and out of bed, then get a hospital bed. Medicare usually covers this cost, but check first. Most companies will let you know and will deliver it to your home.
- Get rid of all clutter and supplies that remind your dad he's sick, such as adult briefs, bed pads, gauze and bandages. Put them in the closet.
- Set up a table next to the bed where he has easy access to fresh water, the telephone, the remote control for television, his glasses and anything else he needs to use frequently. But try not to clutter it.
- If there's enough room, set up a little visiting area with a table and chairs so people can visit with him and get him out of bed.

- Purchase an egg-crate mattress (you can get these at most discount stores for under $20). Make sure he repositions himself every two hours to prevent bedsores.
- Give your dad the security of being able to contact household members by purchasing a room monitor (such as a baby monitor) so he can call without yelling or ringing a bell, which plays on anyone's nerves.
- Hopefully, your dad's bedroom is next to a bathroom. If not, you can get portable commodes through a health care equipment company. Medicare usually covers this expense. You can even purchase a decorative screen so that it's not in full view.
- Place a few plants throughout the room, and if he likes the sound, get him one of those small fountains or waterfalls. You could be more adventurous and get a goldfish or aquarium.
- Place a large clock and calendar in the room, because it's very easy to become disoriented when you spend so much time in one room. If your dad has dementia, it's helpful to have a Magic Marker board where you can write down things like what he just had for lunch or dinner, or what time you're coming back.

And, of course, there's nothing like fresh bedding, soothing curtains and pillows to give a room a warm feeling. Make sure the designs are quiet and subtle rather than loud and dramatic. Large, bold patterns may confuse or aggravate him if he has dementia.

I've seen some families redesign the downstairs dining room to make it into a bedroom for their parent for two reasons: It's less isolated from the hub of family life, and there are no steps. Most families today aren't using the formal dining room and find it an easy space to convert.

There is a national Family Caregiver Support Program that helps qualifying families with a onetime grant for home modifications when they care for an elderly relative. Call your local Area Agency on Aging, (800) 677-1116, to see if you qualify.

Q: **How can I help my mom come home and recuperate from her hip fracture?**

A: I'm sure that your mom can't wait to get home. Be thankful. One in four older people who suffer a hip fracture remain institutionalized for an entire year. People who've had a hip fracture are more likely to have another, so she needs to be very careful. Your mother is already counted among the 338,000 hip fractures of last year. Let's not make her a repeat statistic.

Research has shown that the most common hazards include tripping over rugs or something lying on the floor, absence of stair railings or grab bars, slippery surfaces, unstable furniture and poor lighting. One-half to two-thirds of all falls occur in or around the home and usually from a standing position.

So given that "home sweet home" is where Mom will most likely fall, you need to go throughout the house and remove all throw rugs, declutter walkways, add nonslip mats in the bathtub and on shower floors, install handrails on both sides of stairways and increase the lighting throughout the home.

There are also a number of devices you can purchase. Before you buy any, check with a local medical equipment company and ask if the purchase is covered by Medicare. Here is a list of things to consider:

1. Purchase a bathing chair designed for showers. Make sure it has rubber, nonskid tips on the legs and is adjustable.
2. Install a handheld showerhead to easily control the flow of water so your mom can bathe in the chair.
3. Buy a "reacher" that can help her "grab" things that are either too high or too low for her to reach.
4. Make sure that her shoes are easy to put on and are sturdy.
5. She might need a walker to steady her. There are several types available, some of which offer a folding seat so that she can take a rest whenever needed.
6. Get her a long shoehorn so she won't have to lean forward and lose her balance when she puts on her shoes.
7. Install a sensor light on the bed stand, or buy a lamp that lights up simply when it's touched, so her pathway will be lit if she gets up in the middle of the night.
8. Purchase a toilet seat with sidebars so that it will be easier for her to get up.

Besides making changes in her environment, make sure that she follows the exercise routine recommended by the physical therapist prescribed by her physician. I'd also ask her physician if Medicare will cover having an Occupational Therapist make a home visit to help your mother identify risks in the home and advise her on assistive devices to help her with her daily living.

If she's taking a diuretic (water pill), she should take it in the morning. Taking it at bedtime will cause her to get up in the middle of the night, increasing her risk of a fall. It's also a good idea to ask her doctor to review her medications to identify any that can cause dizziness, which could induce her to fall. The most important thing is to keep her spirits up and keep her exercising. For an excellent Web site with all kinds of aids for daily living go to www.abledata.com.

Q:

My mom really needs to see a therapist, but I know she won't go if she has to pay for it. Is such treatment covered by Medicare?

A: If paying for it is the only roadblock you face in getting your mother to a mental health professional, then she's well on her way. All too often, the older generation is embarrassed about needing to see a psychologist or psychiatrist, so they suffer in silence. Yet depression is often mistaken for "normal" sadness due to the losses of aging, and mental illness can go undetected or misdiagnosed for several years.

Generally, if your mother sees a mental health professional who accepts Medicare assignment, then Medicare will cover about half of the costs of her mental health care. Chances are she has a Medigap supplemental policy, which will pick up the other half. Two rules of thumb: She needs to see someone who accepts Medicare assignment, and she needs a referral from a physician. Medicare assignment simply means that the provider seeing your mother has agreed to accept whatever Medicare "assigns" for reimbursement as payment in full.

Now let's get down to the specifics. If your mother needs inpatient care then:

- Part A of Medicare will cover inpatient hospital, skilled nursing facility, and some home health care. Everyone pays a deductible during each benefit period before Medicare kicks in. For example, in 2004 your mom's deductible was $876, after which Medicare covered 80 percent of the bill. Hopefully, she has a Medigap policy to pick up the other 20 percent and the deductible.
- What's a "benefit period"? A benefit period starts when your mom enters the hospital and ends when she has been out of the facility for sixty consecutive days. Don't be confused into thinking that this is an annual deductible.
- Medicare has a lifetime limit of 190 days a patient can spend in an inpatient *psychiatric* hospital. After that, you're on your own! However, there is no lifetime limit on inpatient mental health services received in a general hospital.

If your mother needs outpatient services from a psychiatrist, clinical psychologist, clinical social worker, nurse specialist or physician assistant then:

- Part B of Medicare will cover individual and group therapy, family counseling, psychological tests, diagnostic services and evaluations, occupational therapy, laboratory tests, and drugs that can only be given by injection.

- These services can be provided in an office setting, clinic or hospital outpatient department.
- Part B may also cover partial hospitalizations; however, this must be prescribed by a physician.
- Medicare will cover half of these costs while your Medigap policy will cover the other half. Usually Medigap policies pick up your 20 percent co-payment but when it comes to mental health services, they are required by law to pick up the remaining 50 percent of the bill.

To keep your mother's costs at a minimum, make sure that whoever provides care to her accepts Medicare assignment. Medical professionals who accept assignments are called "participating providers," and you can get a list of them by calling (800) 633-4227. If you'd like to learn more about mental health coverage and Medicare, go to www.medicare.gov or www.MedicareEd.org and enter the keywords "mental health services."

Your mom is far from alone—nearly one in five people over fifty-five years of age experience a mental disorder not associated with aging. Regretfully, only one in two people who acknowledge their condition ever seek treatment. And fewer numbers still receive the specialized psychiatric help they need. Let's help your mom beat the odds.

Q: What's the best way to research cancer so we know what to ask and do?

A: Most physicians will welcome the opportunity to fully explain the diagnosis and the options that your parent should consider. I find that it helps, however, if you have a basic understanding of the disease beforehand, so that what you're being told will make more sense. It also means that you'll be better able to ask educated questions. How you share information with the doctor and ask questions can help set the tone for your relationship.

Share information with the physician in a spirit of respect. Explain that you and your parent want to better understand the disease and treatment. You're not there to second-guess him with your newfound "medical degree"—you want to establish a partnership.

Here are three basic steps to a crash course on cancer:

1. **Tried and True Web Sites.** It's important to know who is sponsoring the Web site. Go to the "About Us" navigation bar and determine if it is sponsored by a group that has something to gain from what it recommends. For instance, a number of drug companies

sponsor very good educational sites, but you need to keep in mind that they benefit from the drugs they recommend for treatment. Sites with a .com at the end of their name are commercial businesses, whereas those with .edu are academic and educational institutions. Those with .org are usually nonprofit organizations and .gov are government-sponsored sites.

The Oncologist, a journal on cancer, hosts an excellent Web site at www.theoncologist .org and their editor, Karen Parles, M.L.S., has compiled the following list of cancer-related Web sites along with a description of what each offers:

- **CANCER.GOV (NATIONAL CANCER INSTITUTE)**

www.cancer.gov

Extensive patient-oriented information on cancer, including peer-reviewed summaries on treatment, screening, prevention and supportive care. Features a searchable database of clinical trials, with in-depth information on finding and understanding clinical trials.

- **ASSOCIATION OF CANCER ONLINE RESOURCES (ACOR)**

www.acor.org

Not-for-profit organization offering more than 130 online support groups for specific cancers and cancer-related conditions.

- **MEDSCAPE**

www.medscape.com

Commercial Web site aimed at health care professionals. Highlights include conference summaries of major oncology meetings and a weekly e-mail service providing updates of developments in cancer research.

- **STEVE DUNN'S CANCERGUIDE**

www.cancerguide.org

Provides guidance and insight from a patient's perspective on how to find answers to questions about cancer, and most important, how to learn which questions to ask.

- **AMERICAN CANCER SOCIETY**

www.cancer.org

Comprehensive information on cancer. Particular areas of interest include a searchable database of local support services and a "Cancer Survivors Network" community.

- **MEDLINEPLUS (NATIONAL LIBRARY OF MEDICINE)**

www.medlineplus.gov

Consumer Web site provides a gateway to Internet resources, arranged by topic. Covers specific cancers, drug information, medical reference, medical tests and procedures, and directories to doctors and hospitals.

• **CANCER CARE**

www.cancercare.org

Not-for-profit organization providing support services for cancer patients and care-givers. Offers useful information on coping with cancer, its treatment, and effects. Provides practical advice on managing insurance and financial issues.

• **AMERICAN SOCIETY OF CLINICAL ONCOLOGY (ASCO)**

www.asco.org (ASCO Online)

www.plwc.org (People Living with Cancer)

ASCO Online maintains two excellent cancer Web sites, one for its membership and one aimed at patients.

2. **Read a Few Books and Gather Material from the Doctor's Office.** Go to your local bookstore or library and spend some time scanning through the wealth of books on cancer. Choose one or two that speak to your needs. You can also visit an online bookseller and conduct a search on cancer. It's a great way to find out what's available and read reviews of books. Most doctors' offices have educational videos that are really worth watching. Also take the free booklets on the type of cancer your parent has.

3. **Talk with the Doctor.** Your physician is your primary source of information, and he or she will be interpreting all of the test results and making an educated recommendation on the best treatment for your parent, given his or her unique set of circumstances. After you've had a chance to do your homework, set up a consult visit where you can review all of your parent's options. It's always smart to prepare a list of questions ahead of time and to take notes during the visit.

Q: **My dad needs to be screened for colon cancer. What kinds of tests are there and what does Medicare cover?**

A: Colorectal cancer occurs in the colon and the rectum and is often referred to simply as "colon cancer." The colon is the large intestine and the rectum is the passageway that connects the colon to the anus. Your dad shouldn't fool around by ignoring the opportunity to have a colonoscopy. Colorectal cancer is now the second leading cause of cancer death in the United States, but many experts believe that one in three of these deaths could be avoided if people were properly screened to catch the cancer in its early stages.

The cancer usually starts from polyps in the colon or rectum. Polyps are little growths that are foreign; in other words, they shouldn't be there. Screening tests can find the polyps and remove them before they even become cancerous.

You can have colorectal cancer without experiencing any symptoms. That is why screenings are so important. By the time you do exhibit symptoms, the cancer may well be too far advanced to cure. Symptoms include blood in the stool, aches or cramps in the stomach that are frequent and unexplainable, a change in bowel movements such as stools that are narrower than usual, and loss of weight without dieting.

There are a number of tests to screen for colorectal cancer beyond the colonoscopy. The most basic and primary is the Fecal Occult Stool Test, which you should have on a yearly basis. You receive a test kit from your doctor and smear small pieces of stool on a test card and send it to a lab. In a flexible sigmoidoscopy, the doctor places a short, thin, lighted tube into the rectum to check for polyps. This type of test is recommended every five years. A colonoscopy is the same as a sigmoidoscopy except that it examines the *entire* colon. Physicians can find and remove most polyps and some cancers with this procedure. This test is recommended every ten years, unless you fall into the high-risk category.

Medicare does cover a colonoscopy every ten years if you are not at high risk for colorectal cancer. It sounds like this would be your dad's first, so Medicare would cover 80 percent while his Medigap policy would cover the remaining 20 percent.

If he is at high risk for colorectal cancer (for example, another family member has been diagnosed with the disease), then his doctor can order the procedure every two years and Medicare will cover it.

There are a number of "fine print" loopholes that you should be aware of. If you have a flexible sigmoidoscopy, then Medicare will make you wait four years before a colonoscopy will be covered. And if you have either of these tests done at an ambulatory center or hospital outpatient department, then your Medigap policy will have to pick up 25 percent of the cost rather than the usual 20 percent deductible.

If you have any questions about your dad's coverage for this procedure call Medicare at (800) 633-4227 or visit www.medicare.gov. And by the way, if you're over fifty years of age—male or female—you should sign up for *your* first colonoscopy!

Q: **My dad's vision is getting worse. What eye diseases should he be concerned about?**

A: As we age, the lens of the eye becomes more rigid, which leads to a form of farsightedness called presbyopia, in which the eye cannot focus easily on close objects. One of the first signs is holding your menu an arm's length away.

By the time your parents are in their sixties and seventies this condition becomes more pronounced, and they might notice other changes such as finding glare from headlights blinding, difficulty seeing in dimly lit rooms and hallways, trouble refocusing from light to dark rooms, and finding it harder to distinguish between colors, contrasts and shadows. These vision problems are common in older people, and many can be managed with minor lifestyle changes and glasses.

There are four major eye diseases affecting the elderly that are not normal.

1. **Cataracts:** Most people with this condition will tell you that they feel like they are looking through a cloud. That's because the transparent lens of the eye becomes filmy. All light that enters the eye passes through the lens. So if any part of the lens blocks, distorts or diffuses the incoming light, then vision will be impaired.

Cataracts can also block bright light from being diffused. The result? The trapped light touches off a fireworks display of halos around lights, scattering light and glare. If your dad is diagnosed with cataracts, his physician will probably recommend implanting a plastic or silicon lens. The surgery is usually an outpatient procedure, and you'll need to make sure that your dad dutifully takes his eyedrops at the prescribed times.

2. **Glaucoma:** This is a sneaky disease caused by pressure in the eyeball that increases to such a point that it damages the optic nerve. All too often, you won't hear any complaint from your parent until there has been damage. The pressure is caused by fluid inside the eyeball that fails to drain, leading to a loss of peripheral vision. Treatment can range from medications to laser therapy to surgery.

3. **Macular Degeneration:** The macula is the central, most vital area of the retina. Its main job is to focus on the fine details in the center of the field of vision. If your father's macula degenerates, he might start complaining that straight lines appear wavy. He also might have blind spots that appear directly in front of what he is looking at. My mother has this condition and says it's like seeing around a small black hole. Macular degeneration is categorized as wet or dry. Dry means that a pigment is

deposited in the macula with no scarring, blood or other fluid leakage. If it is wet, then there may be small hemorrhages surrounding the macula. Both eyes are usually affected, though each might be at different rates of progression.

Little treatment to reverse the condition is available. If new blood vessels grow in or around the macula, laser surgery can sometimes prevent them from doing further harm. There are a number of products such as telescopic glasses and goggles that can greatly help people with macular degeneration.

4. **Diabetic Retinopathy:** High blood sugar levels make the walls of small blood vessels in the retina weaker, so they are more prone to deformity and leaks. This leads to blurred vision and, if left untreated, blindness. The major lesson here is to keep those glucose levels controlled and blood pressure levels in normal range.

An annual visit to an ophthalmologist is your dad's best defense against these diseases. Many physicians also recommend wearing sunglasses on sunny days to protect the eyes and taking a daily dose of lutein dietary supplement.

Q: **My mother has cancer, and we're concerned about pain management. What do we need to know?**

A: Your mom will undoubtedly be meeting with a team of doctors. She'll now have an oncologist, a cancer specialist who will coordinate her care with other specialists who may treat her. If she is given chemotherapy or radiation therapy, she will be seeing a different physician for each. If she has other health problems, such as a heart condition, then she'll continue to see her cardiologist. Thus it's very important to make sure that either her oncologist or her primary care physician (if she has one) acts as the "air traffic controller" of her care. She should ask them to decide *who will be her central point of command?* Who does she call when she's in trouble? Who receives all of the results of any tests, lab work and treatments, and interprets them for her? Make sure this decision is nailed down.

Now let's deal with her fear of pain. Her oncologist should schedule her to meet with a pain management team, which usually includes physicians, pharmacists and nurses; they may also be referred to as "palliative care." Their goal is to get your mother through her cancer as comfortably as possible. They are experts in pain management and know how to respond to the various kinds of pain she may experience, including the side effects of various treatments like chemotherapy.

But in order for them to be effective, your mom has to be an active team member. These experts must rely on *her* assessment and description of *her* pain. Not until they understand the nature and degree of your mother's pain can they diagnose and prescribe the best treatment regimen for her.

It will be very helpful to the pain management team and the oncologist if she keeps a diary of her pain. Here are some of the things she should keep track of:

- The time of day the pain hit (does it change during the day or night?)
- Did she experience any symptoms prior to the pain (e.g., flushing, dizziness, nausea)?
- Was she doing anything prior to the pain (e.g., eating, getting out of a chair)?
- The location of the pain.
- Ranking of the pain on a scale of one to ten with ten being the worst. She should ask her doctor for a pain rating scale so they are on the same page.
- How quickly the pain came and how long it lasted.
- Did anything reduce the pain (e.g., ice, heat, massage, medication) and how much did it reduce her pain (using the rating scale).
- How long did it give her relief?
- What did the pain feel like (e.g., stabbing, burning, electric, throbbing, dull, or aching)?

With this type of diary, the pain team is in a better position to pick up patterns and determine the causes of her pain. The diary is also a way for your mom to take some control of her disease and her care rather than feeling helpless.

Palliative care teams frequently tell their cancer patients to be sure to report their pain *early* and not wait until they can't bear it any longer. If you wait that long, it is more difficult to get ahead of the pain and reach a plateau of comfort.

One thing your mom will be cautioned about is "breakthrough pain." This is pain that can break through the pain medication and/or treatment she is receiving. It usually comes on suddenly and lasts for a short period of time; however, it can happen repeatedly during the day. This type of pain can be: triggered by an incident, like getting out of a chair; "spontaneous," coming out of nowhere and for no identifiable reason; or caused by an "end-of-dose failure," when a long-acting drug wears off before it's expected.

It will be important for your mom to tell the doctor which type of breakthrough pain she thinks she is experiencing (incident, spontaneous or end-of-dose failure). This will help her physician know what type of drug to prescribe. There is a wide range of short-acting opiates, and one is available as a lozenge that takes effect within fifteen minutes. If your mom's pain is continuous and can't be controlled any other way, her doctor may prescribe a "PCA," or patient controlled analgesia, pump. This pump continuously dispenses small doses of pain medication intravenously, 24/7. If your mom feels breakthrough pain, she can simply push a button to give her an extra boost of the painkiller. If her pain is severe, the pain team might recommend that the pain medication be delivered directly into her spine (intraspinal) through a pump that can either be placed under her skin or within her body.

The bottom line is that your mom's oncologist has a wide range of devices, medications and resources to keep her as comfortable as possible. If she is under hospice care, these medication expenses should be covered—so costs need not deter her. Help her help herself by making sure she knows *how* to report her pain and that she shouldn't be shy about doing so.

II

NAVIGATING LIFE

1

Staying Well

Can you explain to my dad how he can prevent a heart attack?

A: It's not surprising that your father may need an explanation. All too often, older people feel that heart attacks are due to an aging heart that stops "ticking." Just fifteen years ago, even the medical community thought that the hearts of older people just gave out from the wear and tear of normal aging. But along came this twenty-five-year study by the National Institute of Health. It was quite a shock when they discovered that the hearts of the older guys were pumping blood practically the same as their younger counterparts. Yet 80 percent of the 1,300 people who have heart attacks every day in this country are over sixty-five.

Who's at greatest risk?

- Smokers
- Overweight people
- People with high blood pressure
- People with high cholesterol
- Diabetics
- Stressed-out people (You'd better not be the cause!)
- Couch potatoes
- Anyone with heart disease in the family tree

Nearly everything on this list is something your dad can do something about to stave off a heart attack. Here are two major culprits he can take on:

HIGH BLOOD PRESSURE

Of all the risk factors for heart attack, high blood pressure is the "big one." Imagine your garden hose hooked up to a fire truck. The pressure shooting through the hose would wear it thin in no time. Now imagine a small pump at the end of that hose trying to redirect the high-pressured water through other small hoses.

Any bets on how long the pump can handle the pressure?

In a less dramatic way, this is what high blood pressure does to your parent's heart. It's the continuous, high-pressured rush of blood flowing through blood vessel walls (hoselike arteries and veins) that wear them down to a point where they can tear or leak. Your dad needs to monitor his blood pressure, which is a measure of the force of blood coursing through his arteries.

Blood pressure is expressed in two numbers. Mine usually comes in at 110/80 (unless I've just read my teenage son's report card). The first number is the *systolic* blood pressure, the force of blood as the heart is pumping. The second, *diastolic,* number represents the pressure that remains in the arteries when the heart is relaxed.

High numbers aren't good; hitting 160 on the systolic is a sure sign to get to the doctor. You should check with your dad's doctor as to what's considered high for his age and weight.

Decreasing salt intake can reduce high blood pressure, so be sure to check out the sodium content of packaged and processed food—you'd be shocked at the high numbers. Weight control, managing stress and medications also can bring blood pressure down.

The most commonly prescribed medication is a diuretic, which pulls salt and water from the circulatory system and sends them off to the urinary system. Any medication has to be closely monitored by a physician so that other conditions aren't adversely affected.

No matter what, a salty diet has to go and blood pressure checks should become routine. African-Americans should be on high alert for high blood pressure as their parents are more likely than anyone else to have the condition.

CHOLESTEROL

Back to our garden hose analogy. Imagine fatty, sticky stuff stuck to the inside of your hose; the result would be a dribbling stream of water. Cholesterol is the fatty, sticky stuff stuck to your dad's blood vessels. When this stuff reaches a level that actually clogs the vessels, it's given a name: atherosclerosis. Cholesterol readings can tell your dad how much of this stuff is in his system. He is at more risk if he smokes, has high blood pressure, is diabetic or is obese. If that's the case, he should have an annual blood test to check his cholesterol.

To reduce his risk, a low-cholesterol diet is the way to go. Get him to cut down on fats one step at a time. Cholesterol is found only in animal products: meat, poultry, seafood, organ meats, eggs and dairy products, such as butter and cheese. One egg yolk will just about blow one day's healthy limit of cholesterol. Check out the American Heart Association's Web site at www.americanheart.org for all kinds of cholesterol information, diets and treatment, or call (800) 242-8721.

Q: I worry about my mom during heat waves. What should I do?

A: Your mom might not realize how much her brain's thermostat has started to lose its sensitivity to pick up temperature changes, especially if she is in her eighties. Complicating this are circulatory problems and medications that can throw an older person's "thermostat" out of whack. Your mother is also losing her ability to sweat, which means she's left without nature's protective cooling system. And to make matters worse, older people also lose their sense of thirst, so your mom may not crave a glass of water to cool her down.

So while it is normal for your mom not to *feel* the heat like she used to, it doesn't mean she can *take* the heat. We really need to view heat waves just like we do warnings about cold spells. Most older people respect warnings about not going out in extreme cold, yet seem to happily garden, mow their lawns or walk in ninety-degree heat. It's almost seen as a badge of honor to be able to "take the heat" since their generation grew up without air-conditioning.

Just as you'd check in on your aging relatives during an ice storm, it's good to do the same when the temperature stays in the nineties for more than two days. Here are some things you can do to make sure your mom doesn't suffer from heat stroke, or hyperthermia:

- Make sure she's drinking plenty of fluids. Get her water bottles to help keep track of her intake.
- Make sure she uses air-conditioning but is not sitting directly in front of it—her body could cool off too much and suffer hypothermia.
- If she's using a fan, make sure a window is open to create a draft rather than simply circulating hot air in a closed room. You'd be surprised at the number of older people with air-conditioning who keep it off to cut down on their electric bill. So don't assume she has it on. And you'd be surprised at the number of people who keep the windows closed because they are afraid someone will break in.
- Call or visit twice a day—if your mom starts acting confused, has a headache, is dizzy or nauseous, she's showing signs of heat stroke. Call for immediate medical help.

• If she doesn't have air-conditioning, suggest she spend the day at the mall. If necessary, take her there along with a few of her friends.
• One of the most effective ways to cool down is to take a lukewarm bath.
• Suggest that your mom keep a cool cloth around the back of her neck.

Whatever you do, check in with your parents and reach out to elderly neighbors when the National Weather Service and your local weather station warn of heat waves. They can be every bit as devastating to human life as a tornado. In Philadelphia in 1994 over a hundred people, most of them elderly, died from the heat. In response to that crisis, the governor of Pennsylvania asked me to head up a task force to prevent that from ever happening again. As a result, many Area Agencies on Aging throughout the nation now give out fans, take people to air-conditioned senior centers or malls, and have identified at-risk elders through their home-delivered meals programs to reduce the incidence of heat-related deaths. You can call (800) 677-1116 to find the nearest Area Agency on Aging.

Q: **Is a bone density test the best way to screen for osteoporosis?**

A: Several years ago, the U.S. Preventive Services Task Force wasn't sure whether or not bone density tests were warranted. But after a few more years of research, they concluded that getting a bone density test is a smart and effective prevention tool for every woman sixty-five years and older.

Osteoporosis is the abnormal thinning of bone, causing decreased bone mass and density. It's related to aging and the depletion of bone calcium and protein. Women are especially prone to osteoporosis after menopause, and the effects can be debilitating: easily broken bones, spine fractures and hip fractures are common results of osteoporosis. Hip fractures are one of the leading causes of premature loss of home and independence, landing many women in nursing homes.

Your mother is at higher risk if she smokes, is white or Asian, is small-framed, has already had a fracture that wasn't related to major trauma, gets little exercise, drinks heavily, has a poor diet low in calcium, or takes corticosteroids, certain anticonvulsants or excess doses of thyroid hormones for long periods.

So what about the test? There are several ways to measure bone density, but the most reliable test is called dual-energy X-ray absorptiometry (DEXA) of the spine and hip. It is the most expensive, ranging from $125 to $200, according to the task force report. Similar X-ray tests can be used for the wrist, finger and heel at a lower cost. An ultrasound test of your mom's heel for $25 to $35 may also be helpful, especially if she is considered low-risk. All of these are good screening tests, although the DEXA of the spine and hip is considered the gold standard for diagnosis—and Medicare does pay for it.

Usually the referring physician will decide which kind of test your mother needs. None of the bone density tests are invasive or uncomfortable, and they take a mere five to fifteen minutes. Many people are surprised to learn that you don't even have to undress or wear those lovely hospital gowns.

The major benefit of the test is to determine whether or not your mother's condition warrants taking a bone-preserving drug. The options include bisphosphonates (Fosamax or Actonel), the hormonelike raloxifene (Evista), or hormones (hormone replacement therapy or calcitonin). It can also indicate a strong warning to your mom to take steps to prevent the further weakening of her bones, such as changing her diet.

You may need to urge your mom's doctor to prescribe a bone density test. According to a recent survey in the *American Journal of Public Health,* one-third of all postmenopausal women have the condition, yet only 2 percent are ever diagnosed and treated.

Medicare has been covering bone density tests under Part B since 1998. Of course, there are guidelines and restrictions. According to Medicare:

- Bone mass measurement is covered for certain people at risk for losing bone mass.
- Bone mass measurement tests are covered by all Medicare health plans, including managed care plans.
- Deductible and co-payments apply.
- Medicare will only pay for this test if ordered by a physician or qualified practitioner.
- Medicare will cover tests every two years, or more frequently if medically necessary.
- Doctors consider a patient medical history and risk factors in deciding who should have a bone density test and the type of test.

Given the results of this new study, and Medicare's coverage of the test, it makes perfect sense to have your mom ask her doctor to prescribe it. If she's smoking, try getting her to stop; encourage weight-bearing exercise and a healthy diet with plenty of calcium and vitamin D. With more than 1.5 million fractures a year caused by osteoporosis, the odds are if she does nothing, she'll become one of these statistics.

Q: Is it true that staying socially active prevents dementia?

A: The most amazing reason to keep up our social contacts was recently uncovered by a major research study revealing that people who had at least five social relationships and kept regular contact reduced their risk of Alzheimer's disease by almost 40 percent. Social interaction causes people to remain involved in the affairs of daily life and to continue to grow emotionally, and it requires making decisions—all of which are good for the mind.

This twelve-year study was conducted by the *Harvard School of Public Health* and involved 2,800 people past age sixty-five. Those who had monthly visual contact with three or more relatives or friends, and yearly nonvisual contact with ten or more relatives or friends, staved off mental decline much better than those who had little contact. So, if your parents are motivated by staying well and have worried about getting Alzheimer's, this bit of news might encourage them to make the effort.

They also might be interested in knowing that, according to Dr. Lawrence Katz, coauthor of *Keep Your Brain Alive,* the mental decline that we associate with aging isn't due to the death of nerve cells but rather of the connections among them. And using the senses in new ways is how to maintain these connections.

The bottom line is that engaging in activities such as meeting new people, taking up a new hobby, learning how to use e-mail, mentoring young people or taking classes will actually nurture a healthy mind.

Just as your body needs to be toned with exercise, so does your brain. Some of the best brain exercises are old standbys such as reading a good book or a challenging magazine article, playing Scrabble and doing crosswords.

Though TV is a form of connecting, it in no way replicates the benefit of actually getting out and about. If your parent is no longer driving or is finding it too much of a hassle to drive (be aware that he or she might not admit it), it's a good idea to create a schedule where you, a friend or a family member make it routine to come over at least once a week with the understanding that it is to take Mom or Dad wherever they want to go.

Q: I'm worried about my mom being a "fire risk." What can I do?

A: According to the U.S. Fire Administration, older adults represent one of the highest fire risk groups in the nation. People seventy-five years and older are three times more likely than the national average to die in a fire. Many elderly fire victims come into physical contact with the source of the fire, such as a faulty space heater, the stove or a cigarette. In fact, falling asleep while smoking is the leading cause of fires among the elderly. Older adults account for nearly one-third of all fire deaths at home.

Why are the elderly so vulnerable to fire deaths and injuries? Limited sight and mobility may make it difficult for an older person to exit quickly. Impaired vision can lead to accidents while cooking. Memory lapses and mild forms of dementia can cause someone to forget to turn off the iron, oven, toaster oven or stove top. Medications that cause drowsiness or confusion may make her less aware of her surroundings, so she won't pick up smells or sounds that alert her to a fire.

So, yes, you should be worried. Here are a number of fire safety steps you can take to reduce your mother's risk of fire:

- If your mom insists on using a space heater for added heat, look for one that will automatically turn off should it become overloaded or too hot.
- Don't overload electrical outlets or extension cords.
- If your mom cooks, tell her not to wear loose clothing (especially long sleeves) around the stove. If she has impairments that pose a risk near the stove, encourage her to use the microwave.
- Buy a simple, loud timer to remind her to take food off of the stove or out of the oven.
- If she doesn't have an iron that automatically shuts off, buy her one.
- Check all of the fire alarms whenever you come to visit her. Make sure there is one on every floor. Chances of surviving a home fire double with the initial warning from a smoke alarm.
- Identify exit routes for every room of the house and make sure the path is well lit and cleared. Install sensor lights in the hallway.
- If your mom lives alone and has difficulty negotiating steps, consider relocating the bedroom to the ground floor. She'll have a much greater chance of escaping a fire than if she has to negotiate stairs to exit.

If your mom is using space heaters to reduce her high utility or oil bills, see if she qualifies for financial assistance for her energy bills through the nationwide Low Income Home Energy Assistance Program (LIHEAP). Home owners and renters are eligible to receive energy grants from their state's Department of Welfare if they are on a low or fixed income. If she is eligible, LIHEAP will make a payment directly to her utility/fuel company and credit the bill. For information and applications call the National Energy Assistance Referral (NEAR) office toll-free at (866) 674-6327 or go to www.Govbenefits.gov and enter the keyword "LIHEAP."

Q: **How can I get my mom to exercise?**

A: I'm going to offer you four tactics to help get your mom into shape. Here we go:

1. **Scare Tactic.** Plenty of research has shown that people who do *not* exercise:

- Are much more likely to acquire Type 2 diabetes.
- Lose roughly 15 percent of muscle mass in their sixties and another 15 percent in their seventies.
- Land in nursing homes much more quickly since leg strength is the best predictor of whether someone will require institutionalization.
- Have twice the risk of severe intestinal bleeding associated with colon cancer.
- Are much more likely to have heart attacks, high blood pressure, strokes, osteoporosis, and arthritis and suffer from depression and dementia.

2. **Feel Good Tactic.** Exercise is the closest thing we have to the Fountain of Youth, despite what the Botox crowd will tell you. Consider this:

- In a landmark study by Tufts and Harvard universities of eighty- and ninety-year-olds, after a six-week program of exercise a number of subjects were able to ditch their canes, and they all increased their muscle strength by 180 percent!
- Another study found that after five months of light exercise training, 75 percent of participants said that the exercise was just as effective at relieving their depression as medication.
- She'll feel better about herself, as she'll also lose weight and feel like she's in charge of her body rather than the other way around. Every ten years your body loses 7 percent of its metabolism. No wonder those pounds add up.

3. **Life's an Adventure Tactic.** Every decade offers new phases in life, and now your mom can finally focus on *her.* Chances are she's spent a lifetime caring for kids, a husband, parents, grandkids, coworkers and a boss. Now it's her turn. You might need to help her redirect those energies to nurture her body and spirit. Here's how:

- **EASE INTO EXERCISE.** Start a daily routine of just stretching: neck stretches (slowly tilt head from side to side and front to back), arm circles, and trunk twists (slowly turn upper body to one side, then the other). This can even be done sitting in a chair.

• **WALK.** How about going to the mall? Go in the early morning or around two p.m., after the lunch crowd leaves and before teens descend after school. The mall, with its air-conditioning, is particularly nice during the summer.

• **TAI CHI.** A study at Northwestern University found that elderly who practiced this slow-moving Chinese martial art significantly reduced falls and balance problems in just twelve weeks. Many senior centers offer classes in tai chi and yoga. If she won't go, buy a video and do it with her, and get one of her girlfriends to join in, too.

• **GET AN EXERCISE VIDEO.** There are exercise videos tailored to just about everyone's fitness ability. For example, *Armchair Fitness* is a one-hour, gentle session that is set to big band music (call [800] 453-6280). If your mom uses a walker or is in a wheelchair, order the *Exercising with Dorothy* video by calling (800) 779-8491. You can also visit Collage Video, which specializes in all levels of exercise videos, at www.collagevideo.com. Go to their "specialty workouts" and click on "Seniors" or give them a call at (800) 433-6769. There's also a nice "Exercise Guide for Older People" from the National Institute on Aging. Call for a copy at (800) 222-2225.

• **CHECK OUT A SENIOR CENTER.** Many senior centers today offer excellent programs on healthy lifestyles and exercise programs. Just call your local Area Agency on Aging at (800) 677-1116 and ask for the senior center coordinator to find out what programs are available in your area.

4. **Just Do It Tactic.** Enough with "I'm too old, too tired. It won't make a difference" excuses. Get off the couch, turn off the television and start flexing! It could very well save your parent's life or, at the very least, make it worth living.

Q: Could my dad's watching the news all day be making him depressed?

A: Daily news reports continuously remind us that we're living under a cloud of war and terrorism, with experts telling us how vulnerable we have become. Yet we tend to go about our daily lives acting as though life is normal.

Your dad and many of our parents who are retired don't have the diversion of getting on with life as usual—even if it is just a pretense. They don't have school to go to, homework to get done, young kids to get to practice, deadlines to make at work, orders to fill, or customers to please. They've also gone through a war. They know the pain and the hardship that it entails.

Older people who aren't active in their community or family, who have health problems or have experienced the loss of a job, friend or family member, are significantly vulnerable to depression.

But what do you look for in depression and just what is it, anyway? Depression is an illness of intense sadness that interferes with the ability to function, feel pleasure or maintain interest. Researchers have discovered that biochemical imbalances in the brain go hand in hand with depression.

It might follow a recent loss or sad event, but the intensity of the feeling and its duration persist far beyond what is healthy. Remember that, because this isn't just psychological, it's also biochemical; you can't simply tell your parent to "just snap out of it" or "look on the bright side."

The National Institute of Mental Health offers this checklist of symptoms of clinical depression:

- Persistent sadness, anxiety or feeling of emptiness
- Loss of interest or pleasure in ordinary activities, family or friends
- Decreased energy, listlessness, fatigue, feeling slowed down
- Changes in sleep patterns
- Eating problems and changes in appetite
- Difficulty in concentrating, remembering or making decisions
- Feelings of hopelessness, guilt, worthlessness and helplessness
- Thoughts of suicide or death
- Irritability
- Excessive crying, sometimes without reason
- Recurring aches and pains, such as headaches and backaches that don't respond to treatment

If you think your dad exhibits these symptoms, get him to his family physician to rule out any other physical problems. Studies show that a combination of psychotherapy and carefully prescribed medications can be 80 percent successful in treating depression among the elderly. Antidepressants are powerful drugs, however, and they should be prescribed very carefully and in conjunction with other mental health services. Two Web sites that are valuable resources on depression are www.nimh.nih.gov and www.depression.org.

Lifestyle changes including good nutrition, vitamins, exercise and getting out with family and friends are vital to a mentally fit life. I'd also suggest that your parents, especially if they are retired and not very active, limit how much televised news coverage they watch. A constant stream of visuals that reinforces how vulnerable life has become—in addition to the vulnerabilities they feel from an aging body—is simply not healthy. So turn off the TV!

Q: Should I be worried that my mom's becoming an alcoholic?

A: If your mother is drinking alone throughout the day, withdrawing from friends or keeping a supply of alcohol readily available, then, yes, be worried. Particularly if she is grieving over the death of a loved one or other major loss in her life, she could be trapped in the vicious cycle of taking a drink to "drown her troubles."

What complicates the problem for your mom and other older people is that her aging body is more sensitive to the effects of alcohol. Studies show that a sixty-year-old will have a 20 percent higher blood-alcohol level than a twenty-year-old drinking the same amount. Add to this a mix of medications and decreased food intake common among the elderly, and someone who didn't have a problem with alcohol can certainly have one now. Current research shows that nearly one in five older adults is affected by alcohol and drug misuse. Yet few primary care physicians are picking it up. No one wants to ask and no one wants to tell. Many families feel it's too late for the chronic alcoholic, and others are in outright denial that their parent could have a drinking problem.

If your mother answers yes to any of the following questions (known as the CAGE questionnaire), then she has symptoms of alcoholism:

- Have you ever felt you should **C**ut down on your drinking?
- Have people **A**nnoyed you by criticizing your drinking?
- Have you ever felt bad or **G**uilty about your drinking?
- Have you ever had a drink first thing in the morning to steady your nerves or get rid of a hangover (**E**ye-opener)?

There are a number of resources that can help you learn how to approach your mom and her physician to help her gain control of her drinking problem. Part of the strategy should include getting her physically and mentally fit. Your mother might be depressed, and the alcohol will only depress her more. Her treatment plan must include getting at the root of her need to drink.

Reach out to the National Council on Alcoholism and Drug Dependence Hopeline at (800) 622-2255, find a family support group by calling Al-Anon at (888) 4AL-ANON or research the latest information at the National Clearinghouse for Alcohol and Drug Information's Web site at www.health.org.

Whatever you do, don't be afraid to address the issue with your mom. Looking the other way or hoping she'll just stop on her own denies both of you a healthy, happy relationship with each other, let alone her grandchildren. Alcoholics are at great risk for cascading health problems, hospitalization and an early death. Act on your worries.

Q: How can I get my father to eat better?

A: If your dad is anything like mine, he grew up in a meat-and-potato household (with lots of gravy). Most of our parents were raised on great ethnic cuisine that was heavy on sauces, spices and salt. America's interest in low-fat food and light fare has been relatively recent, so getting your dad interested in foods that are user-friendly for his older body might be a real challenge.

But this is a challenge we've got to meet head-on. According to a report by AARP, four out of five older adults have chronic illnesses that are affected by diet. One out of eight suffers depression with a subsequent loss of appetite, one in four drinks too much alcohol, one in three lives alone and doesn't feel like cooking and most take medications that require a nutritionally sound body to be effective. Far too many older people are in a rut, eating the same thing day after day.

Tufts University Center on Nutrition recently came out with a modified food pyramid for adults aged seventy-plus. They made two major changes to the typical food pyramid we're used to seeing: The bottom of the pyramid "floats" with eight glasses of water and the top has a flag promoting supplements in calcium, and vitamins D and B-12. What's with the floating base? Dehydration is a major problem among the elderly. While the rest of us are running around with trendy water bottles, our parents are actually losing their sense of thirst.

Let your dad in on that fact. Otherwise he'll just say he's not thirsty. Without enough water, kidney problems, constipation and complications from medications that deplete the body's water supply will quickly take hold. You might want to stock his refrigerator with small bottles of water, so you can get your dad into the habit of drinking it.

The age seventy-plus food pyramid also has little f-plus signs everywhere. These stand for fiber, and our parents need plenty of it to keep their digestive tracts humming along. Nutritionists will tell you to:

- Talk with your parent's physician to see if any of your parent's medical conditions warrant a special diet.
- Try serving small, frequent meals if your dad has lost his appetite. Or serve him the larger meal of the day when his appetite seems to peak.
- If your dad can't see well, use plain white plates and lay out his food on the plate as if it were a clock. Tell him, for example, that the rice is at nine o'clock, the chicken at noon and the green beans at four o'clock.
- Make mealtime a special event, with nice silverware and colorful napkins.

If your parent lives alone, organize a visiting schedule among family and friends to have lunch or dinner with your parent. Eating alone, day after day, is a prime factor in older folks not eating well. Home-delivered meals are a terrific way to mix a friendly visit with a meal. To find out about the nearest one, call the local Area Agency on Aging or the Eldercare Locator at (800) 677-1116. And if your dad has physical difficulty eating, call Able Data, (800) 227-0216, or Independent Living Aids, (800) 537-2118, and ask for catalogs of eating utensils and devices.

For excellent nutritional advice online, go to:

• **Mayo Clinic's Health Oasis** (www.mayohealth.org). This fun, easy site offers a virtual cookbook that takes recipes and makes them less fattening. On the navigation bar click on "Healthy Living Centers," then go to "Food & Nutrition."
• **The Tufts University Nutrition Navigator** (www.navigator.tufts.edu). This site reviews and rates a zillion Web sites on nutrition and hyperlinks you to them. (Tip: enter "aging and nutrition" on the search bar.)

Q: **What preventive health screenings should my parents have?**

A: Most of our parents grew up with the adage "A stitch in time saves nine." So perhaps you can convince your mom and dad that the same principle applies to their health. A few preventive stitches here and there can save quite a few later—literally. Many of today's health advances are credited to people taking better care of themselves by eating well, exercising and by getting regular checkups to screen for diseases that frequently affect the elderly. Just consider these statistics:

• **Osteoporosis,** or porous bone, is a disease of low bone mass and structural deterioration of bone tissue. This leads to fragile bones and an increased susceptibility to fractures, especially of the hip, spine and wrist. Nearly ten million Americans have the disease, and women are four times more likely to have it.
• **Colorectal Cancer** (cancers of both the colon and rectum) is the second leading cause of cancer-related deaths in the United States. Nearly 131,000 Americans will be diagnosed with colorectal cancer and 56,000 will die of it this year.
• **Type-2 Diabetes,** often referred to as adult-onset diabetes, affects over eleven million people, half of whom don't know they have the disease. Nearly one in twelve people over the age of sixty-five becomes diabetic, and one in four people over eighty-five.
• **Breast Cancer** incidence increases with age. Nearly three out of four invasive breast

cancers occur in women over age fifty while the average age at diagnosis is sixty-four. Based on the current life expectancy for women in the United States, one out of nine women will develop breast cancer in her lifetime.

• **Cervical Cancer** incidence has decreased significantly, in large part because of screening for (Pap smears) and treatment of precancerous cervical lesions. However, an estimated 13,000 new cases were diagnosed and 4,100 women died of the disease in 2002. Older women are at higher risk, as they tend to stop getting annual Pap smears.

• **Prostate Cancer** is diagnosed nearly every three minutes, accounting for 190,000 new cases each year. It is the most commonly diagnosed cancer in America among men. More than 30,000 American men lose their lives to prostate cancer each year. One in six American men is at lifetime risk of prostate cancer. If a close relative has prostate cancer, a man's risk of the disease more than doubles.

• **Flu** hits between 10 percent and 20 percent of U.S. residents each year, causing an average of 114,000 people to be hospitalized. About 36,000 Americans die annually from the complications of flu; many of them are elderly.

• **Glaucoma** is now the leading cause of blindness in the United States, affecting nearly three million people. African-Americans, diabetics and people over the age of sixty are at high risk for the disease, which slowly and quietly causes fluid buildup that damages the eye.

Medicare pays for screenings and tests on all of the above conditions. If your parent has a Medigap policy, they won't have any out-of-pocket expense. So there really is no excuse not to take advantage of all of these preventive health services offered by Medicare.

Have your parents take this list to their next appointment with their primary physician and ask him or her to get these scheduled. The doctor's office should know the eligibility rules surrounding each test.

Q: **Is West Nile virus something my parents should fear?**

A: If you've had a wet spring, then you'll be in for a tough time with mosquitoes, as they love hot, wet environments. And more mosquitoes means more cases of West Nile virus (WNV) in humans. Mosquitoes are carriers of the disease, usually picking it up by biting infected birds. In 2003, the Centers for Disease Control (CDC) reported that the nation saw over 6,800 cases, killing 264 people. To put this in perspective for your parents, imagine if the CDC just announced that nearly three hundred people died of SARS in the United States. I'm sure it would get their attention. Bottom line: Yes, your parents should be concerned, but it doesn't mean they need to give up gardening or feel terrorized whenever they hear the buzzing of that pesty blood-sucking insect. Overall, contracting the disease is rare. However, people over the age of fifty are at the highest risk for developing severe West Nile virus. Most of the deaths during 2003 were among those over fifty years old, while the greatest number were over seventy-seven. Few children contract severe WNV. There's a common misperception that only people who are already in poor health are susceptible, but many healthy older adults who like to exercise and spend time working outdoors found themselves just as sick from the virus.

So Just What Does WNV Do to You? The virus affects the central nervous system, with symptoms appearing between three and fourteen days after being bitten. About eight out of ten people will never even know that they have been infected as they'll exhibit no symptoms. Others will experience fever, headache, and body aches, nausea, vomiting, and sometimes swollen lymph glands or a skin rash on the chest, stomach and back. These will last a few days.

About one in one hundred and fifty people infected with WNV will develop severe illness, potentially causing high fever, headache, neck stiffness, stupor, disorientation, coma, tremors, convulsions, muscle weakness, vision loss, numbness and paralysis. These symptoms may last several weeks, and may result in permanent neurological damage and even death.

What's the Treatment for WNV? Right now there is no specific treatment, according to the CDC. Those with mild symptoms will simply get better on their own. But those with any of the severe symptoms should immediately seek medical attention. Some will need to be hospitalized to receive supportive treatment that may involve intravenous fluids, assistance with breathing and nursing care. People with chronic conditions like heart disease or diabetes, or who have suffered a stroke, will be especially vulnerable to further complications caused by WNV.

So What Can Your Parents Do to Protect Themselves? Most state departments of health issue alerts when the disease is reported in a region. Many post these on their Web sites and give you directions on how to report the disease. You can also find your local health department listed in the blue pages of your phone book.

Here is a list of action steps that Pennsylvania's state health department recommends to minimize your parent's risk of being exposed to WNV.

REDUCE THE BREEDING GROUNDS OF MOSQUITOES BY:

1. Disposing of tin cans, plastic containers, ceramic pots or similar water-holding containers that have collected on your property.
2. Get rid of discarded tires. Mosquitoes love breeding in the stagnant water found in tires.
3. Drill holes in the bottom of recycling containers left outdoors.
4. Clean clogged roof gutters, as they can produce millions of mosquitoes.
5. Turn over plastic wading pools when not in use.
6. Turn over wheelbarrows and don't let water stagnate in birdbaths.
7. Aerate ornamental pools or, better yet, stock them with fish. Water gardens can become major mosquito producers if they are allowed to stagnate.
8. Clean and chlorinate your swimming pool even when you are not using it during vacation.
9. Make sure your screens are well fitted to windows and without holes or tears.

PROTECT YOURSELF FROM BEING BITTEN BY:

1. Applying insect repellent (the CDC recommends DEET) every time you go outdoors; even spray it on your clothing.
2. When possible, wear long sleeves, long pants and socks, especially when gardening.
3. Be aware that peak mosquito hours are from dusk until dawn.

If you'd like more information about WNV or you would like to help eliminate breeding areas for mosquitoes in your community, call your local department of health and ask how you can contact your local West Nile coordinator.

Q: **My dad thinks losing teeth is normal in old age. Is it?**

A: I like to tell my teenagers that parents are always right. But in this case, here's a parent who is wrong. Losing teeth is not a normal part of aging. Decay and gum disease are the major culprits in tooth loss, not getting older. All too often, older people think that the annual dental visit is "kid's stuff." However, people over sixty-five have more tooth decay than any other age group. The good news is that many people today maintain their teeth, and as a result, approximately

50 percent of people fifty-five years old or older have at least twenty-three of their thirty-two natural teeth remaining.

According to the Foundation for Health in Aging, a nonprofit organization of the American Geriatrics Society, older people tend to produce less saliva, resulting in fewer protective minerals to help clean teeth; their gums begin to recede, exposing the tooth to decay or infection; arthritis and poor vision make it hard to floss and brush teeth, all of which further complicate daily oral care. The foundation cites five problems common to older people's oral health: tooth decay, gum disease, poor-fitting dentures, dry mouth and oral cancer.

The bacteria found in plaque give off acid that leads to gum or periodontal disease. Pockets often develop between teeth and gums, trapping food that will decay, thus the need to floss. Symptoms include red or swollen gums that bleed with the slightest irritation. A loose tooth or one that falls out could well be a sign of gum disease, so your father should be examined before it advances any further.

Dry mouth comes mainly from the slower production of saliva but can also be linked to medications such as diuretics, antihistamines and antidepressants. Why is this important? People with dry mouth are more prone to infections and tooth decay. Oral lubricants such as lemon-flavored glycerine drops or artificial saliva can help but, again, this is a sign of something going awry and warrants a dental visit.

Oral cancer includes cancers of the mouth, tongue, throat and lips. Red or white spots, sores in the mouth or continuous bleeding are early signs of oral cancer and should be seen by a dentist pronto. Ninety-five percent of cases of oral and throat cancer occur in people forty and over, and the average age at diagnosis is sixty. Oral cancer accounts for nearly 4 percent of all cancers, and it's no surprise that the leading cause of oral cancer is smoking.

In terms of preventive dental care, here are some things your dad can do after he makes an annual visit to the dentist:

- Use a medium or soft brush and brush daily. Hard brushes don't make teeth cleaner and can actually be harmful. Long handles are easier to use. Buy a new brush every three months and after a major illness.
- Floss. If it's too difficult, buy the small floss holders with the plastic handles.
- Rinse the mouth throughout the day with warm water (add a teaspoon of salt).
- Stop smoking.
- If he has dentures, he should remove them at least six hours per day (most people do this before bed), brush dentures every night, and make sure they fit well. If he has problems with them, don't hesitate to see the dentist, dental hygienist or denturist.

Poor oral health can lead to poor nutrition, which brings on a whole new set of problems. Your teeth, gums and saliva are your first contact with food and start the process of healthy digestion. If your dad is sending bacteria along for the ride down his digestive tract or he shows signs of losing his appetite because it's too painful to crunch and munch, then his oral health will jeopardize his entire body.

My guess is, your dad didn't get a few dollars from the tooth fairy for his lost tooth. But she gave him a better gift—a warning. Tell him to take heed.

Q: How much water should elderly people drink?

A: Water can save your parents from a whole host of health problems, especially those related to kidney disease. Tufts University Center on Nutrition has become so convinced of the health benefits of water for the elderly that they have redesigned the USDA's Food Guide Pyramid. Now, the base of the pyramid "floats" with eight glasses of water pictured on the bottom. Why the floating base? Dehydration is a major problem among the elderly.

While Gen-Xers run around the country with trendy water bottles in hand, their grandparents are losing their sense of thirst. Some experts have even found that our sense of thirst isn't the best indicator that our body needs water. As a result, the older generation is having kidney problems, urinary tract infections, constipation and other health conditions linked to a chronic state of dehydration.

The elderly are especially affected by dehydration because many of the medications they take may further deplete the body's water supply without their ever realizing it. All too often, we forget that nearly three-fourths of our body is water. Thus, we need to keep a healthy amount of fresh fluids flowing in and out of our bodies. Water flushes out wastes, regulates our body temperature, carries nutrients throughout the bloodstream, reaching vital organs, and supports chemical balances. Staying well hydrated can boost energy and keep the skin moist, which is especially helpful for dry, aging skin. Signs of dehydration include dizziness, weakness, muscle cramps and general feelings of weakness.

So how much water should your parents drink? Most experts recommend eight glasses of water (eight ounces each) per day. Some refer to it as the "8 by 8" rule. The nationally known integrative physician Andrew Weil, M.D., believes this general rule of thumb makes good sense. The Mayo Clinic Women's Health Source suggests that people should drink half an ounce of water for each pound of body weight, so if your mom weighs 120 pounds she should drink 7.5 glasses of water a day while your dad, who may weigh 200 pounds, will need 12.5 glasses.

Does it have to be pure water? Not necessarily. Your parents can achieve this higher fluid intake with juices, milk, and teas or coffee without caffeine. Some foods also include water, like soups, yogurt, fruits such as watermelon, apples, oranges, tomatoes and vegetables like lettuce, carrots and cucumbers. But don't think that all fluids are created equal: alcoholic beverages don't count in your daily intake—they get a big fat zero. In fact, alcohol inhibits the body's antidiuretic hormone (ADH) so your parents will actually *lose* fluids. Black tea, green tea, caffeinated sodas and coffee are also known to have a dehydrating effect, so some experts like Marianne Woods Cirone, M.S., R.Y.T., suggest that you count each ounce of this type of beverage as only half an ounce toward your daily fluid intake goal.

Most physical fitness experts recommend starting your day with water. During the night your body becomes dehydrated and can greatly benefit from water first thing in the morning.

Figuring out your parents' best source of water requires a bit of exploration. Would they like to drink bottled water as a way of measuring how much they drink each day? Do they feel their tap water is safe to drink? If not, they could purchase a simple water filter to attach to the faucet or buy a water pitcher with a filter. According to Steve Meyerowitz, author of *Water, the Ultimate Cure*, simple carbon filters in a pitcher or on a faucet are very effective at ridding organic compounds, pesticides and some metals from tap water. Or perhaps your parents would like a water cooler system, with water being delivered each month. This might make a nice gift from the family and induce them not to "waste" all that fresh water being delivered to their doorstep. To make their water intake more interesting they could add slices of lime or lemon.

Before they start on their new water venture, be sure to check with their physician to see if they have a kidney condition or other medical condition in which fluid intake should be monitored. Also take the time to figure out if there are other reasons that your parents are steering clear of water. You might find that your dad is lowering his intake because getting to the bathroom is a hassle, or your mom may be cutting down her fluids because she fears incontinence. These indicate other health problems that will only be exacerbated by limiting their fluid intake. So find out what's going on first and then create a hydration strategy that suits your parents' needs and lifestyle.

Q: Are flu shots free and are they really necessary?

A: The answer to the first part of your question is yes. If your father carries Medicare Part B then he can receive a flu shot from a Medicare provider and pay no coinsurance or deductible. Most Medicare HMOs actually *require* their subscribers to receive a (free) flu shot. Besides physicians, many senior centers and public health centers offer flu shots.

Most Area Agencies on Aging (AAA) throughout the nation offer free flu vaccines. You can track down your local AAA by calling (800) 677-1116. Remember that October and November are the prime months to receive flu shots.

Now, for the second part of your question, are flu shots really necessary? If your dad doesn't want to be counted among the estimated 45,000 people who die every year from influenza, then it's best he take the shot. Ninety percent of those who die from the flu are sixty-five and older. Why? Because many older people have other medical conditions that easily become exacerbated by the flu. People with heart disease, lung conditions and diabetes are particularly susceptible. The Centers for Disease Control (CDC) reports that there are about 142,000 influenza-related hospitalizations every year.

Influenza is an extremely contagious respiratory condition easily spread from person to person by sneezes or coughs. Symptoms usually appear within two to four days of infection and the patient is contagious for three to four days after that. An estimated 10 to 20 percent of the U.S. population comes down with the flu each year. In other words, your dad has a one-in-five chance of being exposed to someone with the flu. Pretty high odds, wouldn't you say?

The reasons your dad needs to receive a new vaccine every year are 1) the virus mutates from year to year and 2) the antibodies produced in response to the vaccine decline over time and are very low one year later.

Most of us know too well the dreaded symptoms of the flu: fever, chills, headache, dry cough, runny or stuffy nose, sore throat and muscle aches. It can also cause extreme fatigue lasting several days to more than a week. One of the clearest dangers for older people is the high risk of the flu developing into pneumonia, which can be life-threatening. For that reason, your dad should ask his physician whether or not he should also receive a onetime vaccination for pneumococcal pneumonia. If his physician prescribes the vaccine, it will be covered by Medicare.

The only people who should not get a flu shot, according to the National CDC Advisory Committee on Immunization Practices, are those who are severely allergic to hens' eggs, have had severe reactions to a flu shot in the past, or developed Guillain-Barré syndrome (GBS) within six weeks of getting a flu shot. Side effects are rare, with the most common complaint being soreness around the injection site.

Q: Other than getting a flu shot, what can my mom do to fight off the flu?

A: Your mom has taken the most effective step: getting a shot. However, according to the Centers for Disease Control, strains of the virus can surface after a vaccine has been created, leaving people exposed to the flu after all.

Before I share with you ways to fight off the flu, let's go over some flu basics. There are two major ways that influenza is transmitted: the first is by *inhaling* infectious particles in the air (usually hurled into your breathing space from a sneeze or a cough) and the second is by *touching* respiratory secretions (such as via a handshake, doorknob or phone) and then transferring them by touching the nose or eyes.

Pneumonia is one of the greatest threats to the elderly who come down with the flu. Each year about 36,000 people die of flu complications, and nine out of ten are over the age of sixty-five. Over 100,000 people will be hospitalized.

So how can your mom fight the flu? Here are Five Flu-Fighting Tactics that may help:

1. **Wash Your Hands—All Day Long!** The flu virus is a mighty little army that can survive on inanimate objects like doorknobs, computer keyboards, phones, cups, and handles of all kinds for up to three hours. It can also survive that long on skin—so that friendly handshake can quickly turn into an unwelcome invasion. I suggest giving your mom several packs of wipes to carry with her throughout the flu season. Use these to clean surfaces too.

2. **If the Grandkids Are Sick—Stay Away!** Okay, this may sound harsh, but you might need to skip that long-awaited visit because children are one of the most fertile carriers of viruses. My family doctor tells me that he always has a surge of elderly patients with the flu right after they've been with grandchildren who were either sick during their visit or just got over a cold or flu. If your parent has a heart or lung condition, I strongly advise family members to opt out of gatherings when they have the flu, just got over the flu, or have been exposed to the flu, so they don't endanger each other.

3. **Stay Clear of Crowds.** Since the flu is contagious, it's smart to stay away from large crowds of people if your parent is especially vulnerable because of other health problems. This may curtail their social life but, given how the flu can turn into a very serious illness for them, it's worth waiting out the flu season. And by no means should they visit friends in the hospital. Send them cards, flowers and give them a call instead.

4. **Maintain a Healthy Lifestyle.** Most health experts agree that doses of vitamin C are helpful, along with a well-balanced diet. Drink plenty of liquids and get adequate hours of sleep, all of which help keep your immune system in top shape.

5. **Keep Your Hands Away from Your Face.** Try to keep your hands away from your nose and eyes, as they act as portals of entry for flu viruses. That's why washing your hands frequently is so important. Always cough into a tissue and then immediately throw it away.

If your mother does start showing symptoms of the flu, she should call her doctor right away. There are several antiviral medications on the market (e.g., Tamiflu, Relenza, Symmetral,

Flumadine) that can reduce the length of the flu and its severity. But don't waste any time getting to the doctor! To be effective these medications must be taken within two days of the first signs of the flu.

Q: What's the connection between salt and hypertension?

A: Not until I started reading labels on food did I become aware of how much sodium (salt) is hidden in foods that I thought were healthy. People are pretty surprised when they learn that a healthy-looking garden salad topped with low-fat dressing can pack in more salt than the hamburger and French fries you dutifully passed up. Two tablespoons of Zesty Italian dressing has more than 500 milligrams of sodium. And who uses only two tablespoons?

To put this in perspective, experts recommend that we consume only 2,400 milligrams of sodium a day, but if you have high blood pressure, your intake should drop down to 1,500. Sodium is not inherently bad. Our bodies need it to regulate our fluids. However, too much of it can cause body fluids to build up.

Picture your garden hose hooked up to a fire hydrant. The pressure shooting through the hose would wear it thin in no time. Now picture a small pump at the end of the hose trying to redirect the high-pressured water through other small hoses. Any guesses on how long the pump can handle the pressure?

This is what high blood pressure does to the heart, which is the small pump redirecting the hoses. In addition, the continuous, high-pressured rush of blood flowing through the blood vessels wears them down to a point where they might tear or leak. This is why high blood pressure is the leading cause of strokes and is a major culprit in heart attacks.

Processed foods, canned soups, sauces, fast food, spaghetti sauces and salad dressing (even low-fat) catapult us over the top on the sodium scale. Experts figure that Americans consume two to three times the recommended limit. Most of us think if we ditch the table salt and stay clear of foods with visible salt on them, such as Saltine crackers and pretzels, we're good to go. But according to Bobbie Mostyn, author of the "Pocket Guide to Low Sodium Foods," "Most of us are unaware of how much salt we actually take in."

The burden shouldn't just be on consumers to detect high sodium amounts; the American Public Health Association is calling on the food industry to cut down on foods with unhealthy levels of sodium.

So, if you're worried that your parents might be taking in too much salt, what can they do? They should try working with the foods they already enjoy and then analyze the sodium levels. If they are too high, search for ways to prepare favorite dishes that are safer for their health.

Expecting older people to dramatically change their eating habits will only set them up for failure. You also might want to pick up a guide to sodium content such as Mostyn's. It's a fast and easy way to check out sodium levels of fast foods, condiments and restaurant cooking, along with products they buy at the grocery store. I know my mother was shocked at how much sodium she was taking in with her favorite salad at a national food chain. She continued to buy the salad but substituted the dressing. You also can check out the author's Web site, with all kinds of smart tips on sodium tracking at www.lowsaltfoods.com. Who knows, your parents might actually enjoy playing "Sodium Sleuth."

Q: My dad isn't sleeping well, but he says older people need less sleep anyway. Shouldn't he see a doctor?

A: It's actually a myth that older people need less sleep. According to the National Sleep Foundation, our sleep needs remain relatively constant throughout most of our lives; for most people, that is seven to nine hours of sleep throughout our lifetime. It's the stages of sleep that will undergo change.

One reason that your dad may be experiencing a drop in restful sleep is that as we age, we experience less of the deep, restorative third and fourth stages of sleep. We also tend to experience less of the fifth stage, R.E.M. (rapid eye movement) sleep—the kind that has your eyes flickering while you're dreaming. All that flickering causes an increased blood supply and the flow of some mighty fine brain chemicals. You can thank these guys for that restored, "go get 'em" feeling when you wake up.

An aging body also produces less melatonin, the hormone that regulates sleep. If your father is in his seventies or eighties, in fact, his melatonin levels may be barely traceable. Other factors that can contribute to poor sleep are getting little exercise, drinking caffeine and smoking.

It's worthwhile to seek ways to help your father sleep more effectively and wake up feeling refreshed. It takes a little work and a bit of reprogramming. Here are some tips to share with him:

- Develop a regular, soothing routine for going to bed, such as listening to music, reading, taking a warm bath or massaging yourself with skin lotion. Send signals to your mind and body that it's time to sleep.
- Stick to the same bedtime and naptime every day. A consistent schedule is critical to setting your biological clock.
- Drink very few fluids a few hours before bedtime so there's no need to go to the bathroom at night.

- Keep daytime napping to a minimum—no more than an hour—and make sure it is early in the afternoon. Watch for dozing off in front of the television.
- Avoid heavy meals close to bedtime, especially spicy ones. Eating at five p.m. will give adequate time for digestion. You might want to consider having your largest meal at lunchtime.
- Don't smoke. Nicotine plays havoc with sleep.
- Avoid alcohol at bedtime. Although it may appear to make you drowsy, you'll actually awaken early without feeling rested.
- Ask your doctor about the side effects of any medications that you are taking. Some will cause sleep disturbances.

If your dad's sleeping problems persist, he should describe them to his doctor. If he's sleeping but isn't feeling rested, it could be a sign of coronary artery disease, lung disease, thyroid problems, depression, anxiety or dementia. A great way of keeping track of sleep patterns that your dad could share with his doctor is to get a copy of the National Sleep Foundation's sleep diary. Call (202) 347-3471 to ask for a copy, or go to www.sleepfoundation.org.

It's very tempting to simply ask your doctor to prescribe sleeping pills to solve the problem. But before any such pill is given, your physician should explore what's causing the problem in the first place. Sleeping pills can assist in the short term and help stop the cycle of fatigue and exhaustion. But they are meant to be taken for a short period of time, and certainly not for the rest of your life. Yet far too many elderly are taking hypnotic drugs as their first line of offense to getting a "good" night's sleep. Taking these pills for the long haul can cause daytime sleepiness, anxiety, depression, decline in cognitive thinking and falls. Getting off the drug must be done very carefully and slowly. So, if your dad's doctor does prescribe a sleeping pill, make sure he takes it responsibly and for the short run.

2

Family Conflicts & Relationships

Q: **All this caregiving is too stressful. How do I get a grip?**

A: There are programs that assist family members caring for an elderly relative to help ease the load. Of course, it takes time and some organizing to track them down, and I'm sure you feel you don't even have the time to find the help.

One of the many pitfalls of caregiving is falling into the trap of "It's easier to just do it myself." By the time you find someone to help, it's too late or just too much of a hassle. You may also find that the person you are caring for becomes dependent on you and only wants *you* to help. You begin to think you're the only one who can do it. Once the cycle starts, it's hard to stop. I know. I cared for my husband's grandmother for a year right after my first child was born. She came to trust me and called me her "manager," making it clear that only Linda could take care of her.

Between Grandma and the baby, I had my hands full. It was too much of a hassle finding a babysitter for the baby and a caregiver for Grandma; I found it easier to simply stay at home and care for both of them. After a while, a good friend intervened and told me enough was enough. She was right. I was running myself into the ground.

So, from both personal and professional experience, here's what I suggest you do:

- Tonight, take the time to list all the tasks you performed today. Then add any other tasks you frequently perform for your parent throughout the week. Can you categorize some of these tasks? What comes under daily personal care (i.e., grooming, toileting, medications or feeding)? Other categories might be transportation, doctor visits, meal preparation, socialization, exercise and supervision. Put a star next to those tasks that you perform daily or routinely through the week.

- Make copies of the list, and share it with all of your family members, friends and neighbors who've asked you at one time or another, "Is there anything I can do to help?" See which items on the list they could do, especially those tasks that routinely have to be performed (the ones with a star). Take them up on their offer to help. You'd be surprised at how people will respond to a specific task that can be made part of *their* routine. Even if just a few people respond, this will give you a chance to create a schedule with some downtime for yourself. Do not use the free time to run off and do more errands for your loved one. The idea is to give *yourself* the time to recharge. Go to your favorite bookstore, walk with some friends, get a massage, catch a twilight movie—do something that makes you feel good.

If you don't have a large enough circle of family or friends, you can reach out to organizations. Here are some more ideas:

- The Interfaith Caregivers Association supports a program called Faith in Action. They will send in volunteers to spend some time with your parent to give you a break. You can find a program near you at www.fiavolunteers.org or call them toll-free at (877) 324-8411. Don't forget to go to your own church or synagogue to ask for volunteers.
- Call your local Area Agency on Aging and ask about the Family Caregiver Support Program. You might qualify for ongoing assistance, and even home-modification funds to make it easier to care for your parent. Call the Eldercare Locator at (800) 677-1116 to find the nearest agency to you.
- Call your local senior center and hospitals to find out if they have any support groups on dealing with stress and caregiving. Talking with others who are going through the same thing can really help you put things in perspective and learn how to cope.
- Consider hiring nonmedical senior care aides who can help you with shopping, watching your parent while you're out, preparing meals and doing many of the nonmedical things that you do all day. Even if they come in once a week, it will give you some free time. You can find them in the Yellow Pages under Home Health Care.
- If you're working, ask your employer about any employee assistance programs they might have to help you out—you might be pleasantly surprised. You can also use the Family Medical Leave Act to take some time to provide caregiving. See page 201.

I know all of this takes some time on your part, and you're already feeling overwhelmed. But doing this will absolutely pay off for you. You must take care of yourself. You can even put making these calls on your list of tasks that you ask help in doing. I've often found that people will help—if you ask and if you give them something specific to do.

Q: **How can I get my sister to help me care for our mom? I've hinted that I need help but she doesn't offer to do *anything*.**

A: The most frequently reported frustration among caregivers is lack of consistent help from other family members. In the National Family Caregivers Association annual survey, three out of four family members felt this way.

It is very common for one family member to gravitate to the central caregiving role. This may be the oldest child, the child nearest the parent geographically, the child without children, the child with a health care background or the child with the most flexible work schedule. It is also common for the central caregiver to begin feeling that no one else can really take care of Mom or Dad. I've heard many caregivers say that despite wanting more help, they're the "only one who really knows" what their parent wants and needs. Or they feel that by the time they explain everything that is needed, they might as well do it themselves. The person who needs the care often feeds into this "only you" syndrome. And so the cycle begins and the caregiver soon becomes worn down and resentful. Many begin to feel that other family members should just "know" what to do and pitch in voluntarily. They resent having to ask for help.

Sending hints to your sister is not enough. She may not be picking them up because she genuinely thinks you have everything under control. In the meantime, you're seething in anger and could eventually take it out on your mother. So let's break the cycle right now.

It is your responsibility to share with your sister exactly what is involved in caring for your mother. Most people don't realize how stressful caregiving is until they've gone through it. Just think of how many of us call our parents after our first child is born and ask in amazement, "How did you do it?"

So create a picture of what it takes to care for your mom. Your sister can't do her fair share if she doesn't get the whole picture. I'd start with a two-column list. On the left-hand side, write down everything you do:

- Making all of her doctors' appointments
- The medications she must take and how often
- The insurance polices and paperwork involved in her care
- The bills you pay on her behalf
- The transportation you provide and must arrange

- Chores that are done on her behalf
- Food and clothes shopping
- Any medical or health care you provide
- Medical and health care you arrange for a professional to provide
- Any daily living needs you must provide her (e.g., dressing, food preparation)

Then, on the right-hand side of the list, identify all of the steps that you take to fulfill each task. I'd also put in parenthesis how much time these tasks take. Now you are in a position to sit down with your sister and share the list. Rather than counting on a look-at-what-a-martyr-I-am approach to throw your sister into guilt-ridden action, start by asking her to help you go through the list and provide input on how the two of you can come up with a care plan for your mother. If she lives some distance away, are there things she can do that don't involve being there? Perhaps she can do all of the insurance work, schedule doctor appointments, pay bills and help research any of your mom's medical conditions. Could she set aside one day a week to relieve you of any of your caregiving tasks? If she can't, could she cover the costs of providing some assistance for that day? When it comes to gifts for Mom, suggest she give gift certificates for home-delivered meals, cab rides, or cleaning service—all of which would assist you, as well.

Once you come away with a care plan, make copies of it so that both of you have it, and be sure to update it as your mother's needs change. I'd also suggest setting up a convenient, weekly phone conversation for the two of you to go over your mother's care—that way your sister will feel more of a partner and remain very much aware of what is involved. You need to begin to relate to your sister differently—as a partner—before she can start acting like one.

Q: Should my dad be driving?

A: Before I answer that question, we all need to remember that driving is directly linked to staying active and independent. So, if your dad must begin to limit his driving, make sure he has alternative ways to stay on the go.

Driving skills vary enormously among all age groups. In general, driving skills do begin to decline from age fifty-five on. Experts believe that 90 percent of the information we need to drive comes through our eyes, especially our peripheral vision. As we age, we need more light to see clearly, we find it harder to adjust to glare from oncoming headlights, and we have difficulty refocusing from light to dark.

Judging distances becomes tougher. Hearing loss makes high-pitched sounds from sirens, horns and train whistles harder to detect. Reaction time is slower, making high-traffic conditions, merging and negotiating busy intersections quite a hassle. Add to all of these physiologic changes medications that many older people take that can cause drowsiness or confusion, and you can quickly see how an experienced driver begins to "slip."

So what can your dad do? First, he can go to school and save money at the same time by taking the AARP 55 Alive driver education course. The benefits are twofold: Besides refreshing your knowledge about driving—including how to assess your driving skills and learning new rules—you automatically get a 5 percent reduction in your auto insurance. The two four-hour classes are taught by trained volunteers and all you pay is $10. To find the class nearest you, call your local AARP chapter, listed in the blue pages of your phone book.

I suggest taking a ride with your father to see if you pick up any of the following warning signs:

- Changing lanes without signaling
- Going through red lights or stop signs
- Reacting too slowly, straying into other lanes or onto the berm
- Showing significant hesitancy at intersections, making jerky stops or starts, or driving too slow or too fast
- Having difficulty making left turns and merging

According to AARP, here are the six most common problems with older drivers: failure to yield the right of way, making improper left turns, negotiating blind spots, getting on and off freeways, backing up, and slow reaction time.

The AARP and the Pennsylvania Department of Transportation offer a number of prevention tips for older drivers:

- Make sure you can easily see over the dashboard.
- Check that your feet easily reach the pedals.
- Adjust the steering wheel, mirrors and seats properly.
- Avoid night driving, rush hour and being on the road in bad weather.
- Limit trips to shorter distances.
- Plan and know the route in advance.
- Have regular medical checkups that include vision and hearing tests.
- Make sure that medications don't interfere with alertness and ability to drive.
- Create more simplified routes to favorite places that avoid challenging merges and intersections.

• Stay a safe distance behind cars to make up for slower reaction time.

• Look ahead to get a jump on trouble by looking down the road.

• Avoid buying cars with heavily tinted windshields and windows.

• Keep your headlights clean.

• Use night glasses to reduce glare.

For more information, readers may check out AARP's Web site at www.AARP.org; on the search bar enter the key words "safe driving." Your parents can take a "Close Call Quiz," track down a 55 Alive course near them and get all kinds of safety tips for older drivers.

The AAA Foundation for Traffic Safety also offers some terrific publications that include a guide for families and a self-exam. You can request a copy by writing to the AAA Foundation at 1440 New York Avenue N.W., Suite 201, Washington, D.C. 20005, or visit their Web site at www.AAAFoundation.org and click on "Free Items." At the "Products" section of the Web site, you can order an excellent video, *The Older and Wiser Driver,* for $19.95. It shows your dad how to compensate for driving skills that have changed with age. You also may order it by phone at (800) 305-7233.

Q: My mother's driving is really terrible. How do I get her to give up the car keys?

A: You're facing quite a dilemma. I'm sure you want your mom to enjoy her independence, but on the other hand, you can't keep looking the other way, knowing others aren't safe with her behind the wheel. It sounds like you're past the point that a driver refresher course will help.

But before she's retired from driving, it's important to have a transportation system in place so that your mom can remain active and not become isolated. The "system" can consist of family and friends who call your mom with frequent invites to take her to the store, the mall, to a friend's house or the doctor's, so she doesn't feel like she's a burden. Don't force her to have to ask for a favor. Be sure to call her Area Agency on Aging and ask them about the shared ride program that offers discounted rides to seniors who share a cab or van, and other transit benefits for seniors. Call Eldercare Locator to find the AAA nearest her at (800) 677-1116.

Now to convince Mom. If you believe her driving is a safety hazard and she will not listen to reason, then here are two things you can do.

First, go to her physician and explain your concern about your mom's driving. Doctors are required by law to report to the state's department of motor vehicles any individual diagnosed with a condition that could impair their ability to safely operate a motor vehicle. The state's medical unit will evaluate the information on a case-by-case basis. They may add or delete restrictions from the license, restore or recall the license, request additional information, such as a medical examination or a driver's test, or they may take no action. Usually, the physician's name remains confidential.

Second, you can write a confidential letter to your state's department of motor vehicles explaining why your mother is no longer able to drive. You must include your name, phone number and signature. Often, the medical unit of the department will contact you to verify that you wrote the letter and discuss the case in more detail. The letter should remain confidential—your mom will not know you wrote it. The medical unit then proceeds the same way as when the physician reports something. Chances are they'll write your mother a letter telling her that they've received information indicating that she has a condition that could affect or limit her ability to drive. They'll ask her for information and could ask her to take a driver and/or physical exam. If she does not answer within forty-five days, many states will automatically suspend her license.

Sometimes, older people hold onto their license because they think it is the only way they can get a check cashed. However, licenses can be issued purely as a photo ID, without driving privileges.

Every state has different laws regulating older-driver licensing, and many now require anyone who reaches eighty-five years of age to renew their license in person. So be sure to check with them before you take any action.

Q: My mom's friend just lost her spouse. What should she say and do?

A: All too often, because we feel uncomfortable with grieving, we tend to shy away from visiting the bereaved, which wrongly sends the message that we don't care. But many people find comfort in being given permission to talk about their loss. You may worry that bringing up the deceased's name is just going to cause tears or unhappiness, so you don't say anything. But never bringing up the spouse will just make the person feel all the more alone.

One of the best gifts you can give someone who is mourning is to share fond memories and stories that you cherish about their loved one. Perhaps your mom could write down a special moment she remembers of her friend's husband as a reflection of what a wonderful man he was—and place it in a card or in a "Memory Box" (such as a small jewelry or keepsake box). She could even collect memories written by other close friends and place them in the box as a gift. This might be nice to bring to her on your visit.

Marta Felber, M.Ed., a grief counselor and author of *Grief Expressed: When a Mate Dies*, offers the following "Do's and Don'ts" for talking to someone who is grieving:

DON'T SAY: "I know how you feel." The person in grief may want to scream, "No, you don't! No one knows how bad I feel!"

DO SAY: "I don't know how you feel, but I care about you and that you are hurting." In this way we validate their feelings.

DON'T SAY: "Just call me if there is anything I can do." People in deep grief can't think straight or focus. They don't know what they need to do.

DO SAY: "Can I get groceries for you or drive you somewhere you need to go?" It's much more useful to offer specific help. Other suggestions: Invite your friend to lunch or dinner, help her with medical or tax forms, or help her go through her loved one's belongings, but only when she is ready.

DON'T SAY: "It will get better." Grieving people know this intellectually, but in their hearts they may feel differently right now.

DO SAY: "It must be so difficult for you. I am thinking about you, caring, loving you" (or whatever you can sincerely say). Remember to stay in the present, where the grieving person is.

DON'T SAY: "Now, now, don't cry." It hurts us to see them cry and makes us sad. But by telling them not to cry, we are trying to take their grief away.

DO SAY: "Go ahead and cry. It's okay. I'm here." Then sit quietly with them. Hold or touch them. If you feel like doing so, cry with them.

DON'T SAY: "Your loved one is waiting for you over there," "God wanted him," "It was God's will," or "God knows best." Imagine how you would feel about God after hearing such comments. Be very sensitive. Know the person's faith, and be in touch with your own.

DO SAY: "Feel God's love," or "I will be praying for you," *if* you sincerely will do this.

Q: My dad came to live with us and now he's taking over! What do we do?

A: As he tries to find his place in a new household, your father seems to be gravitating back to where he is most comfortable—being your dad and being in charge. You'll need to coach him into a new role where he can still maintain a position of respect but can dispense with "giving orders." He also needs to get to know you in a different context, as a parent and a spouse, not just his child. Here are a few suggestions to help him with the transition:

1. Set aside some time to quietly talk with him. You might begin with something like, "Dad, during the rush of the move from your place to here, we really haven't had a chance to talk. We've been living apart for a very long time and each of us has our own routines. What's a typical day like for you?" Be sure to scope out his eating habits and favorite television shows; did he visit with friends, read the paper every morning and so on. Ask him, "Are there things you'd like to be doing that you weren't able to do when you lived alone?"

   Listen very closely. As you begin to learn of his daily life routine, you're in a position to see how well your family's routine will mesh with his. You might also pick up some red flags and begin thinking about ways to accommodate his needs without compromising what's important to your family.

2. Now it's your turn to share your family's routine with your dad. Be sure to have talked this over with your spouse ahead of time so that all of you are in sync. Describe a typical day in your household to your dad, explain how you divide chores, and share with him any ground rules that you've established with your kids. You might want to take the opportunity to share with him your basic principles of child rearing. For example, your dad might be a big tease and think he's just being funny, making jokes about your kids' haircuts, interests or friends. You might need to explain that teasing often drives a child away or into a shell.

   After you've described your household to him, you might want to ask him if he has any suggestions on how he could help support the household culture that you've just described or pitch in with the chores. And you could share how you'll help him maintain the routines important to him.

   In your description of how your household works, I'd include one evening a week that you and your spouse go out (as in, on a date). If he knows this ahead of time, then he won't feel "left out" or that he is being rejected. You could also give him a gentle reminder by saying something like, "Dad, we're going to an event on Friday. Is there anything you need while we're gone?"

3. Talk openly with him about how he'll always be your dad but that you're not a kid anymore. Perhaps you could create a new tradition between the two of you by setting up a weekly outing, or watching a favorite television show together. By doing this, you're setting some boundaries on your relationship while reinforcing it at the same time. He won't have a need to constantly show he's still your father by being in charge.

4. While the move is still new, it might be good to have another discussion on what triggers stress for all family members. Maybe everyone makes a list of their top three triggers and shares it; then the family figures out together how to make life less stressful

for each other. It's best to do something like this now, before real events and real hurt feelings make it tough to have such a discussion that isn't emotionally charged.

5. If your dad isn't a "joiner" you may need to be creative and bring people to him, or become the bridge for your dad to connect to some activity or person. If you're active in church or synagogue, that would present an excellent opportunity, or take him to events where he might meet people, like school performances, or host a small "welcome to the neighborhood" party and invite potential friends. Just like every other member of the family, he needs outside interests so that the household doesn't become his entire world.

6. How you design space in the house for your dad is extremely important. He needs to have his private space so that he can respect the private spaces of other family members, too. For example, he might enjoy having a small refrigerator and microwave for *his* snacks in *his* room along with *his* own television. But, of course, you don't want him to feel physically isolated from the rest of the family. It should be a pleasant space and a personal refuge to recharge—something that every family member needs.

7. And finally, you, your spouse and your father need to discuss who is going to pay for what. Finances, all too often, become the lightning rod for unresolved emotional conflicts. So, even though the topic may feel uncomfortable, do it *now*, before you're in the midst of a family feud.

Hopefully, this will ease the transition for all of you and you'll come to treasure the benefits and joys of a three-generation household.

Q: What do you do when siblings disagree on where their mom should live?

A: One of the toughest things to balance is an older person's independence with their ability to safely live alone. Rather than the family focusing on the solution—e.g., assisted living vs. remaining at home—I'd suggest taking a step back and asking yourselves, "What are we trying to fix?"

All of you, including your mother, should make a list of what she needs. For instance, does she need help with shopping? Paying the bills? Transportation? Cleaning? Getting around the house? Making lunch and dinner? Taking her pills? Is it difficult for her to see? It will be interesting to see if your mother's assessment is similar to those of the rest of you. Creating an objective list that all of you can focus on allows you to explore a wide array of options rather than getting caught up in an "either/or" scenario. It also allows all of you to gain a better perspective on how each of you—and your mom—perceives her needs.

Then review your mother's medical needs and health conditions. Ask her primary care physician to identify any special needs of your mother. It can also be very helpful to get a geriatric assessment, in which a whole team of physicians, nurses and social workers conduct a holistic assessment of your mother's medical, physical, social and mental health needs. You could then share your list of perceived needs and have them help you determine how well your mom can function living alone.

You might also want to go through your mom's house and identify any safety hazards, especially with regard to lighting, stairs, hallways, the kitchen and bathroom. Once all of you have done your homework regarding her needs, secured her medical and mental health assessment, and reviewed the physical state of her living quarters, then you're in a good position to sit down as a team and review all of your information.

Try making two columns on a sheet of paper. On the left-hand side list all of her needs that you can agree upon. (If you can't agree on a certain need, then skip over it and work on the ones that you all do agree on.) On the right-hand side of the paper, brainstorm how each need can be met. For example, say your mom has difficulty taking a shower and one of your siblings thinks this means she belongs in assisted living. To solve this particular problem, you could:

- Buy a shower chair
- Install a long, handheld showerhead
- Place railings in the shower
- Sign up for a personal alert service so she could press a button and have someone arrive to help her if she did fall

Keep going through the list, staying focused on her needs. For ideas on services to help you meet some of your mother's needs, call the local Area Agency on Aging—find yours at (800) 677-1116—they may even send someone out to assess your mother's needs. If you want some professional help to accurately assess her needs you might want to hire a geriatric care manager, found in the Yellow Pages under Home Health or Social Services. You could also call the National Association of Geriatric Care Managers at (520) 881-8008 or visit their Web site at www.caremanager.org to locate someone near your mom.

At the end of the day you may discover that your mom requires such a myriad of services that assisted living may make more sense. On the other hand, you may find that the solutions you've all come up with have alleviated the concerns of those of you who didn't think your mother could continue living alone.

The important thing is to not get caught up in an "all or nothing" debate. There are quite a few options, and professional people available who can help you assess your mother's needs so that all of you can rally around on what's best for her.

Q: My mom wants to extend her stay (she's been here a month), but my husband wants her to leave. What do I do?

A: Well, I'm no Dr. Phil, but let me give this a try. Any change in the status quo of family life can prove stressful. Most of us are creatures of habit and enjoy the comfort zone we establish in our households. Even parents who suffered the pangs of the empty nest give a sigh of relief when the kids go back to college after their summer of renesting.

Here are a few approaches; choose one that feels comfortable for you.

For whatever reason your mom may want to test you and put you in a position of choosing, "Who do you love more—me or your husband?" Maybe she isn't doing it consciously, but tell her that this is how it feels to you. You may want to say, "I won't be placed in this position. I love both you and my husband. Mom, we've welcomed you and enjoyed our time together over the last four weeks." Then mention some of the nice things you've done together and be sure to include some that also involved your husband.

It might then be helpful to tell her that you and your husband had made plans based upon her departure date that you can't change now. You could say something like, "I'm sure you understand, given how active a life you lead, so I'll be taking you to the airport on (the date you had all agreed upon when she came to visit)." If that doesn't seem to work, then how about you and your husband making plans for a little getaway vacation, and tell your mom that if she plans on staying you'll really be thankful for her to house-sit while you're away. This strategy might break the impasse.

If no other family member has ever visited that long then you can tell her that this isn't about "her," it's about how you and your husband conduct your life. In fact, that is why, when you visit her and any other family members, it's never for longer than (say how long).

Another approach may be to ask her, "What's really going on, Mom? You've always been such an independent person, this is so unlike you . . . is there something you're not telling me?" And see what happens.

And finally, you could say that you and your husband also value your space and being independent, just like her. You want this visit to be a memory of good times, so all of you need to stick with *her* original departure date. By identifying the date as the one she chose, you'll give her a sense of ownership, and by using the term "departure date" you'll make this less confrontational. You don't want to descend into just telling her to "leave."

The bottom line is that this is your home and, even though she's your parent, she doesn't have carte blanche to come live with you on her terms. Next year, when the topic of a visit comes up, set the parameters around you and your husband's schedule, and limit it to what works well for the both of you.

Q: **My dad is so impatient with my mom, who has Alzheimer's. What can I do?**

A: One of the hardest things for some family members to understand is that someone suffering from dementia is not deliberately acting difficult. Far too often—perhaps because of past history, unresolved conflicts or old patterns of behavior—spouses or adult children react to the person with Alzheimer's with a heightened sense of frustration. They find it difficult to give the disease the benefit of the doubt. And so they strike back as if the aggravation is deliberate.

Because people with dementia can sometimes go in and out of acting normal, it may be hard for some family members to distinguish between when "she really means it" and when her behavior is caused by the dementia. As a result, they begin to think that Mom "knows exactly what she is doing" and "she's just out to get me." To make matters worse, the person with dementia can become easily agitated and in a matter of minutes you're in the midst of a firestorm when your dad adds fuel to the fire with his anger.

Now how do you cope with your dad? Perhaps you could approach your mother's physician and explain the situation to him/her. Ask the doctor to speak with your dad about the disease and its stages, perhaps showing actual pictures of brain scans. Your dad needs a third party to validate what you're telling him.

A medical explanation should help, but it should be accompanied by a description of how the behavior of people with dementia changes. If you can't get a physician to tell him, then try another professional he would trust. It might also be helpful to use analogies to explain the course of the disease in terms that would resonate with your dad (for example, explaining the workings of the brain in "car terms" if he's a car buff).

I'd also suggest that you search for a local Alzheimer's support group, as they will know of the latest medications and treatments that could possibly help to lessen some of your mother's symptoms. They can identify other resources for you and, hopefully, share strategies on how to respond to your mother's behaviors and how to respond to each other.

Just meeting other people who are caring for a loved one with Alzheimer's and learning how they manage can be helpful. Perhaps you will meet someone who could speak with your dad (for example, an older man caring for his wife with dementia, but who's coping with it more functionally).

To find a support group anywhere in the country, go to www.alz.org. Also, feel free to give their twenty-four-hour Helpline a call at (800) 652-2370. An excellent book is *The 36-Hour Day* by Nancy Mace and Peter Rabbins.

Q: How do I tell my sister that Mom is too stressed out watching her kids?

A: Given the results of a study in the *Journal of Public Health,* your instincts are exactly right. In a study of nearly fourteen thousand women caring for grandchildren, epidemiologist Sunmin Lee with the Harvard School of Public Health found that "providing child care just a few hours a day greatly increased risk of heart disease." The risk of heart disease for grandmothers providing as little as nine hours of child care per week is a dramatic 55 percent higher than for grandmas free from the wear and tear of watching the grandkids.

The researchers suspect that the chronic stress from child care is at the root of the problem. In most cases, Grandma's adult child is working and relies on her to watch the children, making visiting with the grandkids a duty, not an option. On days when Grandma doesn't feel well, she still feels obligated to watch the kids so that her daughter or son can go to work. On the other hand, grandparents who are free from the duties of routine child care (routine is the operative word here) get to enjoy spoiling the grandkids on short visits while gleefully handing them back to their parents before the dear cherubim "disintegrate."

In addition, Lee and her colleagues suspect that stay-at-home grandmothers are generally in poorer health than those who remain in the workplace and thus aren't available to offer child care for their grandchildren. Add the stress of child care to common aging health conditions like arthritis, diabetes, high blood pressure and heart disease and you've created a formula for disaster. No wonder they're twice as likely to have a heart attack.

Caregiving grandmas also find it very difficult to make time for themselves. They don't make regular health care checkups or get to their doctor when they're sick. They don't exercise or find the time to follow healthy lifestyle habits.

So where do we go from here? Depending on your relationship with your sister, you may begin the discussion by talking about your mother's general health. The results of a recent doctor's appointment may be very helpful to focus on, so that it's not just about your impression. You may need to enlist the support of your mother's physician, as he or she may not be aware of her stressful lifestyle. Don't blame your sister or act as if she's taking advantage of your mother.

Chances are that your mom isn't letting on as to how stressful watching the kids has become. You could also tell your sister about this study and share a copy with her. (Go to www .webmd.com and search for "Child Care Can Tax Grandma's Health.") Offer to help your sister find other child care arrangements, as this is seldom an easy thing to do. Perhaps your sister can begin by just cutting back your mother's child care duties to two days a week. Of course, you should also include your mother in this discussion. Reassure her that in no way do you feel she's inadequate at child rearing. Instead, you and your sister want to protect her health, and give her the added time to enjoy herself during her retirement. You also want to create opportunities for her to simply enjoy the kids the way most grandmas do, without the daily pressure of being responsible for them.

There's a good reason Mother Nature makes it nearly impossible to bear children after fifty—follow her lead.

Q: **Will we be in over our heads if we bring Mom in to live with us?**

A: To be sure that your solution (Mom moving in with you) is the best move, make a list of the observations that have caused you to reach this conclusion.

For instance, is she acting confused or forgetful, eating poorly or seeming depressed? Is she not taking her medicines properly? Is her personal hygiene deteriorating? Are the bills stacking up along with other mail? Is she physically not able to get around?

Then get your mom to her physician to do a complete geriatric workup and share your observations with the doctor. Why? It's important to find any underlying physical problems that might be contributing to the behavior and symptoms that have alarmed you. Her confusion might simply be due to a medication she is taking. If this is rectified, living independently may still be an option for her.

Once you are better informed, I suggest making a list with three columns. The first column is for the activity involved in caring for your mother. In the second column, estimate how much time it will take to perform that activity, and in the third column identify who will do it (e.g., you, your husband, a relative, a friend or a paid person).

Here is a list of activities that you should consider:

1. **Eating.** Will you have to prepare all meals? Is she able to feed herself? Is she on a special diet?
2. **Bathing.** Will she need assistance in showering? Help with daily grooming?

3. **Using the Toilet.** Will she need help going to and from the bathroom? Is she incontinent?

4. **Dressing.** Can she get dressed on her own?

5. **Medications.** Will she need to be reminded, or will you need to administer them?

6. **Transportation.** How often will she need to see a doctor or therapist? Will you do the scheduling?

7. **In-Home Therapies.** Any daily therapies? What daily medical care does she need?

8. **Finances.** Will you be taking over all of her finances? Bill paying?

9. **Supervision.** Can she safely be left alone or is she confused, prone to wander or fall? Does she not sleep at night?

There are also ripple effects to these activities that require time and resources, such as extra grocery shopping, more laundry, more trips to the pharmacy and more cleaning. Be sure to take these into account as well.

Once you've done your "assessing" on both counts—your mom's needs and your ability to provide the time and resources—then you are in a good position to make an informed decision as to whether it is in everyone's best interest for your mom to come and live with you.

Remember that you may also qualify for support services to help you with your caregiving. See page 123 to learn more about it and who to contact.

Caring for your mother is a wonderful thing to do. Just make sure that your expectations are realistic and that you and your spouse are prepared for the venture.

Q: **How do you talk to someone who has Alzheimer's disease?**

A: I believe that Alzheimer's is one of the most devastating diseases any individual or family can face. The disease makes sufferers feel like they are in a constant state of being lost—nothing is familiar to them; not the room they live in, the furniture, the faces they see every day, their daily routines and even their own family members. Imagine how you feel when you're driving along and realize you're lost. At first you may feel angry and frustrated that you can't figure out the directions; you may feel irritated with the unfortunate "backseat driver" who tries to help out. And then there's the fear that grips you when you've steered your way into parts unknown, threatening danger at every turn.

For someone with Alzheimer's, the analogy is all too real. They feel frustrated, confused and fearful in a world of strangers doing things to them or giving them "backseat" directions. It's no wonder they exhibit anger or appear agitated.

So how do you talk to them? How do you break past the fear, the anger and the confusion? *Talking to Alzheimer's* by Claudia J. Strauss is full of terrific advice. It would have been a great help to me during the year I cared at home for my children's great-grandmother. Here are some of Strauss's suggestions, which you can offer all of your family members when they visit your loved one with Alzheimer's:

1. Calm down before walking in to visit. Your goal is to get yourself emotionally ready and to be at ease. Take some deep breaths, envision your favorite quiet place or call up the feeling of someone rubbing your shoulders or back. Relax. Why? You'll want to convey a sense of peacefulness and readiness to enjoy your loved one when you enter the room. You're creating an oasis during your visit. You'll want to give off "good vibes," as that's what he or she will pick up. It's best to enter the room with something like, "Hi, Dad, it's me, Linda, your daughter," so he won't have to guess or be embarrassed.

2. Your loved one's reality has changed. Setting him straight on facts and dates is not helpful. It will probably agitate him and remind him that he's losing his grip on reality. If he thinks his mother is still alive or that his son is still small and needs to be picked up from school, simply show that you're listening rather than argue (nod or say, "I hear what you're saying," or give a noncommittal "uh-huh," if you think lying is not helpful).

3. Expect a lot of repetition. Your loved one is struggling to remember the last conversation he had. He lives in the moment. Every time he asks a question, it is new to him, so you must act as if it is a new question to you, too. Answer in a tone of voice that is reassuring.

4. Ask questions that have a yes-or-no answer. An open-ended question like "How is your day going, Mom?" is an exception, as it is in the here and now. The thing you want to avoid are questions that require retrieving information from memory. You don't want to put your family member on the spot so that she becomes embarrassed or angry with herself for not being able to remember.

Strauss's overall message is, "Don't let the person become the disease. Worrying about what you say or do makes it much more difficult to convey love, respect and that you like being with them." The book is full of examples of what to say and how to respond to a great number of common situations. It would make a great gift for any family or friends facing the care of a loved one with Alzheimer's.

Q: When should we tell our grade-school-aged children that Grandpa is dying of cancer?

A: It's natural for parents to want to spare their children from pain. We spend a lifetime trying to protect them from every accident conceivable and our hearts ache as we watch them go through their first breakup. Yet we all know that we do them no favor if we raise them in an overprotective bubble. If we do, they'll be without the protective gear to navigate the rough and tough terrain of life's journey.

Your father's impending death is now part of your children's journey. There is no detour. They'll look to you and your spouse for a compass to guide them along this path. Most experts in childhood bereavement will tell you that children know more than you think. They pick up on your body language, the teary eyes of family members, the whispered conversations, the look in Grandpa's and Grandma's eyes. At your children's age, they need to know what's going on so that none of them will be plagued with "If only I had known, I would have . . ." for the rest of their lives.

To answer your question, I read two excellent books on the subject recommended by the Caring Place, a center for grieving children. The first, *How to Help Children Through a Serious Illness* by Kathleen McCue, tells parents that nearly all children have three universal concerns:

1. Young children may believe that they had something to do with causing their loved one to die. For example, they may have secretly wished them "dead" when they were being inconvenienced or disciplined. As a result, she cautions that children should know that nothing they did or didn't do could have caused what's happening to Grandpa to make him die.

2. Young children need to be told that whatever their loved one has, it is not contagious. They need to know they won't catch it, and that their parents won't catch it.

3. Young children who face the death of a parent also need to know who will take their parent's place. In other words, who will do the "Daddy" or "Mommy" things. In this instance, your kids need to know how your family will function in the face of their grandfather's impending death: how you may be spending more time away from home, how Grandma may come to live with you for a while, how you'll be spending time at a hospital or that when they visit with Grandpa they'll be meeting people from hospice. McCue also recommends giving your children something to do—as she puts it, "they're entitled to help."

In Dr. Dan Schaefer's book, *How Do We Tell the Children?*, he offers a checklist of actions to consider. (For those of you with younger children, please see his book for recommendations during different stages of childhood.)

1. It's better to "control the message" by explaining to your children what is going on; otherwise, they will be confused and anxious, and imagine many things that aren't true. Never lie to a child or make something up so that they'll feel better.

2. Do not be afraid of using the "d" word (meaning death or dying): Terms like "passed away," "gone on," or "left us," cause children great anxiety and confusion. (Is Grandpa on a trip? Is he coming back one day?)

3. Explain death in a simple, straightforward manner, as in, "Dead means that a person's body stops working. He won't be able to talk, walk, move, see, or hear because none of the parts work. He won't feel any pain."

4. Allow the child to ask questions; don't be surprised if they ask a lot of mechanical questions like, "Why is he cold? Where will they put the body? Can he hear me?"

5. Never describe a dead person as "sleeping." Aside from being inaccurate it will frequently cause anxiety about sleep in children.

6. Let them know that it is okay to cry and feel sad—an especially important message for boys.

From all that I've read on this subject, and through personal experience, one resounding message comes through: You cannot protect your children from the cycle of life. Soften the harsh reality with the embrace of love, shared tears and the reassurance that their family circle will help them through this sadness. But sad it will be.

Q: How do we set up a family meeting to decide what's best for our mother, who just had a stroke?

A: Sharing the decision-making is a smart way of handling such a life-changing decision for your mom and your siblings. Each of you has a different relationship with her, different life experiences and thus different perspectives on how to handle your mom's care. In order to maintain peace among you and avoid conflict down the line, it is helpful to discuss your mother's care openly as a unit. But if your family is already at loggerheads, I'd suggest getting a professional facilitator to hold the family meeting (a social worker, psychologist, priest, rabbi or minister). Even if you all need to pitch in to pay for someone, it will be well worth it.

If you're doing it on your own, here are my suggestions for a productive family meeting:

Everyone Needs to Do Some Homework. You'll accomplish more if everyone brings important information to the meeting. Just like organizing who brings what to a family reunion, each of you needs to volunteer to bring the results of an assignment to the meeting. Someone needs to gather your mom's medical information—type of stroke, her prognosis for recovery, other medical conditions that require care, medications and any other information about her health. Someone else should tackle all of her financial and insurance information, and another research the range of housing options and medical care available to meet her needs. If possible, share the results of your assignments ahead of time.

Create an Agenda. Each of you should identify the three most important things you'd like to discuss at the meeting. Organize the agenda around these issues. Chances are you'll find some overlap.

Identify a Facilitator. One of you should be in charge of organizing the agenda and keeping the discussion on task.

Everyone Attends. If all of you can't get together in one place, it's worth setting up a conference call. If your family is small enough you can easily do a three-way call, which is much cheaper than travel.

Chances are most of you have had experience in being part of meetings, so you're aware of the following basic rules (it might feel a little strange to be somewhat formal with each other, but a few ground rules do help):

- Follow the agenda that you all agreed upon.
- No cutting in. Wait until someone is finished talking.
- No accusations (as in "you always side with him").
- When you have something to say, it should reflect what you think, not what you think others think. So start the sentence with "I."
- Stay focused on your mom's needs. Rally around what's best for her. So that means you need to leave old scores behind.

- If you're not clear on a point your sibling has made, ask him to clarify it. (Don't stay silent, assuming he meant something he didn't.)
- If you want to make sure you've understood him, try something like "This is what I heard you say [then repeat what you think you heard]. Is that right?"
- Create next-action steps as you complete each item on the agenda. Identify any other information you need to make a decision. Wrap up the meeting with everyone clearly understanding what you've decided as a group and who will be responsible for what, going forward. Create a list of those duties and share it before you disband.

Functioning as a group will make it much better for your mom and easier for all of you to work as a team. If all of you are online, take advantage of the convenience to exchange information on Web sites, send pertinent attachments, and e-mail each other and the staff in charge of your mother's care.

This will be a very trying time for all of you, but if you openly communicate with one another then emotions of anxiety, guilt, grief, anger, or frustration won't be able to play havoc with your relationships.

Q: My uncle is suicidal and I think he's being seriously neglected by his sister. What do I do?

A: If you suspect that he is being seriously neglected then you are the one person who can make a difference in your uncle's life and, hopefully, make it worth living. Let me offer a few steps to consider.

First, give a call to your local Area Agency on Aging and ask to speak to the Protective Services caseworker. Explain the situation and stress how concerned you are that your uncle will harm himself. If you can, cite the dates on which he has threatened suicide. You will be filing a "Report of Need" that remains confidential and allows the Protective Services team the right to intervene. The Protective Services caseworker will likely go and meet with your uncle and aunt. They will be able to assess his needs (both physical and mental) by arranging for a comprehensive geriatric assessment to determine whether or not he has dementia or any other health issues affecting his ability to live on his own.

The Area Agency on Aging will also be able to sort out the legal and financial issues surrounding your uncle. If he is capable of making decisions for himself, then he can decide whether or not to seek supportive services to remain living at home, or explore assisted living. The geriatric assessment may determine that he actually needs nursing home care, which can also be arranged. If his sister has power of attorney, allowing her to handle his finances, the Area Agency on Aging will work with her to make the financial arrangements. However, if he is considered competent by the social workers, then he does not need his sister to make these decisions and the power of attorney can be revoked.

Second, I'd also let the Protective Services caseworker know that you believe that your aunt is negligent about caring for him. This places his health and well-being at risk and could be assessed by the caseworkers as "caregiver neglect" on the part of his sister.

Third, if you do not want to call Protective Services you still have the flexibility to intervene. Even if your aunt has his power of attorney, she can't prevent him from seeking care. So go visit your uncle, build some rapport with him and see if he would go to a doctor's appointment with you.

Once a physician assesses your uncle's mental and physical state you are in better position (along with a Protective Services team) to make an educated, compassionate decision about his care. It would also make it difficult for his sister to prevent anyone else from providing the care he needs, once a professional medical opinion is rendered.

Fourth, you could also talk to an elder law attorney and ask what options you have, but I'd start with Protective Services workers at the Area Agency on Aging.

No matter what you do, get involved.

Q: Can my sister use her health care power of attorney to prevent us from visiting our mother?

A: The short answer is no. Your sister can't use health care power of attorney to restrict your visits. She is, however, empowered to make health care decisions on behalf of your mother *anytime* she becomes incompetent. The key word is incompetent. The health care power of attorney kicks in when your mother is incapacitated to make health care decisions on her own. It is valid only *during* her incapacity. People usually grant this type of permission to a loved one whom they believe will make good medical decisions *when* and *if* they become incapacitated. Typically, health care power of attorney is used to make decisions on admissions to and discharges from health care facilities, organ donations, moving the patient, home health care and accepting or refusing medical treatments.

For the durable health care power of attorney to be legal, your mother had to be competent when she signed it. Many states have laws that spell out procedures for determining when someone is legally competent. You don't need to be a lawyer to be granted a durable health care power of attorney. The word attorney simply means "designated agent."

However, it sounds to me like something else is going on with your sister. Perhaps she feels like she's losing control of her household with everyone (no matter how well intentioned) coming and going as they please to see Mom. There might be unresolved conflicts between her and the rest of the siblings. She might perceive that surprise visits agitate your mother because they disrupt her routine. Rather than argue over whether or not she has the *right* to restrict visits, try exploring what your sister is trying to accomplish by restricting your visits and focus on what's best for Mom. Your mother should be included in this discussion.

Offer to set up a visiting schedule that, besides allowing you to see Mom, gives your sister a break to do whatever she'd like. Ask her to make a list of how each of you could be of assistance. Could one of you take Mom to a doctor's visit, the hair stylist or to church? Let your sister know that you do want to respect the privacy of her home, but you'd like to find a happy medium so that all of you can share in the role of being good sons and daughters, just like her.

Hopefully, in time, your sister might not hold to such a rigid schedule and find that a few impromptu visits now and then lift your mom's spirits—and that's what all of you should be working toward.

If you're still having difficulty being able to visit your mom, then seek some outside help to work this out with your sister. You may need to reach out to a minister, rabbi, priest or counselor. It's in everyone's best interest to develop a healthy way of communicating with each other now, because down the road the decisions are likely to get tougher and the stakes will be higher. It will be a lot easier on everyone if you're acting as a team working from the same playbook.

3

Lifestyle

Q: **We'd like to bring my dad on vacation despite his health problems. How do we make this work?**

A: The best vacations are usually the ones where you've taken the time to plan and do your homework. So let's begin researching your vacation options. First, all of you must *want* to go on this vacation. If your dad is being dragged into this, chances are you'll have a dismal time. If he really wants to stay at home, then make a list of all the tasks that you would expect someone to do in your absence, such as shop, make meals, make sure he takes his medications, go to doctor's appointments, and assist with physical therapy—whatever you do now. Then call a local home health or senior care agency, describe what you need and have them identify the properly skilled person to care for him. If his care is light, then perhaps a reliable family member or friend can come and live with him while you are away.

If you, your husband and Dad want to make a go of it, here are some things to keep in mind:

- Find a place where the weather is agreeable for all of you. It's best to look for moderate climates.
- Cruises make for a great family vacation that can meet each individual's needs and those of a whole family. There are cruises that will accommodate a wide range of medical needs. In fact, there are cruises that are fully equipped and medically staffed for dialysis patients, diabetics, and those who are oxygen dependent. Some cruise lines offer nursing and attendant care. A Web site that can help you identify such cruise line packages can be located at www.medicaltravel.org or call them at (800) 778-7953.
- All three of you should make a list of the kind of activities you'd like to do on the

vacation. Be sure to share your likes and dislikes. Use this list as a guide to develop a mutual itinerary, and also to identify ways that everyone can go off on their own sometimes. You don't have to be a constant threesome.

- Family resorts offer another alternative for a vacation package catering to multiple generations. Most travel agents or the American Automobile Association will know of such family-friendly resorts. They often have individuals available who can stay with your dad while you and your husband enjoy other activities.
- Take all of your dad's medications, check if you'll need a refill during vacation and fill it before you leave. If you are flying, be sure to store them in a *carry-on* rather than risk their loss if the luggage is detained or stolen.
- If your dad needs a scooter to get around, a wheelchair or other cumbersome equipment, ask the hotel where you'll stay if they can provide or rent it for you. Or call medical equipment companies listed in the Yellow Pages in the area where you'll be staying to find out how you can rent whatever you'll need.
- Be sure to notify hotels of any conditions that your dad may have and ask to have the room near the elevator or one on the first floor.
- Choose activities and a vacation length that aren't too physically demanding.
- Take the time to call ahead to restaurants and hotels to make sure they are handicap-accessible.
- Take breaks—whether driving a long distance or planning a long day—and pace the day for your father.
- Check with your dad's health insurance and find out if there are any policy restrictions when he is out of the service area.
- Be sure to buy trip insurance in case you need to cancel at the last minute.

Some families, if they can afford it, bring a caregiver on the vacation to attend to their parent. Or they make arrangements with a home health service in the area where they will vacation. Some geriatric care managers will do all of this for you; find them, and home health agencies anywhere in the country, at www.eldersearch.com.

Q: **My husband and I want to go on vacation but we cannot leave his mother alone. Any suggestions?**

A: If your mother-in-law would like to stay at home while you are away, then make a list of all the tasks that you would expect someone to do in your absence—shop, make meals, make sure she takes her medications, go to doctor's appointments, assist with physical therapy and/or bathing—essentially whatever you do now. Then call a local home health agency or senior care agency and describe what you need, and they'll identify the properly skilled person to care for her. If her care is light, then perhaps a reliable family member or friend can come and live with her while you are away. But make sure this individual is up for the task.

You could also set up "mutual vacations" wherein she takes a "vacation" at a quality assisted living facility while you and your husband go out of town. Many assisted living facilities are delighted to have a short-stay guest. She may enjoy all of the attention and dining out every day along with the security of having her physical needs met. Just make sure this option is okay with her, and you both should visit the facility ahead of time. She should not feel like she is being abandoned or "set up" for eventual placement in what she may consider a nursing home.

Here's how one person described the experience of vacationing this way:

We personally visited several retirement communities, eliminated some on sight and others because they did not provide the flexibility we needed. The one we ultimately chose had neither a minimum nor a maximum period for so-called "respite" care.

We planned our loved one's vacation so that she entered the facility a day or two before we left town, and extended two or three days on the other end. That way, if adjustment problems arose, or medication problems surfaced (that happens!) we would be around to see to the problem. At the other end of the vacation period, we had a couple of days to unpack and "reenter" without coping with caregiving needs.

During the vacation period, we made arrangements for drop-in visits by friends of the family. We also planned the mailing of cards so that the week was pretty much covered by mail each day. We arranged for the newspaper to be delivered to her so that she had her own paper for crossword puzzles, etc. We arranged with a local florist to have a fresh arrangement sent at midpoint to cheer up the room and remind her that we were thinking of her. (For a man, some florists will make up and deliver "snack baskets" with little boxes and bags of this and that.)

A refundable deposit is required by most facilities, depending on the length of stay. This can be left on deposit, however, providing a very convenient way to assure a place and ease in making arrangements if an emergency arises or an unplanned trip opportunity necessitates a home away from home.

As a bonus, when the time came for her to enter assisted living full-time, she related to her very pleasant "vacations" rather than feeling threatened or, worse, abandoned.

Thus, with some thoughtful planning and homework, you can enjoy a vacation while your mother-in-law is safely cared for. Taking a break from caregiving, whether it's a vacation or simply enjoying an afternoon to yourself, is far beyond a luxury—it's essential. Have a great time.

Q: **Ever since our dad died, we feel Mom could really use the companionship of a pet. Is a dog a good idea or just too much of a hassle?**

A: There's plenty of research heralding the benefits of interacting with pets: people are less depressed, pets offer a welcome distraction from pain, talking to and caring for a pet reduces loneliness and walking a dog encourages exercise. Sure, their love and affection requires some work, but you can make this easier than you may think.

First, it makes more sense to get her an older, housebroken dog; you'll also want to make sure that the dog is used to a crate, so that when she goes out during the day she won't have to worry about her new friend wreaking havoc throughout the house. Older dogs can be found through newspaper ads, the Humane Society and nonprofit pet adoption groups listed in your phone book.

Your next step is to make sure that walking the dog won't become an athletic or hazardous event for your mom. Get her a dog whose size she can manage and make sure that where she walks the dog is obstacle-free. You might want to build a long handrail alongside a walkway. Or install a dog-door (a small, secure opening that is cut into an existing door) that leads to an enclosed backyard. That way, if your mom isn't feeling up for a walk, the dog can easily go in and out without her. These are pretty inexpensive and you can find them at most discount retail and pet stores. You can also make life easier by keeping your mom stocked with twenty-five-pound bags of dog food to save her from frequent shopping trips and heavy lifting.

Your mom might be worried that, if she becomes hospitalized or wants to take a short vacation, no one will be around to take care of the dog. She might not realize that there's a relatively new service known as "Pet Sitting." I've used it myself and it's a great way to leave your best buddy behind, feeling safe and happy in his own home. You can find them in the Yellow Pages of your phone book under Pet Sitters or go to the Web site of Pet Sitters International (www.petsit.com) and search for one of their members by ZIP code. Here's what to ask and look for in a good, reliable pet sitter:

- Are they insured and bonded?
- How long have they been in business?

- Are they a member of any professional association, e.g., Pet Sitters International (PSI)?
- Do they have any formal training in caring for pets? Do they own pets?
- What kind of background checks and training do their employees have?
- Do they have customer references? (Take numbers and call.)
- Do they have a formal relationship with a veterinarian in case of an emergency? Is there a veterinarian who recommends them?
- Do they come to your home before the first pet sitting assignment to meet the pets and gather detailed information about their care?
- If so, watch how they interact with the pet and how much attention they give to finding out details on how to care for your pet.
- Do they write up daily reports on each visit and will they leave messages on your voicemail on how well your pet is doing?
- Do they run their service as a professional business, e.g., presenting you with written materials and contracts?

On average you'll pay ten to fourteen dollars per visit and two dollars for each additional pet. Perhaps you and other family members can tell Mom that you'll chip in for the service or give her gift certificates.

Your mom may also be worried that she'll become attached to the dog and then have to give him up if she needs to move into an apartment or assisted living. But there are facilities that welcome pets as long as the resident is able to provide the care. Even nursing homes today have dogs and cats that either live on the premises or visit as part of pet-assisted therapy programs. All in all, with a little bit of planning, there really isn't that much of a hassle in your mom having a dog, but you do need to make sure that this is something she wants. The rewards of owning a warm and cuddly companion are pretty darn high. If she's not up for a dog, consider a cat or even a chatty bird. Of course, this advice comes from a pet lover.

Q: How can my parents downsize their home?

A: Remember when you first looked at a college dorm? Downsizing all of your worldly possessions into a tiny room seemed insurmountable. Now fast forward to your mom or dad's life as they try to downsize from the family homestead to an apartment or assisted living facility.

It's not just the emotional transition but also the practical challenge of downsizing that makes the move so daunting. There's so much "letting go": deciding what to sell, what goes to Goodwill, and what's given to family and friends. Then there are the innumerable choices.

How will the furniture fit into the room? Where will the pictures hang? Just the thought of making all of these decisions stops many people dead in their tracks. They stay put even if they're unhappy or have become hostage to a very large house.

With good old necessity being the mother of invention, a relatively new service has emerged that can help your parent make all of these decisions and many more. "Professional Organizers" will certainly help in downsizing from a full house to apartment living.

Finding an expert might prove a bit difficult, as this is a rather new field. Some realtors now offer real estate consultants who can organize the move, sell the furniture and help your parents assess just how much space they will have in their new apartment for new and old furniture. You can also call the National Association of Professional Organizers at (512) 206-0151 for a referral, or visit their Web site at www.napo.net. Also try the Yellow Pages under Organizing Services.

I asked professional organizer Alice Winner if she'd share some of her tips on how to help parents downsize their homes to make a smooth transition into new, smaller living quarters. Here's what Alice recommends:

- First, your parent must *want* to do this. Don't launch a decluttering, downsizing attack without their full support. Initiate the topic gently by asking if they'd like some help in getting ready for the move.
- Begin by asking your parents to make a list of what they want to keep, give away or perhaps sell. Place stickers on the backs of items noting if they are to be sold, given to someone or be part of the move. Don't criticize their list, even if it appears unreasonable.
- Start with what's in the basement. Chances are they don't have strong emotional ties to what they've been storing down there.
- Break down moving tasks into small segments over a reasonable period of time. Rather than set aside a whole day to clean an entire area of the house, clean out one kitchen drawer, one closet, or one dresser drawer in an afternoon. If you tackle small projects throughout a week, you'll accomplish more.
- Begin getting rid of paper clutter. For example, check with your accountant on how long your parents need to keep canceled checks and start shredding what they no longer need. Newspapers, magazines and books can be recycled or, if valuable, given to local senior centers and libraries.
- Separate financial and legal records from memorabilia. Don't worry about identifying or categorizing the memorabilia. Just put it in boxes.
- If they have lots of pictures on the wall and will soon have less wall space, have them identify those that would look nice in a good photo album.

- If there's a large piece of furniture they can't quite bring themselves to part with, ask if they can envision it stored temporarily in someone else's home until they can make a final decision on what to do with it.
- Take photos of furniture that has special meaning but will be given away or sold.
- Ask your mom or dad to tell you the story behind pieces of furniture, glassware, vases, or paintings that are being passed down to other family members. Write each on a piece of paper and place it inside the item or tape it to the back of it. Now other generations can enjoy the story.

A very helpful book is *Making the Move: A Practical Guide to Senior Residential Communities* by Lettice Stuart. She recommends that your parents choose five of the most important pieces of furniture they must have to feel at home in their new place. (I can see Frasier's dad sitting in his beloved duct-taped rocker!) Another great book is *Living Transitions: A Step-by-Step Guide for a Later Life Move* by Sue Ronnenkamp. You can order it through her Web site at www.livingtransitions.com.

Q: Any tips on getting my mother to go online and use e-mail?

A: Believe it or not, seniors are one of the fastest-growing groups signing up for Internet service. So perhaps some of your mom's peers might be your best bet to convince her that she's missing out on something. Find out how many of her friends are using it and talk with them.

Senior centers, community colleges and neighborhood groups are offering classes on using computers and the Internet. Many of these programs offer free classes on how to use a computer, send e-mails with attachments (including family photos) and use the Internet. Anyone can walk in and get help in setting up a free e-mail account.

Darlene Simmons, who never used a computer before she took a class, can't say enough about how it changed her life. "It's a whole new highway of communication for me," she says. "I'm now e-mailing my grandson, and I've learned how to send electronic greeting cards. My daughter is living in Germany and e-mail has been a godsend." She has also enjoyed more contact with other relatives, convinced eighty-year-olds in her church to sign up for classes and posted her own poetry on the Internet.

Having a close relationship with her grandkids of all ages (especially those in college) might be the incentive to get her involved. When she's visiting, have your kids sit down and show her what they could do together, for example, play games (such as checkers) over the Internet or have her help them with homework assignments. I recently ran into a grandmother who was thrilled at finally finding a way to connect with her teenaged granddaughter through e-mail; kids at that age are much more likely to e-mail news about their life than to telephone.

Research has shown that many seniors just aren't convinced that the Internet is relevant to them. Perhaps you could tap your mom's interest in a hobby and show her what she can do on the Internet to further her talent. Or, if she takes quite a few medications or has a health condition, you can show her how to access helpful information online. And then there's the shopping!

One way to start her off might be to get her and a friend to sign up for a class at a local senior center where she won't feel threatened. Or you might acquire an older computer with a modem (or purchase an external modem) and bookmark a few sites of interest. A good site that is easy to navigate is the AARP's at www.aarp.org. Show her how to use e-mail using a free, trial account so she doesn't have to worry she'll be throwing her money away.

Besides computers, there are "Internet Access Products," of which WebTV is one of the most common. Some people find these extremely easy to use, but others have told me they're cumbersome. It's best to go to an electronics store and test them out for yourself. These are less expensive than computers and allow you to search the Internet, e-mail, join chat rooms and Instant Message. However, you might not be able to send attachments or family photos, so if that's important to you, be sure to ask. Given the way prices keep coming down, it might be just as well to get a computer.

Q: Are Continuing Care Retirement Communities a smart move?

A: If your mom and dad can afford it, CCRCs (also known as life care communities) are a great housing option. They usually offer the total range of care on one campus: independent living apartments and homes, assisted living apartments, and intermediate and skilled nursing care.

Your parents will be offered a wide range of activities: golf, swimming, exercise equipment, physical therapy, banking services, educational courses and transportation. If they become ill, they're able to receive most of their health care on-site, and once they recover, they can go back to their original residence. For people who like living in a community of folks their own age and like the security of a one-stop approach to long-term care in a campus setting, a CCRC is a perfect match.

So what should your parents be looking for? First, they need to check out the CCRC's financial solvency. Since your parents will be investing most of their life savings into the CCRC, you'll want to make sure that the company has a solid past and a strong future. In many states, the department of insurance regulates and licenses CCRCs.

CCRCs must give prospective residents a "disclosure statement" containing information about the financial status and operation of the facility. It should include the names and addresses of all persons responsible for the operation of the facility, financial statements showing assets, liabilities and operating expenses, clear details of all fees, and its association with any other organizations. Be sure to ask for it along with a copy of their latest inspection report.

CCRCs basically offer three types of agreements:

1. **Extensive Contract:** This includes unlimited long-term nursing care for little or no substantial increase in your parents' usual monthly payments.

2. **Modified Contract:** This includes a specified amount of long-term nursing home care. Once your parent has used the limit then he or she is responsible for paying the bill in full. Remember: Medicare doesn't cover nursing home care.

3. **Fee-for-service:** This covers independent and assisted living services only. No nursing home coverage is included; your parent is required to pay the bill out-of-pocket or carry long-term-care insurance.

Your parents will be asked to sign a very detailed contract. It's smart to have both a lawyer and a financial consultant read it over for you. But before they get that far, your parents should spend some real time at the CCRC: going there for lunch and dinner, attending events, and staying overnight for a few days to really get a feel for the community.

Here are some questions your parents should ask:

- Who makes the decision as to what level of care I'll need, if I should become ill?
- What kind of refund policy do you offer and under what circumstances?
- Are there health insurance requirements (e.g., will the CCRC purchase long-term-care insurance on my behalf? With what company?)?
- What is the payment schedule? Will I own or rent my residence?
- Are you accredited by the American Association of Homes and Services for the Aging? This is voluntary—not all CCRCs opt to go through the accreditation process—however, it's a good quality marker. You can view a list of accredited CCRCs in the country by going to www.ccaconline.org (Continuing Care Accreditation Commission).

If you'd like a directory of all the CCRCs in the state, contact your state's insurance department as they will likely provide you with a complete directory with a brief description of each facility, their entrance fee and monthly fees, along with contact information. Check out your state's government home page to see if their department of insurance provides a directory online.

Q: How can I handle caregiving when my parents live in another state?

A: First you need to go to where your parents live and do a little advance work. It's sort of like advance teams for political candidates. It's their job to scope out the town, know the hot-button issues of the locals, get everybody's name right, know who to invite and brief the candidate. They can really make or break an event. Think of this as a campaign to help your parents make it on their own. They're the candidate, and you're the advance team. Here are some pointers:

Get to Know the Neighbors. You'd be surprised at how much neighbors do for each other. On your next visit, go over to the neighbors and give them your contact information, and ask for their phone number. If you're lucky, these are folks who knew you when you were growing up, but chances are, either the neighbors or your parents have moved. Ask the neighbors to check in with you if they become concerned about your parents, especially if they live alone. Stay in touch with those neighbors, even if it's just a matter of sending them cards on the holidays.

Get to Know the Mail Carrier. Now here's someone who probably knows more about your parents' routine than you do. Getting the mail for many older people is the highlight of the day, and they wait for a quick chat along with their mail. If Mom's not there, seems disoriented, or her mail piles up, it's her mail carrier who will pick up the warning signs and take action. If you'd like the mail carrier to pay a little extra attention to your parents, contact their local post office and let them know you'd like them to keep an eye out for your folks.

Get to Know the Bankers. It's probably a good thing that many parents are part of a generation that hasn't taken too fondly to automatic teller machines. An ATM sure won't give you a call that Mom just took out a large sum of money or that a stranger has been accompanying Dad to the bank. Introduce yourself to the bank manager and ask him or her to alert you of any concerns.

Get a Phone Schedule Going with Your Siblings. A friend of mine happened upon an idea to keep up with his mom, who lives several hours away. He noticed when he talked to her on Sundays that she'd often just heard from his sister and brother, too. Rather than get a triple dose of her kids in one day, he thought it would make more sense if each of his siblings agreed to call on separate days throughout the week. Now their mom gets a call just about every day from one of them, which is more fun for her as well as providing a frequent checkup on how well she's doing.

Get to Know Your Parents' Best Friends. Your parents' friends can let you know if something's up and that, perhaps, you should look in on them. My mother lives in Phoenix, and I've gotten to know her buddies pretty well. We've shared phone numbers, and I try to stop by and say hello when I'm out there. One time I called one of them to look in on my mom when she had the flu. My mom didn't want to bother anyone, but I knew she needed someone to get her medicine and good old chicken soup. Friends are your best eyes and ears, and they'll likely have your parent's best interest at heart. Take the time to nurture your relationship with your parents' friends.

Get to Know the Home Health Services Network. Be sure to scope out the home health services and nonmedical senior care agencies in your parents' community, so that if you need them, you can spring into action. This can buy some time, just in case you can't get there right away. You'll want to explore the levels of care they provide, the costs, and what is covered under what circumstances. Find out if they can send a nurse to assess your parent's situation and let you know if more medical attention is needed. This could be especially helpful if you think your dad has more than a regular case of the flu or you're worried that his diabetes has gotten worse.

Bring Home the Phone Book. A good advance team has everybody's phone numbers, so next time you're visiting your parents, bring back an extra copy of the local phone book. You'll find the yellow and blue pages of government and social agencies especially helpful. If you're online, you can always check out www.yellowpages.com.

And finally, get to know the staff at the local Area Agency on Aging. They can help you track down a host of human services for your parents. To find the agency in your area, call the Eldercare Locator at (800) 677-1116 or go to www.eldercare.gov.

Q: How can I adult-proof the house so my mother won't injure herself from a fall?

A: Remember when you ran around the house covering wall outlets, removing cherished breakables from coffee tables and barricading steps so your toddler wouldn't have an accident? Welcome to adult-proofing—it's the same concept as child-proofing, only now you want to create an accident-free environment for your parent. And this time, instead of creating obstacles, you're removing them.

Studies show that simple changes in the home can prevent one out of every three home accidents among the elderly. Falls, especially, can be dangerous, with the possibility of a broken hip and a long period of recuperation. Besides making environmental changes to prevent falls, your mother should: exercise, have her vision checked, take her time getting out of bed in the morning, and talk with her physician and pharmacist regarding any medications that make her dizzy.

Now on to making her home accident-proof:

IN THE KITCHEN:

- Replace standard dials on the stove with large, easy-to-read dials. Make sure the off button is very visible (consider marking it red).
- If your mom is using small towels or an apron to grab hot pots and plates, go get her real pot holders and have them easily accessible.
- Make use of lazy Susans so that dishes, pots, pans and cooking materials that your mom uses most frequently are easy to reach. You don't want her reaching too high or too low, which may throw her off balance.

IN THE BATHROOM:

- If she uses a shower, make sure that the shower curtain isn't held up by a tension rod—if she grabs for it, she'll fall with it. Install a rod that's bolted to the wall.
- Install grab bars in the shower and/or tub. If she is having trouble getting on and off the toilet, get a raised toilet seat and install handrails alongside the toilet.
- Attach a liquid soap dispenser in the shower so that Mom won't slip and fall when she tries to retrieve a bar of soap she's dropped.
- Make sure the water temperature is set at a safe temperature (120 degrees or lower); many older people lose their sensitivity to temperature and scald themselves.
- Place rubber, nonskid strips on the bathroom floor and nonskid bath mats in the tub and/or shower.

THROUGHOUT THE HOUSE:

- Get rid of throw rugs. Unless we're talking about some great family heirlooms, they need to go. (How about making them into a wall hanging?) Even with carpet tape, it's still too easy for someone who scuffles along the floor to slip a shoe under the rug and trip. It also throws off your parents' depth perception as they refocus from bare floor to carpet.

- All stairways should have handrails on both sides.
- Place brightly colored adhesive tape on the edge of each step, so Mom can see the contrast and know she's at the edge of the step. If the steps are carpeted, consider pulling it up if it's old, easy to slip on or frayed.
- Install sound- or movement-activated lights that go on and off automatically when Mom gets up in the night to go to the bathroom.
- Get rid of clutter and cute little tables in the hallways.
- Make sure that all cords and wires are close to the wall or tape them down so she won't trip over them.
- Move items in kitchen cabinets that are most frequently used to shelves that are easily reached.

Your mom should also be advised to wear sturdy shoes that have thin, nonslip soles. Stay clear of sneakers that have thick soles that will cause her to trip.

These are just a few things you can do to make living at home both safer and easier for your parents. Is it worth it? You bet. Nearly 1,000 people a *day* break a hip, according to the Academy of Orthopaedic Surgeons, and nearly 9,000 die every year as a result of their fall.

For a great checklist, readers may visit the AARP's Web site at www.aarp.org. On the home page, use the search bar and enter "Home Design," or write to AARP Fulfillment, 601 E Street NW, Washington, DC 20049 and ask for "How well does your home meet your needs?" (D16270). They'll send it for free.

Q: How can I help my dad track down his old military buddies?

A: If you saw *Band of Brothers, Saving Private Ryan,* or a host of similar movies, you certainly understand how meaningful it would be for your dad to reconnect with the guys in his unit. My dad, who was stationed in Italy, had been talking for years about trying to find his buddies. By chance he saw a reunion announcement for his unit in the *Legion* magazine. He went to the reunion, and when he returned showing us pictures of his old buddies, it unleashed a flood of stories from the war that he'd never told us before. The event meant the world to him.

The U.S. Department of Veterans Affairs has made it pretty easy for you to help your dad pursue his quest. Go to the VA's Web site at www.va.gov. On the home page go to the Burial and Memorial Benefits section and click on the sidebar: "Locating Veterans." The site will give you directions on how to write a message to your dad's comrade(s) and then send it to your VA regional office. The regional office will take the next step and forward it to your dad's buddies. (Because of privacy requirements, the VA can't simply release the information directly to you or your father.)

At the Web site you can also view a complete list of all the reunions being held for each military branch throughout the country. Besides using the VA's resources, try www.switchboard.com—all you'll need is the full name of your dad's military buddy to get an address. You might have to write to everyone who has the same name because your dad might not know what town his buddy lives in, but it's well worth the postage.

If you're interested in doing a World War II oral history of your father or having him listed on the electronic World War II Registry, see below and page 161.

Q: **How do we get my father to talk about his experiences in World War II? I think it's important to have a record for the family.**

A: Since the attack on September 11, 2001, we've come to appreciate the real meaning of "hero." The glitz of sports heroes pales before the true heroism of firefighters and police officers who fought to save lives and died trying. But chances are you have heroes in your own family circle and what better way to celebrate their contribution to our freedom than to create an oral history to pass down to your children and theirs.

Tell your dad that the Veterans History Project, which was passed into federal law in October 2000, directs the American Folklife Center at the Library of Congress to collect and preserve audio- and videotaped oral histories, along with letters, photos, diaries and maps of veterans of America's wars for all branches of service. Their seasoned interviewers report that it's best to have a list of questions that you work from, and to simply tape the interview on audiocassette.

If you're pleased with your oral history, they would love to have a copy of it. Give them a call at (202) 707-4916 to find out how to send it in. You can also visit their Web site at www.loc.gov/folklife/vets for a list of questions to ask and full details on the project.

I looked over their list of questions and the Oral History Workbook of the Nieman Enhanced Learning Center. Here are some questions from these two excellent sources that will set you on the right track:

GETTING STARTED

- What were you doing just before you joined the armed services?
- Were you drafted or did you enlist?
- How old were you?
- Where were you living at the time?
- Why did you join?
- Why did you pick the service branch you joined?
- Do you recall your first days in service?
- What did it feel like?
- Tell me about your boot camp/training experience(s).
- Do you remember your instructors?
- How did you get through it?
- Did you make buddies at boot camp?
- What were they like?

WAR EXPERIENCES

- After boot camp, where exactly did you go?
- Do you remember arriving and what it was like?
- What was your job/assignment?
- What were your rank and serial number?
- What were your living conditions like?
- Did you see combat?
- Were there many casualties in your unit?
- What was the objective of your unit?
- Tell me about a couple of your most memorable experiences.

DAILY LIFE IN THE WAR

- How did you stay in touch with your family?
- What was the food like?
- Did you have plenty of supplies?
- What equipment did you use?
- How did you handle fear?
- Was there something special you did for good luck?

- What did you do when on leave?
- Where did you travel while in the service?
- Do you recall any particularly funny or unusual event?
- What did you think of officers or fellow soldiers?
- Describe some of your buddies in the war.
- Did you ever think we might lose the war?

LIFE AFTER SERVICE

- Do you recall the day your service ended?
- Where were you?
- What did you do in the days and weeks afterward?
- Did you work or go back to school?
- Did you make any close friendships while in the service?
- Did you continue any of those relationships? How long?
- Did you join a veterans' organization?
- What did you go on to do as a career after the war?
- How did your service and experiences affect your life?
- What do you want your grandkids to know about this time in history?

For great examples of interviews, stories and other links to World War II oral histories and projects, visit www.tankbooks.com. Don't let next Veterans Day come and go without recording your hero's contribution to world history.

Q: How do I get my dad onto the World War II Memorial Registry?

A: If you want the whole nation to know what your dad did in the war, here are two ways to do it: the World War II Folklife Project sponsored by the Library of Congress and the World War II Memorial Registry. Here is how *your* dad can go down in history as being part of the Greatest Generation:

WORLD WAR II MEMORIAL REGISTRY

You can easily enroll your father in the World War II Memorial "Registry of Remembrances" by phone or by going online. I registered my dad by phone and was extremely impressed by how easy it was. Just call (800) 639-4992 and wait to speak to a customer service representative. She'll want to know your veteran's branch of service, rank, where he served, his hometown, and when he went into the service. You can also add a few words about his activity during the war.

If you're online, go to www.wwiimemorial.com and click on the WWII "Registry" side bar and then on "Register an Honoree." Any U.S. citizen who contributed to the war effort, whether he or she was a veteran or back on the home front, is eligible for the registry. So if your mother was also active on the home front, register her, too.

At the World War II Memorial in Washington, DC, there are four computers at the Pacific Arch, where you can look up your honoree's name and a short bio will appear. Of course, you can also see it online by going to www.wwiimemorial.com. (It takes a few weeks for them to verify the information before it is viewable on the Web.)

For a fee of $10.00 you can also have his photo displayed. Send a photo digitally by going to www.wwiimemorial.com/photo or mail it to World War II Memorial Processing Center, P.O. Box 305, Calverton, New York 11933. Write on the back of the photo the ID number and account number you received when registering your father.

THE VETERANS HISTORY PROJECT

This project is operated by the Library of Congress at the American Folklife Center. Their mission is to collect and preserve firsthand stories of veterans who fought in wars of the twentieth century, with a special emphasis right now on World War II vets. They are also very interested in accounts from civilians who were actively involved in the war effort, such as USO workers, flight instructors, industry workers and medical volunteers.

If you have access to the Internet you can download their Project Kit, which will help you assemble all of the material the Library of Congress would like to receive (e.g., photos, audiotapes, letters and official papers). Go to www.loc.gov/folklife/vets/ to find out more information and download the kit. You can also call (202) 707-4916 to get the kit. The Folklife Center submits the names of all those who submit their histories to the National Registry of Service. The Center plans to digitalize all of the submissions and make the findings available to historians.

Q: Is a personal alarm system a good idea and how does it work?

A: Many people fear, when living alone, that they won't be able to get to a phone to call for help. If this concerns your parent or he has a condition that raises the likelihood that such a situation could occur, then looking into a "personal medical alert or alarm system" might be a good answer. Most of these systems are listed in your Yellow Pages under Medical Alarms. An Internet search using key words "personal alarms" and "elderly" will bring up a good number of services.

There are essentially two options: Your parent can sign up for a monthly service plan or purchase a system outright. Here's a brief overview on how each system works.

MONTHLY SERVICE PLANS

Most of these systems operate using two primary components: a small wireless waterproof pendant and a base console connected to your parent's phone line. Most people wear the pendant around their neck so their hands are free, while others like wearing a wristwatch-type pendant. The pendant should be waterproof so it can be worn in the shower or bathtub where accidents are common.

In the event of an emergency, your parent presses the activation button on the wireless pendant. This activates the console to immediately phone an emergency response center operated by the service he subscribes to. Within seconds, a two-way, hands-free conversation is established between your parent and the company's emergency operator via a highly sensitive two-way speakerphone. Some also offer digital service with 900 MHz capacity, similar to your cordless phone.

The emergency operator has preprogrammed information on your parent, including medical history, prescribed medications, location, preferred hospital and who else should be contacted (family, neighbors, doctors). If the operator is able to talk with your parent, the operator can be directed to call a series of contacts (you, a neighbor, a friend) who can come over immediately. However, if the operator is unable to make voice contact or thinks the situation requires medical help, he will contact emergency personnel.

With most of these plans, you will pay a monthly fee ranging from $30 to $80, depending on what options you choose. Many companies also charge a onetime installation fee. You don't own the console and need to return it when you deactivate the service.

Here are some basic questions you should ask:

- What kind of training has the staff had who receive the calls?
- What formal relationships does the service have with the local emergency response services in the community?
- If English is a second language for your parent, do they have an interpreter?
- What is the company's average response time?
- If the operator places calls to nonemergency contacts, to a family member, for example, how long do they wait for a response?

- Do they maintain contact with your parent until someone arrives?
- Is there a trial period for the service? Or a minimum contract period?
- What kind of range will your parent have with the system? Can he activate the system from his mailbox? How far in the yard? What about the basement?
- How long has the company been in business? Would you be able to speak to a few customers?
- If you're not satisfied with the service, are there any advance notices or deactivation fees?

Be sure to test the system to determine its range throughout the house and how far it can be used outdoors.

BUYING THE EQUIPMENT

There also are companies that will sell you a system that your parent will own. It usually comes with two components: a transmitter and a phone dialer. The transmitter is the usual waterproof pendant; when the button is pushed, it sends a radio signal to the phone dialer, which will dial preprogrammed numbers of first responders (you, a neighbor and/or 911). If no one answers the first call, it automatically goes to the next number.

With this system, your parent prerecords a message stating that help is needed and giving name, address and basic medical information. So even if your parent is rendered speechless by a heart attack or stroke, the emergency operator will still have all the information he or she needs to respond. These systems usually come with a speakerphone to activate a brief, two-way conversation. Prices vary depending upon how sophisticated a system you buy. All of these systems offer a variety of features, and with technology changing every day, be sure to research the latest advances to meet your parent's particular needs and budget. It can certainly offer you and your parent peace of mind—and besides, it makes a great gift for the holidays or a birthday. My mother has one and it has definitely given her a sense of security.

Q: What should my parents have in their Disaster Supply Kit?

A: Other than being prepared should our nation face a Red Alert, it is wise for older people to have a Disaster Supply Kit for other events as well: an evacuation of their home, apartment or high-rise due to a fire, weather disaster or chemical spill. Having extra food and medicines stored can also be helpful if your parents live alone and in an isolated area—a bout with the flu could incapacitate them enough to not be able to leave the house. In other words, you do not have to appear paranoid of terrorists to get you and your parents motivated to prepare such a kit. It's really just common sense.

The American Red Cross, the Federal Emergency Management Agency (FEMA), and the Centers for Disease Control all offer checklists of what you need to include in your Disaster Supply Kit. To make this easier, I've created two categories: supplies your parents need to take with them in the event of an evacuation, and those they need to have on hand if they need to "shelter in place." I've given special attention to items relevant to an older population. The goal in both instances is to have enough supplies to remain self-sufficient for a short period of time.

EVACUATION SUPPLIES FOR YOUR DISASTER KIT

It's best to store these items in a duffel bag, backpack or a light travel bag with wheels that will be easy for your parents to transport. The items in the evacuation bag, of course, will also be used if your parents are told to remain in their homes. It is recommended that they have a week's supply of the items in the evacuation bag. However, I recommend that your parents have a thirty-day supply of their medications. During a disaster stores may be closed, transportation shut down or supplies may be limited. Ask your pharmacist how these medications should be stored and your physician about prescribing an extra thirty-day supply.

LIST OF SUPPLIES FOR THE EVACUATION BAG

- Small battery-operated radio with an extra set of batteries
- Cell phone (If your parents don't have one, it might be a good idea to purchase a basic phone with a simple plan for emergencies)
- Flashlight and extra batteries
- A manual can opener
- Extra set of eyeglasses and/or contact lenses and cleaning supplies
- Hearing-aid batteries
- Extra wheelchair batteries or other special equipment
- Supplies for dentures

- Three-day supply of food that won't spoil (e.g., ready-to-eat canned meats, fruits, or vegetables, smoked or dry meats such as beef jerky, canned juices, bouillon cubes or dried "soups in a cup," canned or powdered milk, peanut butter, jelly, crackers, nuts, health food bars, trail mix, cereals, cookies)
- Plates and utensils
- Three-day supply of water (one gallon per person per day) and pack of water purifying agents
- Insulin supplies and dietetic foods, if appropriate
- One change of seasonal protective clothing and sturdy shoes
- One blanket or sleeping bag per person
- A first aid kit (buy a prepackaged kit with a first aid manual)
- Sanitation supplies (e.g., towelettes, prescribed ointments for skin, personal hygiene items that you use every day)
- Extra set of car keys
- Cash, credit cards or traveler's checks
- A whistle
- Nonprescription drugs: aspirin and nonaspirin pain reliever, antidiarrhea medication, antacid (for stomach upset), syrup of ipecac (used to induce vomiting if advised by a poison control center), laxative and vitamins
- Place the following lists in a Ziploc plastic bag: style and serial numbers of medical devices such as pacemakers, doctors and emergency contacts, prescription medications including dosage, allergies and medical conditions
- Place copies of medical insurance and Medicare card into Ziploc bag

ACTION STEPS TO PREPARE FOR AN EVACUATION

- Identify an out-of-town contact person for family members to call and share messages. (It may be easier to get calls out of the disaster area.)
- Plan how you will evacuate or signal for help.
- Plan emergency procedures with home health care agencies or workers.
- Tell others where you keep your emergency supplies and evacuation bag.
- Teach others how to operate necessary equipment.
- Label equipment like wheelchairs, canes or walkers.
- Shut off water, gas and electric if instructed to do so.
- Keep the fuel tank of your car full and a signal flare in the car.
- Use emergency routes specified by authorities (shortcuts could be hazardous).

SHELTERING IN PLACE SUPPLIES

This list is in *addition* to the supplies previously cited for your parents' Disaster Evacuation Bag. It is based upon the assumption that your parents would remain homebound for at least one week without electricity, gas or water.

LIST OF SUPPLIES FOR SHELTERING IN PLACE

- Same type of foods cited for the Evacuation Bag; however, have enough stored for at least a full week and place in containers (e.g., trash or Rubbermaid bins) to keep them cool and dry.
- One gallon of water per day per person. (Half for drinking and half for bathing and food preparation.)
- Shutoff wrench to turn off household gas and water.
- Plastic sheeting and duct tape to secure a safe room. If this would be difficult for your parents to put up, perhaps you could do it now (except for the door). Of course, this should *not* be a room that is being used now.
- Flashlights with extra batteries. (Consider keeping a flashlight in each major room, e.g., the kitchen, living room, bedroom and bathroom.)
- Camping type of stove or grill for cooking in case going outside is not restricted.

ACTION STEPS FOR SHELTERING IN PLACE

- Your parent should know how to turn off the water, gas, and electricity.
- Determine a safe room to be sealed off with plastic and duct tape.
- Replace stored food and water every six months.
- Exchange numbers with a neighbor who would be willing to look in on your parents.
- Make arrangements for pets or have enough supplies in place for them.

For great information on how to prepare for each type of disaster go to the American Red Cross Web site at www.redcross.org or call your local chapter, located in the phone book.

Q: We'd like to help a coworker who is caring for her mother, but what's the best way?

A: I've often thought that there ought to be some sort of "Lamaze" movement for families when they take care of older relatives. We heap all kinds of information, good wishes and tips on expectant parents for bringing in a new life, but when we're bringing in a "wisdomed" life—we're on our own.

How about you and your coworkers hosting a "caregiving shower" for your friend during a lunch hour? Make it festive, with a cake and refreshments. Here are some ideas for gift-giving:

GIVE HER GIFT CERTIFICATES FOR:

- Taxi services so that next time she has to take Mom to the doctor's office she doesn't have to deal with the hassle of parking.
- Cleaning services so she can go home to a clean house without doing the work.
- Take-out dinners from restaurants on her way home from work.
- A massage, manicure or other appointment with her favorite beautician. (Include a coupon that offers your time. You'll watch her mom while she's being pampered.)
- Home health or homemaker services that will provide an aide to spend time with her mother so she can leave without worrying.
- Phone cards for long-distance calling if she has siblings and needs to involve them in decision-making. Or her mother can use them to call out-of-town friends and relatives.

DO SOME HOMEWORK FOR HER BY:

- Calling around and finding local pharmacies and grocery stores that deliver to her home. If there is an extra charge for services, pay it in advance.
- Checking out what senior services are available by calling the local Area Agency on Aging at (800) 677-1116. They'll probably have a guidebook on services, so be sure to pick one up. Prepare your findings in a nice notebook and present it to her.
- Buying her some helpful books on caregiving (you can go to my Web site for a list of books and my Caregiver Kit at www.lindarhodes.com).

GIVE HER COUPONS FOR YOUR TIME:

- to come to her home and sit with her mom for a few hours while she does whatever she wants.
- to do helpful tasks such as calling to set up appointments, Internet research on various health conditions, or organizing her mom's contact and medication list.

All too often, caregivers are not aware of the many services available to them, partly because they have no idea where to look and partly because they don't have a moment's peace to do so. Your colleague will be forever grateful that you gave some time and effort to help her get through the maze of health and aging network services—not to mention some TLC.

Q: We are holding a family reunion, and I want to create an oral family history. Where do I begin?

A: What a great idea! A family reunion poses a perfect opportunity to sit down with older members of the family and ask them about how things were "back in the day." Most of them will love telling stories about their childhood, how they learned to make a living, raise a family and overcome obstacles along the way. They relish being asked to pass down some words of wisdom to the younger generation, and the mere act of asking them about their life story allows them to feel valued. The act of creating an oral history is just as valuable for you, the interviewer, as you develop a sense of roots to their past.

Now how do you go about it? It's best to have a series of questions prepared ahead of time. If you're able to send these out before the reunion to those you'll interview, even better. At the very least you'll want them to have an idea of the topics you hope to cover. You might also suggest that family members bring memorabilia to display on a table.

You can use a tape recorder or video recorder. Of course, video allows you to be more creative. Besides just individual interviews, you'll find that trading memories *among* family members can also be fun. For example, you could tape an exchange between aunts and uncles about particular family events, or what life was like growing up with their parents or grandparents. You could film them looking at old photographs while they tell the stories behind them; include a shot of the actual photo or some other memorabilia, such as a piece of jewelry, documents, ethnic dress or a family Bible, that becomes a focal point for discussion.

I recently went back home and videotaped my father showing us around the old family farm and telling us about what it was like growing up there. Thanks to software for us amateur videographers, I was able to scan an actual photo of the barn being built in 1896 onto the video and have it fade into a shot of the same barn today. There are plenty of videographers who will do the same for you and it really isn't that expensive. A family history video that blends interviews with old photos makes a perfect birthday gift for your parents. And if videos aren't your thing, a lovely scrapbook can achieve the same goal.

There's a very nice, easy-to-use book, *How to Tape Instant Oral Biographies* by Bill Zimmerman, that's designed for young biographers but is appropriate for all ages. Here are some questions that he recommends asking beyond the typical fact-finding ones:

1. Is there a story behind how you were given your name?
2. Who were the first family members to settle in this country?
3. What brought them here?
4. Do you know of any stories about what life was like for them?
5. How did your parents meet?
6. How did your parents make a living?
7. Is there any particular hardship that they faced?
8. Was there any special "saying" that your Mom or Dad used? What did it mean?
9. What beliefs did your parents try to teach you?
10. Are there any special traditions we celebrate in our family?
11. Do you recall any special home remedies that your mom or grandmother used?
12. What was your hometown like when you grew up? What do you miss most about it?
13. Did you have a nickname and how did you get it?
14. How do you think your friends would describe you as a teenager?
15. If married, how did you meet your spouse?
16. How did you know your spouse was "the one"?
17. Any suggestions on how to enjoy a long marriage?
18. What goals did you set for yourself in your twenties? How did those change and why?
19. Did you go to war? Where were you stationed? Can you describe the day you were called up?
20. If you've had children, what are the three most important things you've taught them?
21. What would you say are your major accomplishments in life?

22. Any big surprises in your life or special hardships? How did you get through them?
23. What should we pass on to the next generation about our family?

Creating an oral history is truly one of those gifts that keep on giving. You'll never regret taking the time and effort to do one.

Q: **I think my dad would feel better if he volunteered, but where should he start looking?**

A: Not only can volunteering help your dad feel better about himself, it can be downright life-saving. Turns out that, in a study reported in *Psychological Science* by researchers at the University of Michigan, older people who give social support and help others have a higher survival rate than people who don't get into the act of giving. Sure proves that you can't argue with the old saying, "It is better to give than receive."

Now that we know volunteering might be "just what the doctor orders" for your dad, the next step is figuring out who you call and how you find a great volunteer experience. But before he even picks up the phone, he'll be ahead of the game if he spends some time thinking about answers to the following questions:

1. Would I like to learn something new and try something totally different?
2. Would I like to apply my current knowledge, experience and skills?
3. What are my strengths, skills, experience and natural gifts?
4. What is it that I really enjoy doing and what is it that I dislike doing?
5. Do I like working on my own or with a group of fellow volunteers?
6. Would I be able to take a hobby and turn it into a volunteer experience?
7. Do I want a variety of volunteer experiences or just a consistent one?
8. What would make me "jump at the chance" to volunteer?
9. Am I willing to travel to where I'll volunteer, stay close to home, or stay at home?
10. How much time do I want to give, what days and time of day?

Most volunteer coordinators will ask him similar questions to find the best match for him. The following three "gold standard" volunteer agencies are found nationwide. These groups will also connect you to other volunteer programs.

RSVP (RETIRED SENIOR VOLUNTEER PROGRAM)
(NATIONAL: (800) 424-8867)

This program has been around for decades and is very experienced at placing retirees (people fifty-five years plus) in volunteer opportunities with hundreds of local groups within any community. They also provide their volunteers with supplemental car, accident and liability insurance while they are on assignment. If necessary, they'll even help out with transportation needs. When your dad calls RSVP, he'll be asked where he lives so they can connect him to his area coordinator, who will either talk with him on the phone or set up a face-to-face interview. Carol Oman, a director of an RSVP program, describes her volunteering match service this way: "We specialize in making dreams come true. If you've been a desk jockey all of your life, never want to see another piece of paper, and want to get out in the open, we'll have you monitoring streams in our environmental program. If you want to do something new, we'll give you the training."

Their goal is to customize the volunteer experience to create something meaningful for each volunteer. RSVP has volunteers ranging from dispatchers, friendly visitors, environmental monitors, tax preparers, health insurance reviewers, and hospital aides to mentors, tutors in schools, computer refurbishers and trainers. If your dad thinks he's too old, think again—hundreds of their volunteers are over eighty-five.

THE VOLUNTEER CENTER (THE UNITED WAY)
(NATIONAL: (800) 595-4448)

Heidi Neuhaus, as a director of a Volunteer Center sponsored by the United Way, recommends volunteers "do something that's close to their heart." She also advises them to shop around, meet the people they'll be volunteering with and for, and then decide what they'd like to do. "With budget cuts that nonprofit agencies have faced, the need is even greater for volunteers," beckons Neuhaus. Programs like the Contact Helpline and the Domestic Abuse Hotline are staffed by volunteers. Unlike RSVP, their program is open to all age groups. They, too, will interview your dad to find the best match.

THE AREA AGENCY ON AGING
(NATIONAL: (800) 677-1116)

Thousands of older people throughout the nation volunteer by distributing home-delivered meals. "They deliver a lot more than just a meal," claims Shirley Gallagher, a retired Area

Agency on Aging director. "They're our eyes and ears whenever someone living alone needs help." Besides offering home-delivered-meal opportunities, the Area Agency on Aging can have your dad volunteering as an ombudsman's assistant in nursing homes to help resolve complaints, a friendly visitor to elderly living alone, in nursing homes or personal care homes, a driver, a dispatcher, a recreation director at a senior center, or an Apprise volunteer helping people sort out their health insurance. Just like the other volunteer agencies, the Area Agency on Aging will tailor something to meet a volunteer's needs or refer them to someone who can. When your dad calls, tell him to ask for the Volunteer Resource Coordinator.

And finally, don't forget your local newspaper; most have a "Volunteer Connections" section listing all kinds of volunteer opportunities.

Q: How can my parents give away their "good stuff" to good causes?

A: My husband was recently confronted with disposing of fifty years' worth of his parents' saved checks, receipts and financial papers. A realtor told him that there's actually such a thing as a "shredding company." Presto. What would have meant an entire day bending over a personal shredder was handled in one hour. With a little homework, you'd be surprised at the number of businesses and organizations there are to deal with or that want your "stuff."

A great book by Bette Filley, *How to Dispose of Your Stuff: Heavenly Uses for Earthly Goods,* is jam-packed with great ideas on how to give away items that will do your heart good and earn a tax deduction along the way. It contains hundreds of innovative and specific instructions about what can be done with all kinds of things, and how to find exactly who can use whatever you've got. The author encourages older people to "do your giving while you're living, then you'll know where it's going."

Here are some tips that I found especially helpful. Perhaps, as you help your parents wade through their years of accumulation of things, you'll find that their stuff can be a treasure for someone else.

1. **Reader's Digest Condensed Books** are welcomed by the Book Project in care of the World Bank Loading Dock, J Building, 1775 G Street NW, Washington, DC 20433. Call them before you ship at (202) 473-8960. Be sure to send them at book rate through your local post office to save money. They give these books to the Peace Corps to distribute in developing nations.

2. **National Geographic Magazines** are too beautiful to throw out, so send them to Bridge to Asia at 450 Mission Street 407, San Francisco, CA 94105. Call them at (415) 356-9043 before shipping. They send these to students in Vietnam, China and Cambodia.

3. **The One Shoe** project of the National Odd Shoe Exchange provides shoes to amputees and people with different size feet. Contact them at (480) 892-3484 and send to 3200 Delaware Street, Chandler, Arizona 85225.

4. **Old Cell Phones** will gladly be taken by CollectiveGood, Inc. Send them to CollectiveGood, 4508 Bibb Boulevard, Suite B-10, Tucker, Georgia 30084. They send the phones to sixty countries and they are given to people who have never had the benefit of modern telecommunications.

5. **Hearing Aids** can be sent to Hear Now, a national nonprofit organization that recycles used hearing aids and gives them to hard-of-hearing persons with limited financial means. Place the aids in a box or padded envelope and send to: Hear Now, 9745 East Hampton Avenue, Suite 300, Denver, Colorado 80231-4923 or give them a call at (800) 648-4327.

6. **Eyeglasses** can find a new home by sending them to Vision Habitat. After being run through a lensometer to read the glasses' prescriptions, they are sold for $1 to $2 a pair overseas. This money is then used to build houses in the country where the glasses were sold. Mail them to Vision Habitat, 121 Habitat Street, Americus, Georgia 31709. They can be reached at (912) 924-6935.

7. **Frequent Flyer Miles and Camcorders** are in demand by the Making Memories Breast Cancer Foundation, which arranges memorable occasions for women who are dying from breast cancer. If you have a time-share you'd like to give up, frequent flyer miles, or a video camera, give them a call at (503) 252-3955. Making Memories Breast Cancer Foundation, PO Box 92042, Portland, Oregon 97292-2042.

8. **Warm Winter Coats** can be sent to Russia through the Coats for Russia project at 200 E. Frank Phillips Boulevard, Bartlesville, Oklahoma 74003. (800) 747-0085.

These are just a few unique ways that you can give away your "stuff" to good causes. The book also identifies a wide range of ways to sell your goods, organize your downsizing and hire companies to help you in the process.

Q: We are moving away. How can my parents make long-distance grand-parenting work?

A: According to a survey by AARP, 66 percent of grandparents have at least one grandchild who lives more than a day's drive away. And that has *me* worried. I just told my son, who is in college in San Diego, my new rule: "You're allowed to be three thousand miles away from me while you're single, but when a grandchild enters the picture—it's three *blocks!*" I now live in fear of West Coast relationships and send him not-so-subtle articles about the wonders of East Coast girls. But as we all know, we live in a very mobile world and it is rare for all of us to remain in our hometowns.

So it's going to take some creativity and disciplined effort for your parents to maintain a close relationship with their grandchildren. Thanks to land phones, cell phones, the Internet, the ancient art of letter writing and the good old post office, they can stay in touch and even create new traditions to make this move a positive adventure.

First of all, Grandma and Grandpa need to reassure your children that they'll find new, fun ways to stay close and, of course, they can look forward to great visits together. The children will be anxious enough leaving their school and friends behind, so they don't need their grandparents to add to the anxiety. They've got to be strong and positive. (Someday, someone may need to remind me of these words!)

Here are a few ideas for your parents to share the journey and cross the miles:

- If they don't have a computer and don't know how to use the Internet, now is the time to jump into their grandchildren's world of communication. It's a myth to think that seniors don't "get it." AOL reports that seniors are one of the fastest-growing population segments using the Internet. Many senior centers and community colleges have classes on how to use e-mail and surf the Net. My seventy-eight-year-old mom was one of the first in Sun City West, Arizona, to get a computer and shocked her college grandkids when she started Instant Messaging them. I'd tap your parents' motivation to stay in touch right now, and you, the kids and the grandparents go off together to a computer store and get set up.
- Set up a routine of a weekly or biweekly call so that the children can look forward to talking to their grandparents.
- Read stories to each other over the phone. My nephew and I love reading his favorite series, *Captain Underpants* (I'm not making this title up), over the phone.

- Get a digital camera and e-mail pictures of daily life, from showing off a homework assignment, to something the dog did, to just making a funny face to scare Grandma. The same goes for them. If digital isn't their thing, buy them a bunch of single-use cameras and have them mail each one to you to develop.
- Write letters. Despite all of the high-tech ways of communicating, there is nothing like getting mail from those you love—especially from grandparents. Have the children create a colorful letter box to collect their letters from your parents.
- Be sure to make pictures or copies of homework assignments and artwork to mail to Grandma and Grandpa to put on the refrigerator.
- Most schools have assignments where you need to interview someone and write a report. Grandparents are a great source.
- At your local electronics store, you'll find picture frames that can receive digital photos via the Internet. If you're savvy with the Internet and a digital camera, your parents will love getting new photos.
- You can also buy clocks and picture frames that have chips on which your kids can record their voices saying hi to Grandma and Grandpa. And your parents can do the same for the kids.
- When your parents visit, schedule a trip to school so that your children can show off their new school, new teachers and friends. Take pictures.
- Grandparents can send care packages with some of the kids' favorite candy, books, articles in magazines—little things that let them know they're thinking of them every day.

All of you can make this work. But you'll need to make a conscious effort to create and sustain new ways of communicating before you slip into a routine of typical biannual visits, usually filled with too much activity and too little one-on-one time for your parents and children to really get to know each other.

It's been said that "absence makes the heart grow fonder." Let this absence make their hearts grow fonder still.

Q: How can we make the outside of my mother's house safer?

A: Your first step is to help your mom identify whatever makes her feel insecure when she leaves and reenters the house. It might be helpful for you to come home with her from an outing so both of you can identify what is making her feel less safe about her surroundings. Perhaps there's poor lighting along the walk to the house, it takes too long to use the key to unlock the door, or overgrown bushes make the entrance too dark and provide a hiding place for an intruder. Some of her safety concerns may come from feeling vulnerable physically. The fear of falling and breaking a hip plagues many older women. And no wonder; more than 300,000 people break their hips every year. Icy sidewalks or steps can pose a very grave threat to your mom.

Once you have a better sense of what makes her feel insecure, and after you've surveyed the environment outside of her home, here are some things you might consider:

Movement-Sensitive Lighting. Perhaps it's time to install new lights that are sensitive to any movement directly outside her entryway. For any would-be intruder, the automatic light makes them think someone is at home and aware that they are in the driveway. The other advantage is that, even if your mom forgets to turn on the lights before she leaves, the light will be on for her when she comes home. She should also have timers that control outside lights, and one in the bathroom throughout the night so that anyone casing the house will think someone is up. Timers offer an inexpensive way to burglar-proof the house and they are easily installed by plugging them into an electrical outlet.

Clearing the Way into the House. If your mom's driving and has a garage but she's without an automatic door opener, now would be a good time to get her one. (Having siblings who will pitch in will make it even more affordable.) There are also systems that turn on a radio a few minutes before she enters the house so that the noise will alert a burglar to escape. Wherever she parks the car should be well lit; this can also be activated by remote control as she enters the driveway. Make sure that the pathway to and from the house is clear of any obstacles so that she won't trip over them. This may be the time to finally repair or lay a new sidewalk, and to add a railing along the walkway so she won't have to fear falling. Even though she may love bushes surrounding the house or along a pathway, you may need to relocate them to another part of the yard if they create too good a hiding place for an intruder or block safe lighting.

Take a Cab. If your mom likes to go out in the evening but doesn't like coming home alone, or doesn't like driving at night, perhaps you can treat her to cab rides so they can pick her up and take her back home. Most cab drivers, if asked, will wait until she is safely in the house before they leave.

Keyless Entry or New Locks. Make sure the lock to the door can open easily and quickly. She may become nervous if she has to work with a lock or a key that's become difficult to negotiate, perhaps because of arthritis. You can install a keyless lock, available at any hardware store. (Make sure she's able to remember the code.) Keyless locks are also great for opening and closing the car door.

Security Systems. If you're able to afford it, investing in a security system not only protects your mom but also provides her with peace of mind. You'll need to make sure, however, that she can easily operate the system so she's not constantly triggering the alarms and causing herself undue fear. Be sure to be part of this decision so she isn't sold something more complicated or extensive than what she needs. And don't forget the simple things, like installing a peephole in the front and side doors, an intercom so she won't have to open the door to any stranger and decals on the windows to look like she has an alarm system.

In cold weather, always make sure that she's well stocked with rock salt to tackle icy sidewalks. Better yet, hire a service or responsible neighbor to maintain her driveway and sidewalk throughout the winter.

III

NAVIGATING LEGAL & MONEY MATTERS

1

Benefits & Resources

Q: **How does my mom apply for Social Security benefits?**

A: The traditional way is to make a visit to your local Social Security office, but the process is much easier on the Internet (see below). There are 1,300 offices nationwide and you can call (800) 772-1213 to find the office nearest you. If you go to the local office to apply for benefits, you and your mom should bring her:

- Social Security card
- Birth certificate
- Proof of U.S. citizenship
- Spouse's birth certificate and Social Security number if she's applying for benefits based on her husband's record
- Marriage certificate
- Military discharge papers if she served in the military
- W-3 form from last year, or her latest tax return

The time to apply for benefits is four months before the date she qualifies. Presently, early retirement can begin at age sixty-two. If your mom was born before 1938, her full retirement age will remain at age sixty-five; however, the full retirement age is moving up for those born after 1938. Be sure to check with the Social Security Administration as to her full retirement age based upon her birth date. (For example, Baby Boomers born between 1943 and 1954 will not reach full retirement age until they are sixty-six years old.)

If you have access to the Internet you can go to Social Security's excellent Web site at www.ssa.gov. The SSA has been in the forefront of offering a range of services on the Web. If you lose your Social Security card or Medicare card, you can apply for new cards online. You can e-mail questions and add your name to a list to be updated on the latest rules, given a topic of your choosing. You can even submit a request to receive a Social Security statement identifying all of your contributions throughout your working life and what you can expect to receive upon retirement at different ages. You can also search for your full retirement age based upon your birth date.

Here are a few guidelines for submitting your mom's Social Security retirement application online: You'll need a printer because, once you've entered the information and sent it to SSA, you'll also need to print the application, sign it and mail it to the address provided. The Internet service isn't available 24/7 but close to it, so be sure to check the hours listed on the benefit application page before you start. You must agree to direct deposit (a good idea) to make an online application, so have your mom's bank account number on hand. You'll need to know her earnings for the past and current year.

You'll also need to enter other basics, such as her married name, Social Security number, and date of birth. SSA lists what you'll need to know before you start the online application. As with all applications you will need to mail in some original documents that SSA will mail back to you.

The Web site can answer just about every question on Social Security and benefits. (If you're a teacher, note that there's a terrific Kids' Page.) You'll also find a Women's Page filled with financial tips and benefits advice for women of all ages.

Q: Are VA benefits automatic or do you have to enroll?

A: Several years ago, Congress passed the Veterans Health Care Eligibility Reform Act stating that any veteran who wants to receive VA health care services must now enroll. Your dad needs to fill out Form 10-10EZ and there are three ways he can get it:

1. Visit, call or write a local VA care or benefits office listed in the blue pages of the phone book under "Federal Government."
2. Call the VA Enrollment Center at (877) 222-VETS.
3. Simply download the form and file it electronically by going to the VA Web site at www.va.gov.

Hopefully, your dad kept his Honorable Discharge Certificate (DD-214) because he'll need to give them a copy. Once your dad enrolls, he'll be assigned one of two eligibility categories:

must-do or may-do. The VA must provide hospital and outpatient care to veterans in the "must-do" group, consisting of veterans who have a service-connected disability, former POWs, World War I veterans and low-income veterans. Depending upon funding, the VA may also offer some nursing home care to this group.

The VA may provide health care services to the "may-do" group, depending upon the resources available to the Department of Veterans Affairs. These veterans will have to pay a co-payment for the care.

In addition to an eligibility category your father will be assigned to one of seven priority groups. Vets with a service-connected disability that is 50 percent or more disabling are given priority one status. Most veterans of World War II fall into priority group five—they don't have a disability connected to the war but their annual income and net worth are low income as determined by the VA system. Those who have higher incomes can still receive services, but they pay a higher co-pay.

Veterans accepted for enrollment in the VA health care system can receive inpatient and outpatient services, including preventive and primary care. Prescriptions are covered when veterans receive their treatment from a VA medical facility. Most of the time the veteran will be asked to pay a $2 co-pay.

If your dad qualifies, he could receive primary care from outpatient clinics, community-based care, some nursing home care, home-based primary care, adult day care, rehabilitation, diagnostic and treatment services, and hospital (medical and surgical) inpatient care. If the VA doesn't operate a facility where your father lives, they can send him to one located nearest to him or subcontract with another provider to give him the service. It's certainly worth the effort for your father to enroll and find out what kind of health care he could receive in return for his service.

Q: What are some of the best Web sites dealing with aging parent issues?

A: The Internet is downright amazing, if not overwhelming, when it comes to spewing out all kinds of information on just about every topic imaginable. As baby boomers age and become Internet savvy, the sites on aging are popping up faster than the speed of light. A simple keyword search on "eldercare" will call up an easy 58,000 hits. Where to begin? Here are my six favorite Web sites that will get you well on your way to navigating the resources that await you in cyberspace:

NATIONAL COUNCIL ON AGING "BENEFITS CHECKUP"
www.benefitscheckup.org

Simply fill out an online questionnaire and immediately find out if your parent qualifies for benefits and prescription discounts. The site provides forms and contact data once you know you're eligible for a benefit.

MEDICARE
www.medicare.gov

Medicare is the centerpiece of your parents' health care. What's covered and what's not are always changing. But the feds did a nice job in making it understandable by putting up an online guide with just about every question you might have on Medicare. They also provide "Nursing Home Compare" so, if you're looking for a nursing home, you can find the results of the latest inspection reports on every nursing home in the country! They also provide comparisons of Medigap policies and home health care, and provide links to Social Security and other federal sites.

LOCATING ELDERCARE SERVICES NATIONWIDE
www.eldercare.gov

If you're looking for community-based services in another state, this site is a one-stop shop. Go to their "Quick Index" so you can easily hyperlink to all of the services offered by the Administration on Aging. You can track down the Area Agency on Aging closest to your parent(s) and access other caregiving Web sites.

THE "GRANDDADDY" OF AGING INFORMATION
www.elderweb.com

This award-winning site is an excellent resource for a wide range of topics related to aging. It's updated daily to provide the latest news affecting seniors in such areas as health care, legislation, and consumer alerts, along with the links that connect you to the resources you need.

HEALTHFINDER

www.healthfinder.gov

A gateway to consumer health and human services information from the U.S. Department of Health and Human Services. The Web site offers a directory of services and links to agencies and databases. Great site and easy to use.

AARP

www.aarp.org

Even though this is a commercial site, when it comes to senior issues it is top-notch in giving you easily understandable consumer information from A–Z. They provide you with the latest news, helpful links and printable versions of many of their excellent publications. You don't have to be a member of AARP to use it.

I'd love to give you more sites, but if you visit any of these they all act as portals to hundreds of other age-related Web sites that are of excellent quality. And you can always visit my Web site, www.lindarhodes.com, which features hyperlinks to sixty other age-related sites.

Q: What is an Area Agency on Aging?

A: I'm waiting for the day when social services are run like food courts: If you "feel like" Chinese, Mexican or good old McDonald's, it's just a few steps and a food tray away. Wouldn't it be nice to walk into a food court with every service your mom or dad could possibly need right in front of you—home health care, home-delivered meals, doctors in every specialty, adult day care, senior centers, Medicare and Social Security offices, pharmacies and physical therapists?

While we're waiting on an enterprising developer, there is a great place to start: the "Triple A." No, not the American Automobile Association but the Area Agency on Aging. Chances are there's one close to you, as nearly every county in the nation is covered by an Area Agency on Aging. Usually, they're either part of county government or they are a nonprofit agency. Their job is to plan for, organize and provide aging services for their local community. They're as close as it gets to the "food court" for aging services.

Here are just three of the major ways you can take advantage of your local Area Agency on Aging:

Information Hub. Since the agency is responsible for planning aging services for the whole community, they'll know just about every program in the region. Many of them offer guidebooks of all the services available. Most have Web sites—find them by going to www.eldercare.gov; enter your parent's county and click on "General Information and Assistance" on the search bar. The local AAA can tell you what services are available, advise you on eligibility criteria of various programs and give you contact information.

Family Caregiver Support. This is a terrific program funded by the state and federal governments for caregivers and care receivers (sixty years plus) who are related by blood or marriage and live together. So, if your mom lives with you and you're caring for her, you may qualify for financial help to cover out-of-pocket expenses, and a grant to modify your home or purchase helpful devices to meet your parent's needs. Some families have used the money to install a stair climb or modify a bathroom. The age restriction of sixty plus is removed if your parent suffers from dementia. The program operates on a sliding fee scale; it's not a poverty-restricted program. You can receive a family consultation, legal advice, needs assessment, respite care, caregiver education and training, and help with out-of-pocket expenses.

Care Management. If your parent has a modest income, he or she may qualify for a caseworker and a team of professionals skilled in geriatric social work and nursing (provided either by the Area Agency on Aging or one of its subcontractors) to help manage care. They'll assess your parent's needs and bring together the services required to take care of your parent and help him or her remain in the community. The Area Agency on Aging also provides geriatric assessments to determine whether or not your parent needs nursing home care or assisted living.

You can track down your Area Agency on Aging by calling the Eldercare Locator, (800) 677-1116, or look them up in the blue pages of your phone book under Aging or Senior Services. You can also go to www.eldercare.gov and find your local agency online.

Q: **Is there a one-stop shop to find out what benefits my parents can get?**

A: For many benefits, sixty-five is the magic number for eligibility, but you should be aware that some benefits can be secured as early as age sixty. Here are three major resources to navigate your search for benefits:

The National Council on Aging (NCOA) offers a great questionnaire at www.benefitscheckup .org that only takes ten to fifteen minutes to complete. You'll enter basic information on your parent, including his income, all of which remains confidential. Once you've entered the data, the "Benefits Checkup" will search thousands of benefits against your parent's information. Within seconds you'll receive an "Eligibility Report" that will identify potential benefits for which your parent may be eligible. The report will include all of the information that you will need to contact the local agency to determine whether or not your parent actually qualifies. You will be given local names, addresses and toll-free phone numbers, along with application forms that you simply download and send in to the appropriate agency. This resource is a great time-saver. So, if you don't have Internet access, it's worth a trip to the library to get online.

The NCOA Web site also offers a benefits search for prescription drugs: "Benefits Check-upRX." This takes only five minutes to complete and you'll find out if your parent qualifies for any of the 240 public and private prescription savings programs that cover nearly 800 prescription drugs. In addition, thirty state-funded pharmacy programs are included. Again, you'll be given contact information to make an application to determine whether or not your parent qualifies. The Benefits Checkup Web site is especially helpful if you live in a different state than your parents, as it searches thousands of programs by state and gives you local numbers to make contact.

Finally, the Area Agency on Aging (AAA) is another valuable resource for advice on what services are available and if your parents qualify. You can find your parents' local AAA by calling the Eldercare Locator at (800) 677-1116. (See page 185 for more on Area Agencies on Aging.)

Q: How can my mom apply for handicapped parking tags?

A: Your first step is to contact your state's department of motor vehicles, as each state has its own laws and regulations governing parking tags. Most states now refer to these as a *Person with Disability Parking Placard*.

In general, the following people qualify for this type of placard, allowing them to park in the handicapped parking spaces with the wheelchair symbol. Anyone who is:

1. Blind.
2. Does not have full use of an arm or both arms.
3. Not able to walk 200 feet without stopping to rest.
4. Not able to walk without the use of or assistance from: a brace, cane, crutch, another person, prosthetic device, wheelchair or other assistive device.
5. Restricted by lung disease (usually specified levels measured by a spirometry test).

6. Using portable oxygen.

7. Affected by a cardiac condition to the extent that the person's functional limitations are classified in severity as Class III or Class IV according to the standards set by the American Heart Association.

8. Severely limited in his or her ability to walk due to an arthritic, neurological or orthopedic condition.

If your parent has a 100 percent service-connected disability that is certified by the U.S. Veteran's Administration, or the same disabilities as listed above but they are service-connected rather than due to aging or injuries, then your parent can apply for a "Severely Disabled Veteran" placard, which provides the same benefits as the Person with Disability placard.

So how do you go about getting a Person with Disability placard?

Many states now allow you to download copies of their application forms, or you can go to a local motor vehicle office of the state department of transportation. If you are a member of the AAA (American Automobile Association), they, too, have copies of the forms and some can help you apply and process your state's application. In most cases, the applicant must be the person with the disability—not you, even if you were going to be driving her everywhere in your car. In other words, the placard is for the person, not the vehicle.

Your next step will be to take your state's form to your mother's physician. He or she must certify which conditions make her eligible for this parking privilege. Her doctor must sign the form and enter his or her medical license number.

In some states, a police officer may also certify that someone is eligible if the applicant "does not have the full use of a leg or both legs, or is blind," as evidenced by use of a wheelchair, walker, crutches, cane or other prescribed device. Once a physician or police officer certifies that your mother is eligible and signs the form, she may need to get the form notarized.

If your parent is applying for a "Severely Disabled Veteran" placard, then the Veterans Administration Regional Office must certify and sign the form.

According to most states, a placard is to be used only when the vehicle in which it is displayed is parked and is being used for the transportation of the person with the disability. You don't get to use it if your mother is not in the car. The placard qualifies you to park in areas designated for use by persons with disability only. It does not give you license to park where parking is prohibited.

Q: Are there tax credits for caring for an elderly parent?

A: Yes, there are federal tax credits available to you if you are providing more than half of the support of your parent (or parent-in-law), they live with you during the tax year and they have not filed a joint income tax return for the same year that you claim them.

According to the IRS's Publication 503, titled "Child and Dependent Care Expenses," you can claim up to $3,000 in expenses (2003) for dependent caregiving expenses. The elderly person's gross income, however, cannot be more than the personal exemption amount ($3,050 in 2003). Social Security retirement benefits and tax-free interest on investments are not included in calculating the dependent's income.

So what kind of expenses can you claim?

Paid Help. If you pay someone to care for your loved one so that you can work, you can claim the expense of paying for this care. You'll need to provide the name, address and taxpayer identification number of the care provider. If this is an individual, give the IRS their Social Security number, and if it is a company, then ask for the Federal ID number. You cannot pay someone to provide the care who you claim as a dependent, or a child under nineteen years of age.

Medical Expenses. If the caregiver or the care receiver incurs medical expenses that exceed 7.5 percent of their adjusted gross income then your medical expenses are deductible. Here are some of the medical expenses that the IRS defines as acceptable according to their Medical and Dental Expenses Publication 502:

- Capital improvements to the home (e.g., ramps, stair climbs, widening hallways) to accommodate the medical condition of the disabled person.
- Cost of devices used in diagnosing and treating illness and disease. For example, blood sugar test kits to monitor blood sugar levels.
- The cost of a hearing aid and the batteries you buy to operate it.
- Insurance premiums you pay for policies that cover medical care.
- Premiums you pay for Medicare B are a medical expense. If you applied for it at age sixty-five or after you became disabled, you can deduct the monthly premiums you paid.
- Amounts paid for premiums for qualified long-term-care insurance contracts.
- Amounts you pay for prescribed medicines and drugs.

- Cost of medical care in a nursing home, home for the aged, or similar institution, for yourself, your spouse, or your dependents.
- Cost of wages and other amounts paid for nursing services (these do not have to be provided by a registered nurse but are generally performed by a nurse), such as giving medication or changing dressings, as well as bathing and grooming the patient either in your home or another care facility.
- Costs for oxygen and oxygen equipment to relieve breathing problems caused by a medical condition.
- Costs of transportation primarily for, and essential to, medical care (e.g., bus, taxi, train, or plane fares or ambulance service).

There are other medical expenses that can be claimed, so I highly encourage you to go to the IRS Web site at www.IRS.gov and search for their Publication 502 for complete details on the tax credit and how to validate your expenses. You can also give them a call at (800) 829-1040.

Besides the federal tax credits for caring for a dependent older person, half of the states also allow tax exemptions for state taxes. So be sure to check with your state department of revenue to see if your state offers additional exemptions.

As with all tax information, this should not be construed as tax advice. Talk with your accountant or the IRS directly to determine if you qualify for these credits.

Q: My mom keeps confusing Medicaid with Medicare. Just what is the difference?

A: There is a world of difference between the two programs. Medicare is a federal health insurance program for those sixty-five and older: Part A essentially covers hospital expenses, and Part B covers physician and outpatient services. Everyone receiving Social Security at age sixty-five automatically receives a Medicare card. This is Medicare in a nutshell; for lots more on the subject go to www.medicare.gov or pick up a benefits book at your local senior center.

Medicaid is a health insurance program run at the state level for people living at or below the poverty line. The federal government shares the cost with the state. Many older people who qualify for Medicaid are also eligible to receive a federal supplement to their Social Security check known as SSI.

Medicare is automatic and you do not have to meet income eligibility limits. In contrast, Medicaid has stringent income eligibility rules and you must apply. If your mother qualifies she would be able to receive health care services from physicians who accept Medicaid, and her hospitalizations and prescriptions would also be covered. If she's sixty-five or over, she'd receive Medicare as well. The two are not mutually exclusive. Depending upon her financial circumstances, Medicaid may cover her premiums for Parts A and B along with the deductibles.

Most people start looking toward Medicaid when they are facing nursing home costs that can easily reach $5,000 per month. Her state Medicaid program will review all of your mother's "countable income," such as wages, self-employment income, pensions, interest, dividends, annuities, entitlements and benefits. If the countable income is less than the nursing home costs, then your mother would likely pass the income test. But she'll also have to meet medical requirements that prove she needs skilled nursing care in an approved long-term-care facility.

You'll often hear the term "spending down" associated with Medicaid and nursing homes. Many people pay for a nursing home using their savings, assets and income to meet the monthly bill, eventually spending their assets down to a level where they meet federal poverty guidelines. At that point, they apply to Medicaid.

Years ago, people had to spend down to such an extent that the nursing home resident's spouse would be impoverished by the time Medicaid would help out. But, today, federal law protects spouses from becoming impoverished. Medical Assistance Offices calculate a monthly "Community Spouse Resource Allowance," which can be as high as $2,175 per month. If the spouse is living in the home, it will not be considered a countable asset, nor will the household goods or the car. The state Medicaid office will determine the allowance based upon an eligibility formula.

Some people think that they can game the system by transferring all of a parent's income and assets to the children as a way of "spending down" so that the parent will immediately qualify for nursing home assistance. You should know, however, that any assets transferred within thirty-six months prior to nursing home admission are *not* exempt from the asset eligibility test. This is often referred to as the "look back" provision.

The Medicaid program also requires repayment of medical assistance for nursing home care from your mother's estate after she dies, or from her husband's estate if he outlives her. Why? The program is meant to help people of low income and minimal resources; if the estate has anything left of substance, then the idea is that it should help replenish the Medicaid coffers to help other low-income individuals. It's very likely that the state would have paid at least $76,000 toward your mother's nursing home stay alone.

Contact your local welfare office, listed in the blue pages of your phone book, to determine if your mom would qualify. It may also be wise for you to see a certified elder law attorney; you can find one in your local area by going to www.naela.com.

Q: A friend of my mother's rarely has any food in the house, and we know she's not eating well. Do you think she could get food stamps?

A: You've really touched on a topic that many older people either misunderstand or shy away from. The United States Department of Agriculture (USDA) reports that nearly a million and a half elderly households do not have enough of the right types of food needed to maintain their health or simply do not have enough to eat. We've all heard the stories about older people being forced to choose between spending money on their prescriptions or groceries. It's a trade-off they should never have to make.

Yet of all the benefits out there for the elderly, my guess is that food stamps are the most underutilized. A great many people qualify and simply don't know it. Others fear they'll be embarrassed, handing over food "stamps" to a cashier in front of a bunch of judgmental onlookers. But the days of "stamps" are long gone. Your mom's friend would be handing over an electronic card just like a plastic credit card. So who's to know?

If you don't have a problem accepting Medicare—a government-subsidized program—why walk away from this benefit? There are actually five programs available: Food Stamps, Commodity Supplemental Food, Senior Farmers' Market, Congregate Meals, and Home Delivered Meals, also known as "Meals on Wheels." So let's go over each.

> **Food Stamps.** Generally, all persons who live together and prepare meals together are grouped as a "household" under the food stamp program. An adult sixty and older, however, can be considered a separate household even if living with other family members. These "elderly" households must meet the "net income test," which is gross income minus certain deductions, such as medical expenses; and they may have up to $3,000 in assets. The older person's home, lot, and pension funds are not included in the $3,000 limit. Your mother's friend would apply at the local county board of assistance office. If it is difficult for her to go there, she can be interviewed by telephone. To find her local office, look in the blue pages of your phone book under "Government Services."

> **Commodity Supplemental Food.** This program offered by the USDA provides a free box of commodities up to once a month. Anyone at least sixty years of age, with an income at or below 130 percent of the poverty level (approximately $12,103), can qualify. Nearly eight out of ten participants are elderly, so your mom's friend certainly wouldn't be alone. Typical boxes include pasta, rice, beans, butter, cheese, canned meat and poultry

along with canned fruits and vegetables. Oftentimes, the state agency receiving the commodities from the federal government contracts out to nonprofit groups like food pantries to distribute the food. Give your local Area Agency on Aging ([800] 677-1116) a call to find out about eligibility and who distributes the food.

Senior Farmers' Market. This is another program offered by the USDA for folks sixty years and up whose income is less than 185 percent of the federal poverty guidelines (or approximately $17,223 for a single person). If she qualifies, she'll receive coupons worth an overall average of $70, which she can take to local farmers' markets to buy fresh produce. Again, give the Area Agency on Aging a call to see if the program is offered near her.

Congregate Meals. This program is offered at no cost to seniors and there are no income guidelines. Many people, however, give a small donation. Perhaps your mom can take her friend to a local senior center a few times a week to receive a very good hot meal and the added benefit of socialization. Most senior centers will also help her apply for the other food programs described here. Senior centers are listed in the blue pages of your phone book, usually under "Aging Services," or give the local Area Agency a call to track down the closest center to your friend.

Home-Delivered Meals. Chances are the same senior center offering congregate meals will also have a group of terrific volunteers who will deliver meals five days a week. This program is for those elderly who are homebound and is of no cost to seniors aged sixty years and older. There are no income eligibility limits, but because resources are limited there may be a waiting list and most people who use the program do have a modest income.

With all of these resources available, your mother's friend shouldn't be hungry or, worse yet, at risk of being malnourished. Good nutrition is critical to an older person's health. You'll be saving her from a lot more than hunger pains—so trust your instincts and get involved.

Q: What is the Family Caregiver Support Program?

A: One of the most helpful resources for families providing care to a relative is the Family Caregiver Support Program. This federal program is administered by each state's state unit on aging, so if you have friends who are caring for their parents in other states, be sure to let them know about the program, too. For thousands of families this program can spell the difference between their elderly relative staying at home or going to a nursing home.

Each state decides what type of programs they will offer families providing care to an aging relative. The program is basically geared to families with a household income at or below 380 percent of poverty. As of 2004, that would amount to a combined household income of about $44,000. However, some of the services, like educational programs and information and referral, are not income-restricted. So it's in your best interest to call your local Area Agency on Aging to see if you qualify. You can reach them at (800) 677-1116.

In general, you will find that Family Caregiver Support Programs offer:

1. Information to caregivers about available services.
2. Assistance to caregivers in gaining access to supportive services.
3. Counseling and training to assist caregivers in making decisions and solving problems related to their caregiver roles.
4. Respite care to temporarily relieve the caregiver. For example, they can help pay for adult day services, intermittent or overnight respite care during an emergency, or in-home respite care.
5. Supplemental services to complement the family caregiver's role. For example, they can provide funds for home modifications (like putting in a ramp or a stair climb), assistive technologies, equipment supplies, emergency response systems or transportation.

The program also provides caregiver support services to grandparents raising fully dependent grandchildren and older adults raising a dependent disabled (mental and/or physical) adult child.

Some states broaden the income eligibility by allowing family members to share in the cost of services. In Pennsylvania, for example, family caregivers can receive up to $200 per month to help with out-of-pocket expenses ranging from respite care to adult briefs, and a onetime grant of up to $2,000 to modify the home or purchase assistive devices to help care for a frail relative. These families must meet specific eligibility rules and they do share in the cost of services.

Even if all they can do is give you good information on what to do and where to turn, it's worth the call.

2

<u>Legal Issues</u>

Q: **I suspect that the prizes my mom keeps winning are scams. How do I know and what do I do?**

A: You're right to suspect that something might be up—and it's not your mom's luck. There are an estimated 14,000 illegal telemarketing operations fleecing at least $40 billion out of unsuspecting Americans every year. More than half of the victims are among the elderly.

Why older people? They were raised to be polite and, as a result, are very reluctant to just hang up. Many live alone, so they are accessible by phone, and they welcome almost any human contact. The telemarketers are very friendly, polite and act like they're looking out for the older person, or present themselves as nice people trying to make a living to support a family or work their way through college. Many older people have difficulty hearing and so may agree to something they didn't understand.

And like all of us, they're all drawn to winning something.

There are warning signs that you should look for when you visit your mom or dad. The National Fraud Information Center, run by the National Consumer League, warns that your parents might be a target if they are:

- Receiving loads of junk mail for contests, "free trips," prizes and sweepstakes.
- Receiving frequent calls from strangers who promise valuable awards, great money-making deals, or requests for charitable contributions.
- Having payments picked up by a private "courier" service.

- Receiving lots of cheap items (prizes) such as costume jewelry, beauty products, or small appliances. In some cases, your parent might have bought these to, supposedly, win a bigger prize.
- Receiving calls from organizations that say they will recover money that your parent paid to a telemarketer for a fee.

Besides these warning signs, you should be highly concerned if your parent is having trouble paying bills, has written numerous checks or made withdrawals for escalating amounts of money to unfamiliar and out-of-state companies.

Be especially on guard if checks are written to companies with addresses in Canada, as these scam artists operate across the border in an effort to escape U.S. prosecutors.

If you see these warning signs, what do you do? First of all, don't blame your mom or make her feel that she's been foolish or this is her fault. If you do, she might fear that if she tells you everything that has happened, you might take away her financial control.

You'd be surprised at the number of people who fear this, so they might act very secretively about the telemarketer phone calls. Instead, let your mom know that you suspect something and that these people might be taking advantage of her honesty, politeness and trusting nature. Tell her that it wouldn't be surprising if she became a target, because reports show that it's not unusual for an older person to receive twenty telemarketer calls a day!

She needs to know that this is robbery—the thief has used a phone instead of a gun, but he or she has robbed your mom nonetheless.

Now you need to act. Help your mom assemble all of the information surrounding the scam. If you're not sure whether it is a scam, counselors will help you to sort this out at the National Fraud Information Center. You can reach the NFIC by calling (800) 876-7060 or file an "Online Incident Report" by visiting the Web site at www.fraud.org.

You also can call your state's Office of the Attorney General; most have a consumer hotline. Both groups really encourage you to report scams so they can prevent these guys from taking advantage of others.

Once someone has entered one contest, or has taken the bait from one scam, these companies create "mooch lists" and, you guessed it, sell them to one another. So, if your mom has been seriously harmed by these telemarketers or she's receiving far too many calls, you might want to consider equipping her with caller ID, changing her phone number and/or getting her to hang up.

To stay ahead of the game, here's a list of tips from the NFIC to keep your parents out of harm's way. According to them, it's probably a scam if:

• You have to take the offer immediately.

• The caller refuses to share written information before you commit to anything.

• You can supposedly make huge profits in an investment with no risk.

• The caller insists that you send your payment by a private courier who will come to your house and pick it up.

• You get a postcard announcing you've won a prize but need to make payments for processing fees, customs, taxes or any other reason first.

• The caller wants cash.

• The caller wants your Social Security number, credit card number or any other financial information.

• The caller asks for a charitable donation but won't give you any information on how to verify the charity.

• The caller never accepts no for an answer—and keeps calling.

You can also help your mom by getting her phone number listed on the national Do Not Call List by calling (888) 382-1212, or going online at www.donotcall.gov. (See page 216 for more on the Do Not Call List.)

Q: **What are the most common scams targeting the elderly?**

A: The Senate Committee on Aging held hearings that exposed the wide range of fraud and abuse that's being heaped upon unsuspecting elderly throughout the country. The National Association of Adult Protective Services estimates that there are more than a half million such cases each year. This number doesn't even include all of the consumer fraud complaints that are often filed with state attorneys general for telemarketing fraud.

Your parents are susceptible to a wide and ever-growing range of ways to swindle them of their life savings. Here's a brief rundown of some of the more common ways that scam artists are making their mark:

• **Stock Offerings.** Your parents may receive a call from a telemarketer telling them of a great chance to buy stock in a small, promising company just before it goes public. They'll be told that by getting in on the ground floor of this "Initial Public Offering" (IPO) they'll yield high profits with little risks. If your mom or dad is Internet savvy, they'll get these offers via e-mails—they are extremely risky and many are simply bogus.

• **Faith-Based Schemes.** More than 90,000 investors have lost nearly $2 billion in faith-based investments. Swindlers offer investments that prey on the older person's religious beliefs by telling them that their investment also helps a social cause, or that some of the funds will go to a church. Some scam artists scan obituary notices and show up at the widow or widower's door days later with a package in hand. Often it's a Bible or religious symbol they claim the deceased ordered—of course for a high price. (Yes, it was a popular scam back in the Depression and it's still going on today.)

• **Credit Card Insurance.** Cashing in on the protective and cautious nature of many older people, telemarketers will offer them credit card insurance that they don't need (since federal law protects consumer exposure to no more than $50 of unauthorized expenses when a credit card is stolen). Or telemarketers will tell people they've won a prize and a three-year credit protection plan. Once your parent hands over his or her credit card number to be "protected," the telemarketer accesses the account and enjoys a spending spree.

• **Home Repair.** A very common tactic is for a home repair person to approach your parents and tell them that while they were working on someone else's home in the neighborhood they noticed a leaky roof or some other construction problem. Since they have some extra material from their other job, they'll do your parent's at a discount. Sometimes they'll ask for the money up front and never return, or they'll perform poor-quality work and overcharge; once they're in the door they'll sometimes keep "discovering" new things that must be fixed.

Unfortunately, the list of scams numbers in the hundreds, from door-to-door sales, sweepstakes, gifting clubs, travel/vacation offers, and credit repair to loans that are too good to be true.

For an excellent overview of most scams check out the Federal Trade Commission's Web site at www.ftc.gov. You'll find a comprehensive listing of scams, how they operate and how to spot them. Just scrolling through the list gives you an appreciation of what your parent is up against.

Another smart resource is AARP's Web site at www.aarp.org. Click on "Scams" at the home page for nine warning signs, six tip-offs to family members that your parent is being scammed and hyperlinks to five excellent sites on consumer protection related to seniors. You can also call AARP for free publications on the topic at (800) 441-2555. And if you want to check out a business before your parent commits to their service, call the Better Business Bureau at (703) 276-0100 or visit their Web site for a national search at www.bbb.org.

Q: **Is being an executor of my parent's will an honor or just a huge headache?**

A: For many people, being named an executor of an estate is a sign of trust. However, many people will also tell you that being an executor can be hard work and some would say it's more of a headache than an honor.

When your parent dies, you'll need to take his or her will to your local county government office that handles probate. Some counties call these offices probate court, registrar of wills or surrogate's office. You'll need to bring an official copy of the death certificate and your personal identification when you present the will. The court will look over the papers and confirm that they are valid and you, indeed, are the executor. All of the stakeholders of the will—creditors, heirs and beneficiaries—will be given notice that probate has begun. The next step is an inventory and appraisal of the estate. Everyone who is due money must be paid and, as you might guess, creditors and the IRS get first dibs. An accounting of the estate's remains is completed and then the heirs receive their inheritance.

Here's a list of some of the things that an executor does:

- Inventories all of the assets
- Identifies and lists all of the debt
- Arranges to have all assets and debts appraised
- Notifies creditors that they need to file their claims for payment and pays all creditors
- Files claims with insurance companies
- Opens a checking account from which to pay bills and deposit assets
- Closes old bank accounts
- Pays taxes to the state and federal government, and files a final income tax return
- Decides whether or not assets must be sold to satisfy debts
- Distributes the assets as directed by the will

Depending upon how large or complicated your parent's will is, this process can literally take years; most families report that it takes a full year to execute the will. In many states the executor is given some financial compensation out of the estate; this amount is set by law. Some executors hire people to complete many of these tasks, especially if they have a busy career and live out of town.

There's an excellent book on what to do when you're an executor titled *The Inheritor's Handbook* by Dan Rottenberg. A terrific Web site that will also be of assistance to you is www.nolo.com. Just click on "Wills and Estate Planning" and you'll find great resources and answers to frequently asked questions.

Q: **How do I talk with my parents about their will?**

A: Let's start with why people write a will or create a trust in the first place:

- They want to plan ahead for the costs of incapacity—for example, nursing home care—and let others know their wishes.
- They want to pass their assets on to family members rather than let the government take them.
- They want to keep peace in the family by identifying who gets what.

Keeping these in mind should help bring some focus to your conversation. You could begin the discussion with something such as "Dad, I really want to carry out your wishes, but I need to better understand what they are. Do you want to pass down property to the family? Would you like to use money from your assets to help take care of you and Mom if either of you need care? Have you thought of ways to avoid paying high taxes and staying out of court?" This gives you the opportunity to identify what they have or have not done to meet their needs.

Let your parent know that you fully understand that this is their money and that advance planning means they stay in control. If you sense they need to better understand how to protect their assets, recommend they see a professional to guide them through the options that are best for them.

You may also want to broach the subject by sharing strategies you've used to write your own will (whoops, *you do have one, don't you?*). Or you might simply relate some information that you've learned, as in "Mom, guess what I discovered the other day. If I set up a trust, I can . . ." Sharing information during the course of everyday life makes the topic less threatening.

However you approach the topic, remember that an inheritance is a gift, not a right.

For an excellent Web site on general legal issues and frequently asked questions about wills, go to www.nolo.com or give them a call at (800) 992-6656 and ask about their publications.

Q: How do I use the Family Medical Leave Act to take care of my mom?

A: Just as soon as the days of carpooling, PTA meetings and life on the run with the kids are winding down, here comes Mom: runs to the pharmacy, doctor's appointments for every body part and then surgery that's going to require rehab and tender loving care to get her back on her feet.

Up until now you've been piecing it together but, eventually, something slips up: Mom misses a crucial doctor's appointment, you're late on making a deadline at work, time spent on the phone with Mom and all of her specialists becomes noticeable to your coworkers.

Pretty soon you're showing up late for work and your reputation as a top-rate employee starts to take a beating. It's time to take a deep breath, look at your options and go to your boss.

So what are your options? Well, the law's on your side, for starters. You can take advantage of the Family Medical Leave Act, since the law applies to taking care of your parents as well as you, your spouse and your kids. The law states that employers with fifty or more employees must allow them at least twelve weeks of unpaid leave for a family member who is seriously ill (we're not talking a cold).

Grandparents don't count, nor do your in-laws. To qualify, you must have worked for the company a minimum of twenty-four hours a week for at least one year. Your company must continue providing your full health benefits during your leave and you're entitled to get your old job back, or another position with equivalent duties, along with your same salary and benefits. You do not have to take the full twelve weeks off at once. You can break it up during the year. Remember that this is not paid leave, which is the prime reason people don't ask for it, even though they need it.

Many companies provide more than the law requires. Family-friendly companies will even offer geriatric care manager services to help you organize and identify the services your parent needs; others help subsidize adult day services or arrange for care during the day so you can work. Providing you with flex-time or job sharing are other options that a helpful employer may offer.

The lesson? Don't assume your employer will fail to respond or understand. With baby boomers dominating the workforce and finding themselves sandwiched between caring for kids and parents, look for more progressive elder-care benefits to be offered.

Before you go to your employer, however, do the research: find out what vacation and sick leave are owed you, make a list of your parent's caregiving needs and have a frank discussion with the doctor to get a sense of how much time is needed for your mom or dad to recover. Realistically assess what your siblings can do and then determine how much time you'll need to take off.

Your next step is to go through the requirements of FMLA. Go to the U.S. Department of Labor's Web site at www.dol.gov. Click on "Laws and Regulations" and enter FMLA in the search box. They provide all the information you need and a list of Frequently Asked Questions. You can also ask your employer for a copy of the FMLA fact sheet that your employer must display.

Another helpful Web site is offered by AARP; just go to its home page at www.aarp.org and search for "balancing caregiving and work" for excellent tips and resources on juggling your job with caring for your parent.

Whatever you do, don't keep your caregiving demands a secret. Coworkers and employers can be very sympathetic if they know what's going on in your life. Think of all the understanding we shower on parents of a newborn, knowing they haven't had a good night's sleep in weeks and understanding their need to check in with the babysitter every chance they get. Parents with newborns don't keep their caregiver role a secret. Nor should you.

Q: What's the difference between living wills and durable health care powers of attorney?

A: Both living wills and durable health care powers of attorney come under the general heading of "advance directives," as they provide guidance on what people want in advance of a particular situation. Living wills focus on end-of-life decisions enabling your dad to state his wishes about medical care in the event that he develops a terminal condition or enters a state of permanent unconsciousness and can no longer make his own medical decisions.

The living will takes effect when a doctor determines that death is fairly certain or that the person is in a persistent state of unconsciousness. The living will directs a physician to withhold or withdraw life-sustaining treatment that serves only to prolong the process of dying. However, the directive also states that measures should be taken to provide comfort and relieve pain. Most living will documents state whether the individual does or does not want any of the following forms of treatment:

- Cardiac resuscitation
- Mechanical respiration
- Tube feeding or any other artificial or invasive form of nutrition (food) or hydration (water)
- Blood or blood products
- Any form of surgery or invasive diagnostic tests

• Kidney dialysis

• Antibiotics

The living will declaration becomes effective when the doctor receives a copy of it and determines that the patient is incompetent and in a terminal condition or a state of permanent unconsciousness. In most states the document must be signed in front of two witnesses who are eighteen or older.

The living will does not have to be notarized or executed by a lawyer. Be sure to give copies of it to physicians and the hospital. Your dad can also name a surrogate in the living will who is authorized to make end-of-life decisions on his behalf. You can download a free copy of a living will that is accepted in your particular state by going to Choices In Dying's Web site at www.choices. org, or call them at (800) 989-9455. Aging with Dignity offers an excellent "Five Wishes" living will that is very complete and helpful. You can order a copy ($5.00) at www.agingwithdignity.org or call them at (800) 681-2010. Many hospitals also offer copies of living wills at admission.

In some states, a living will is not effective in the event of a medical emergency involving ambulance personnel; paramedics are *required* to perform CPR unless they are given separate orders that state otherwise. These orders are commonly referred to as "nonhospital do-not-resuscitate orders" and are designed for people who are in such poor health that there is little benefit from CPR. These orders should be sought directly from a physician.

Durable health care power of attorney is broader than a living will. It empowers an "agent" appointed by the individual signing the document to make health care decisions on his behalf should he become incompetent. This agent can make decisions on admissions to and discharges from health care facilities, what to do with medical records, whether to make organ donations, whether or not to move the patient, arrangements for home health care, and accepting or refusing treatment that affects the physical and mental health of the patient. These medical decisions come into play at all levels of health care—not just when death is imminent.

You don't have to be a lawyer to be designated as having durable health care power of attorney on behalf of your parent. The word "attorney" simply means "designated agent." The power of attorney does not kick in until your parent is legally incompetent. For example, he may not be able to communicate following a stroke or may be too confused following surgery to make decisions. However, as soon as he has recovered and is competent, he resumes his power to make his own health care decisions. Your parent must sign the durable health care power of attorney when he or she is competent and in front of a witness.

Every adult should have both a living will and durable health care power of attorney. It's far better to thoughtfully and openly consider these issues while you're well rather than in the midst of a crisis.

Q: **Does having a general power of attorney status allow me access to my parents' medical records?**

A: Before we begin this answer, be sure to read page 205 on the Health Insurance Portability and Accountability Act (HIPAA). The Act specifies federal standards that provide patients with access to their medical records and more control over how their personal health information is used and disclosed.

This law requires any individual requesting access to copies of medical records of a family member to have written permission. If the hospital or other medical provider does not have your parent's permission in writing, they cannot give you copies of medical records or orally communicate to you any health information regarding your parent. In an emergency, if you are not at the hospital with your parent, this can pose a real difficulty. That is why writing a letter granting a loved one access to your medical records and medical information *now*, before it's needed, is a very smart precaution.

According to the Office of Civil Rights, which oversees HIPAA regulations, power of attorney given to a person for purposes other than health care (such as real estate or financial matters) does *not* allow them access to medical records.

So the answer to your question is no.

On the other hand, if you have "health care power of attorney" you do have the right to gain access to the medical records of the individual you represent. However, according to HIPAA regulations, when a physician "or other covered entity reasonably believes that an individual has been or may be subjected to domestic violence, abuse or neglect by the personal representative, or treating a person as an individual's personal representative could endanger the individual," the health care provider may choose *not* to treat that person as an authorized representative or grant access to medical records if in their judgment doing so would not be in the best interest of the individual.

Thus, if you have durable health care power of attorney, *yes*, you can gain access to your parents' medical records.

Durable health care power of attorney empowers you to make health care decisions on behalf of the individual you represent any time that individual becomes *incompetent*, for example, is unconscious, in surgery, or too ill to understand what's going on. You can make decisions on admissions to and discharges from health care facilities, medical records, organ donations, whether or not to move the patient, home health care arrangements and what kinds of treatment to accept or refuse. This only lasts during your parent's incapacity. Once they are well, they are back making their own health care decisions.

If you have other questions about HIPAA, go to the Office of Civil Rights Web site at www.hhs.gov/ocr/hipaa.

Q: What is "HIPAA" all about?

A: The Health Insurance Portability and Accountability Act (HIPAA) created the first national standards to protect an individual's medical records and other personal health information. Congress passed this law in response to numerous abuses of personal health information being given (without a patient's permission) to mortgage lenders, credit card companies and employers who, in turn, used this information against the interests of the patient. With medical records moving across hospitals, doctors' offices, insurers, third-party payors and state lines, advocates cried out for national standards to protect health care consumers.

All patients must now receive notification from their doctor and health care provider as to how their office will implement the HIPAA Privacy Rule in their practice. For example, just the other day, my dad received a letter from the Department of Veterans Affairs explaining their Privacy Practices. As a result of the Privacy Rules, consumers have the right to:

- Review their health information
- Obtain a copy of their health information
- Request that their health information be amended or corrected
- Request that their health information *not* be disclosed
- Request that their health information be given in an alternative way (e.g., fax) or at an alternative location in a confidential manner

The Privacy Rule does allow health care providers to impose a reasonable fee to cover copying and postage. If you have a durable health care power of attorney for your parent (or anyone else), you are authorized to receive health information; a general power of attorney will not allow ready access to another's health information.

I recommend that anyone who regularly needs access to their parent's health care information should ask their parent to write a letter authorizing them to receive it. If you're being told that you or another doctor cannot receive your parent's records because of HIPAA, keep prodding. According to the American Medical Association, "Doctors can share protected health information when it is in their patients' best interest."

A word on faxes: It is not against the federal ruling to fax medical records to you; however, the doctor's office must make sure that the fax number is valid and will go to a secure place to reach the authorized recipient. Many doctors' offices will not fax records to patients due to lack of support staff to handle the requirements and the volume of requests.

If you'd like to learn more about HIPAA rules and how they may affect you and your parents, go to the Office of Civil Rights Web site at www.hhs.gov/ocr/hipaa and click on "Frequently Asked Questions (FAQ)."

Q: My dad was just fired. How does he file age discrimination charges?

A: The U.S. Equal Employment Opportunity Commission (EEOC) reports an estimated 84,000 filings a year, of which nearly 20,000 are related to age—and this percentage is on the increase.

The law that applies to your father's situation is the Age Discrimination in Employment Act of 1967 (ADEA), the bedrock to all age discrimination cases. It protects anyone who is forty or older from employment discrimination based upon their age. These protections apply to both employees and job applicants. According to ADEA, it is "unlawful to discriminate against a person because of his/her age with respect to any term, condition, or privilege of employment—including, but not limited to, hiring, firing, promotion, layoff, compensation, benefits, job assignments, and training."

The ADEA applies to employers with twenty or more employees nationwide, including federal, state and local governments, school districts, employment agencies and labor organizations. Another law, the Older Workers Benefit Protection Act of 1990 (OWBPA) amended the ADEA to prohibit employers from denying benefits to older employees. They can, however, reduce the benefits based on age only if the cost of extending the reduced benefits to older workers is the same as the cost of providing benefits to younger workers.

So how does your dad know whether or not he has been "let go" because of his age? Paul Dellasega, an expert attorney representing victims of age discrimination, tells me that there are a number of clues that indicate age discrimination:

1. The employer has recently asked, "When are you planning on retiring?" or has shown an added interest in your retirement plans.
2. The employer replaced you with a younger person who has less experience, fewer skills and/or less education.
3. The employer has recently given you a poor performance evaluation without any basis or, after years of good performance evaluations, all of a sudden finds fault in your work and cites this as a reason to demote or fire you.

Another telltale sign is not sending an older employee to training courses to develop new or updated skills, and then using their "outdated skills" against them as a reason to fire them.

Dellasega has found that employers sometimes believe they will save money hiring younger workers because they'll have fewer health care and Worker Compensation claims, fewer vacation days to cover and lower pension payouts. On the flip side, he has heard employers who hire older workers say that older workers actually cost their companies *less* because they are more reliable, loyal, and punctual, and have higher attendance rates.

So how can your dad file a claim if he thinks he has been unjustly fired because of his age?

He must first file a charge of age discrimination with your state's Human Relations Commission (HRC). You cannot go to court with a private lawyer until *after* you have filed with them. If your dad worked with a company that has more than twenty employees nationwide, then he can file a complaint with a federal agency, the Equal Employment Opportunity Commission. The HRC covers employers with four or more employees and they will file your father's complaint with the EEOC if it is covered by the federal agency. Your dad will need to file his complaint with the HRC's regional office for the region where he works, not where he resides.

You must file your complaint within 180 days of the "alleged act of harm"—in other words, when your dad was fired. The HRC will help him prepare his complaint and he is not required to have a lawyer represent him. Be aware that the commission investigator must be neutral during the investigation. So don't think that the commission's investigator is acting as your dad's legal representative. Employers receive notice of the complaint within thirty days and they must respond thirty days later; however, they can be granted another thirty-day extension. Your dad must be granted a copy of the employer's response to his complaint.

Your dad can file in his local court of common pleas if the HRC dismisses his complaint within one year of the date of filing the complaint or if the complaint is still open after one year.

For more information on filing age discrimination complaints check out the Equal Employment Opportunity Commission's Web site at www.eeoc.gov or give them a call at (800) 669-4000. To find a lawyer specializing in this field go to the National Employment Lawyers Association at www.nela.org or make a written request for your state's listing of lawyers by sending a self-addressed, stamped envelope to NELA, 44 Montgomery Street, Suite 2080, San Francisco, CA 94104.

Q: **What paperwork should I have prepared in the event of a health crisis?**

A: Regrettably, most of us wait until a crisis before we start thinking about caregiving issues facing our parents. Even though the odds are high that some health crisis, like a broken hip, stroke, or heart attack, looms in our parent's future, all too often we adopt the "if it happens, I'll deal with it" philosophy. All the while we're crossing our fingers that "it" never happens.

But making high-stake decisions while your emotions are on overdrive can almost always guarantee poor, uninformed choices.

There are a number of proactive steps that I encourage all families to take to make sure your loved one gets the best possible health care when a crisis hits. It's also a way for your parents to prevent conflicts among you and your siblings since no one will have to "guess" at what Mom or Dad wants when they're in no position to act for themselves.

Here is what every parent should do:

1. Fill out a living will (also known as an advance directive) so that everyone will know what you want regarding end-of-life decisions. Your local hospital can provide you with a copy to fill out, or call Aging with Dignity for their easy-to-understand "Five Wishes" living will at (800) 562-1931.

2. Fill out a durable health care power of attorney. This is broader than a living will. It empowers someone you trust to make health care decisions on your behalf any time you become incompetent. For instance, they can make decisions on admissions and discharges to and from health care facilities, decide on your medical treatment, arrange for home health care—essentially make all of the health care decisions that you would normally make with your doctor. Once you are able to resume deciding for yourself, your "agent" is no longer in power.

3. Make a list of all of your physicians and identify the hospital of your choice in the event of an emergency. Share this list with your family members.

4. Play out "IF" scenarios with your loved ones: IF you should have a stroke or break your hip, what rehab or nursing home facility would you like to go to for your recuperation? IF you're sick and need home health care, what agency should be called? IF it's not safe for you to live alone, what assisted living facility would you like to live in? IF you can't get around and do for yourself but can still remain at home, what kind of services would you like to help you?

5. To help you play out your IF scenarios, go visit assisted living, rehab and nursing home facilities while you are well, and then decide which ones you'd like if you ever need them. Interview home health agencies, and find out what services are available from your local Area Agency on Aging ([800] 677-1116 or [866] 286-3636), from your local church or synagogue, and senior-care agencies. Make a list of your top choices with contact information for each.

6. Create a "Rainy Day Folder" for all of your directives and the results of your research

from steps 4 and 5. Be sure to make a duplicate folder and give it to the family member to whom you've assigned your durable health care power of attorney.

Bottom line? Plan for the unexpected and share your plans with family members *now*. Unplanned decisions are uninformed decisions, and in the heat of a crisis, they are rarely in *anyone's* best interest.

Q: How can I prevent my parents from becoming victims of identity theft?

A: Identity theft among the elderly is skyrocketing: according to the Federal Trade Commission (FTC), in just one year the number of identity thefts among those over the age of sixty rose by 218 percent. Older consumers make great targets because they are likely to have higher credit lines, greater home equity and better financial resources than the rest of the population. Besides shredding unsolicited credit applications, outdated checks, statements and inessential financial information, the FTC and the American Bankers Association offer the following steps that your parents can take to protect their credit identity:

1. Never give out identifying numbers or financial information on the phone unless you prompted the call and know the person or organization being called.
2. Know the due dates of your bills and statements. If a regular bill or statement fails to reach you within a week of the usual time, contact the company to find out why. Thieves often reroute mail to themselves to avoid alerting victims.
3. Stop receiving most prescreened credit card offers by calling (888) OPTOUT ([888] 567-8688).
4. Call the National Do Not Call List at (888) 382-1212 or visit their Web site at www.donotcall.gov and sign up to stop receiving most telephone solicitations.
5. Do not carry your Social Security card in your wallet, put the number on your driver's license or use it for personal identification numbers.
6. It's wise to review a copy of your credit record once a year to see who has been asking about your credit, which can give you an early warning of potential trouble. There are three major companies that provide credit reports: Equifax, (800) 685-1111; Experian, (888) 397-3742; Trans Union, (800) 916-8800. You can also visit their Web sites to receive a copy online for a minimal fee.
7. Do not leave financial information lying out in the open that would tempt hired help or even financially strapped or unscrupulous family members to access your accounts.

And what if your parents are victims? They should act immediately! The Federal Trade Commission's Web site (www.ftc.gov) offers an excellent booklet, "ID Theft: When Bad Things Happen to Your Good Name." Go to the Consumer Protection section of the Web site and then click on "Identity Theft." You can also call them to receive this information or to report a theft at (877) 438-4338.

The FTC recommends three immediate steps. First, contact the fraud departments of the three major credit bureaus cited above. Get them to flag your file with a "fraud alert," requiring creditors to get your permission before opening any new accounts in your name. When fraud is suspected, the bureaus must give you free copies of your credit report.

Secondly, the FTC suggests that you contact all creditors with fraudulent accounts or charges in your name. Ask for someone in the security or fraud division and tell them what you know. Follow up with a letter and be sure to list all charges that you did *not* make.

And third, file a report with the police in your community and/or where the identity theft took place. Keep copies as proof to creditors that you are doing what you can to catch the thief. Under the voluntary "Police Report Initiative," credit bureaus will automatically block the fraudulent accounts and bad debts from appearing on your credit report, but only if you can give them a copy of the police report.

Sometimes, older people don't like going to the police if they suspect that a family member or someone they know might be involved. However, it's a step they really need to take or they could find themselves losing everything.

Q: I think my friend's mother is a victim of domestic violence. Do I report it as elder abuse—and how?

A: Mistakenly, too many people think that "elder abuse" is not connected to domestic violence and that it's something that just happens in nursing homes. But as you are finding with your friend's parents, elder abuse can be a family, domestic matter.

All too often, older women are ashamed and embarrassed to seek help. They frequently live on fixed incomes and feel that they have no option but to stay in an abusive relationship or setting. The numbers are very unsettling. One in three women is a victim of domestic abuse, and nationally 4,000 women on average die every year from domestic violence. Among those victimized by elder abuse, women in their mid-seventies are the most frequent victims, and most of them are injured by a male family member.

According to research on elder abuse, bruises or grip marks around the arms or neck, bruise marks that look old, rope marks or welts on the wrists and/or ankles (caused by tying people to wheelchairs and beds), repeated unexplained injuries, a dismissive or evasive explanation about injuries, and refusal to go to the emergency room for repeated injuries and black eyes are all signs of abuse. If your friend's mother also acts uncommunicative, fearful or suspicious of your interest in her, shows lack of interest in social interaction, and/or becomes isolated by her caretakers, then she might also be experiencing emotional or psychological abuse.

Family situations that contribute to elder abuse include: discord in the family accelerated by illness and care needs, caregiver stress, marital stress and a history or pattern of violent interactions within the family. Sometimes, a woman who may have been abused for years may turn her pent-up rage on her frail and sick husband, or an adult child who has been badly treated by his or her parents now begins to neglect and abuse his parents when the tables are turned.

So what do you do about your concerns and possible suspicions? Inform your friend that you visited her mom and report what you saw. She may have a medical explanation for it. But if there isn't an explanation, then continue to pursue it. If you feel comfortable and the opportunity presents itself, ask her mom what happened and use your judgment as to her response and explanation. Let her know that if she would like to talk to you, you are there to listen and assist her. Professionals advise that you should not confront the alleged abuser, as you may place the victim in a more vulnerable position. If your suspicions are confirmed or you see more symptoms as I've described, then encourage your friend to seek professional help right away. Here's what both or either of you can do:

- Call the Domestic Violence Center hotline at (800) 654-1211 and a crisis advocate will help you assess and respond to the immediate situation. Once the immediate situation is stabilized, they offer counseling for the victim and create a safety plan with her and family members. She could also receive emergency shelter, if she needs to be removed immediately.

- Call the Area Agency on Aging Protective Services program. They guarantee confidentiality and are professionally trained to determine whether or not abuse is taking place. The social workers can also assess the entire situation and help create a less stressful caregiving environment, if that is contributing to the problem. You can find the Area Agency on Aging closest to you by calling (800) 677-1116.

No matter what, don't ignore what you saw. As one crisis advocate told me, "If you, a doctor or family member sees bruises on a woman of *any* age, please ask questions. Let them know you're there for them and so are a lot of resources. You just need to ask."

3

Money Matters & Insurance

A: Long-term-care policies usually offer one or all of the following kinds of care:

• **Nursing Home Care.** This means skilled nursing care at a long-term-care facility. Some nursing homes also provide custodial care and assisted living, which would not be covered under the skilled nursing care provision of the policy. So don't assume that if the care is provided by a nursing home, the care is automatically covered. Be sure to ask for clarification. Nursing homes are licensed by the state and, if the facility accepts Medicare-certified patients, they are also monitored by the federal government. Nursing home care is the major reason most people buy long-term-care policies. It's no wonder. The average annual cost ranges from $50,000 to $75,000 a year.

• **Home Health Care.** These are services provided at home and include occupational, physical, respiratory, and speech therapy; nursing care; social work; and home health aide and homemaker services. This benefit is very helpful as it gives your parent an alternative to nursing home care.

• **Respite Care.** This is temporary care to relieve a caregiver who provides full-time care to the insured person. For many companies, this is an add-on to a regular policy.

Most companies divide care into three levels: skilled care that requires doctor's orders and is provided by physicians, nurses and registered therapists; intermediate care that requires trained personnel who are under the supervision of a doctor or nurse; and custodial care that requires nonmedical personnel to help with the tasks of adult daily living.

If your parent lives alone and does not have family members close by, you might want to consider the benefit of custodial care. She could be recovering from a bad flu and not need a registered nurse, but could use someone to cook her meals, shop, get her prescriptions filled, give her a bath, monitor her health and alert a family member that she needs to get to the doctor.

Custodial care, in many cases, can prevent your mom or dad from going down a slippery slope that could have been prevented. Make sure the agent clearly spells out what the company defines for each level of care and have them tell you who decides if that level of care is needed.

Most companies require that your parent cannot perform at least two activities of daily living (ADL) tasks before coverage kicks in (eating, bathing, using the toilet, walking and dressing). They frequently send out a company nurse to assess your parent's condition. Ask the insurance agent about any restrictions surrounding hiring help (e.g., whether you can hire a relative who is a nurse's aide). And what is the appeal process if you disagree with the level of care decision the company made?

Be sure to get "compound-inflation rider coverage," which means that the daily benefit would increase over time. Say, for instance, that your mother buys a policy today that pays out $110 per day because that's the average cost of a nursing home in her area. In twenty years, if you calculate a modest 5 percent inflation rate, that nursing home cost would rise to $292—over twice the amount she'd receive. With the rider, her premium will cost more, but inflation protection is an important feature.

Also be sure the policy is a tax-qualified one. Federal law now allows individuals to deduct a portion of the premium. Check to see if your state has a thirty-day "free look" provision for a long-term-care policy so you can cancel it within thirty days of enrolling if you change your mind.

One other thing I'd recommend is to choose a policy that allows your parent to redirect his or her benefits from home care to nursing home care and vice versa. For example, if your dad exhausts his nursing home benefit but has untapped home health care benefits, the company should add the home health care amount to his nursing home care.

"A Shopper's Guide to Long-Term Care Insurance" offered by the National Association of Insurance Commissioners (NAIC) includes a nifty worksheet to help you compare policies. Give them a call at (816) 783-8300 and ask them to send a copy of LTC-LP, or e-mail them at pubdist@naic.org. Long-Term-Care Quote is a national resource center and independent agency specializing in long-term-care insurance that offers easy-to-understand, free, comparative quotes to consumers. Check out their Web site at www.longtermcarequote.com or call them at (800) 587-3279.

Q: **I think my mom is getting into serious credit card debt. What do I do?**

A: Your mom certainly isn't alone. Most people are shocked to find out that the fastest growing group filing personal bankruptcy in the country is the elderly. They're the generation known for their thrift but faced with a slow economy, a fixed income, medical bills and the skyrocketing cost of prescription drugs, older people find plastic their easiest way out. Since many older people own their homes and have had a lifelong pattern of living within their means, credit card lenders jump at the chance to give them unsolicited cards.

A recent Harvard study on consumer bankruptcy reported that the number one reason older people fall into bankrupting debt is medical bills. Out-of-pocket expenses and expensive maintenance drugs drive them over the edge.

Others find it tough adjusting to life on a fixed income, so they bridge the gap with plastic. After years of working hard, they feel they deserve to play, go on vacations, and spoil the grand-kids with gifts or to continue the provider role and help pay off expenses that their adult children are juggling. The plastic puts them back in charge. It's all too seductive.

So now what? First, let your mom know she isn't alone and she shouldn't be ashamed. Tackle this as a chance for your mom to cut wasteful, high-interest costs and to strike a blow against the credit card companies that have been luring her on. Show her how they've been taking advantage of her. Don't make it personal or about her mistakes.

Here are some tips from debt counselors:

- Review the bills and her spending patterns to identify where she's overdoing it.
- Create a monthly budget.
- Review the credit card statements and total up what she is paying each month in interest and fees. Chances are she'll be shocked and angry.
- Pick out one credit card for her to keep—it is tough functioning in today's world without one—or better yet, get her a check debit card. Talk with her about what she would use it for and suggest she leave it at home otherwise; it's too tempting to have it with you at all times.
- Stay clear of impulse buying (including TV shopping channels).
- Don't pay off the credit card debt with her "nest egg."
- Shop around for the best rate on cards that consolidate paying off other cards. Go to www.bankrate.com to find comparative rates on the best credit cards for paying off loans, cards that give the best rebates and those that are friendly to folks who pay the entire balance off every month.

• Check the statements every month for errors, penalties and fraudulent billing. Many predators count on the fact that seniors often just look at the bottom line and pay the bill.

• Contact the creditors, explain your mother's situation and set up a payment plan. Most will respond to your initiative to pay off the debt.

Debt counselors often advise that the first step out of debt is preparing a realistic budget. Assess how much money comes in from all of your mom's sources of income and then create a list of fixed expenses such as rent or mortgage payments, car payments, and insurance premiums. Then make a list of her monthly expenses, like food, telephone and utility bills, and prescriptions. Finally, create a list of discretionary expenses such as clothing, gift-giving and entertainment.

If your mom is in serious trouble, then going to a debt counselor is the best alternative. For help finding one contact the National Foundation for Consumer Credit, a national network of nonprofit budget and debt counseling agencies. To find a local agency near you call (800) 388-2227 or visit their Web site at www.ngcc.org. Of course, you can also look in the Yellow Pages for debt counselors in private practice along with other organizations that provide the service.

Q: I worry that my dad has a serious gambling problem. What should I do?

A: Gambling addiction among the elderly is growing nationwide, yet it remains hidden under the innocent guise of "fun, travel and recreation." The New Jersey Council on Compulsive Gambling developed the first senior outreach program in the country and reports that well over half of the revenue Atlantic City casinos earn comes from older adults.

There are several reasons older people are vulnerable to the lure of gambling. For many, it is the first time in their life that they have disposable income. Your dad might feel he deserves to have fun and doesn't have to worry about supporting his family anymore, so what's the harm?

Casinos market heavily to their senior patrons. Your dad will be made to feel important, and he'll be wined and dined. The VIP treatment can go a long way to fill the void of loneliness or provide feelings of power and excitement. For others, who have suffered losses of jobs, spouses, sense of purpose or self-esteem, gambling can make them feel like a "winner," literally and psychologically. Many chase the dream that the next win will be the big win, the one that solves all of the problems caused by a constantly shrinking retirement income.

The elderly, however, face the dangerous consequence of gambling away their life savings without the ability to recoup it in the long run. Research studies indicate that about 5 percent to 7 percent of people who gamble become addicted. However, the growing number of casinos, multistate Powerball lotteries, tourist packages to gambling destinations targeted to seniors, off-track betting facilities, slot machines and Internet gambling sites, all have the potential to pull even more elderly into the gambling addiction ranks.

The National Council on Problem Gambling offers ten warning signs of gambling addiction:

1. Have you often gambled longer than you had planned?
2. Have you often gambled until your last dollar was gone?
3. Have thoughts of gambling caused you to lose sleep?
4. Have you used your income or savings to gamble while letting bills go unpaid?
5. Have you made repeated, unsuccessful attempts to stop gambling?
6. Have you broken the law or considered breaking the law to finance your gambling?
7. Have you borrowed money to finance your gambling?
8. Have you felt depressed or suicidal because of your gambling losses?
9. Have you been remorseful after gambling?
10. Have you gambled to get money to meet your financial obligations?

And here are some questions to ask yourself. Is your father spending an excessive amount of money or time on gambling? Has he lost touch with friends or picked up new gambling buddies? Is he always short of money? Does he have unexplained debts or disappearances? Is he unable to pay for prescriptions and utility bills? Is he secretive about his finances? Does his mood depend on whether he won or lost?

For specific information on how to help your dad, call the National Council on Problem Gambling at (800) 522-4700. It offers a twenty-four-hour confidential Helpline to help you assess the situation and connect you with the resources and counselors nearest you. You can also visit its Web site at www.ncpgambling.org, where you can conduct an online search for a certified gambling counselor. You can look for a Gamblers Anonymous chapter near your father by going to their Web site at www.gamblersanonymous.org or by calling (213) 386-8789.

Q: How can my parents get on the Do Not Call Registry?

A: I'm sure your parents, like many older people, are constantly hit up by telemarketers offering them all kinds of "free" prizes, special deals on vacations, a host of insurance products and "once in a lifetime" offers. One way of protecting them from the constant barrage of uninvited callers is the National Do Not Call Registry.

The registry is managed by the Federal Trade Commission and was created to protect consumers from unwanted solicitations. Once you register, telemarketers have up to three months from the date you registered to stop calling you. So do not expect this to take effect immediately. Many states have their own registries, usually operated by their Attorney General's office with the states sharing data with the national registry; so if your parents were registered with the state, chances are they were also placed on the national directory.

To register, simply call (888) 382-1212 and follow the prompts. You must call from the phone number you want on the registry, so you'll need to call from your parents' phone if you want to register them. You can also register online at www.donotcall.gov. It's very simple and has the benefit of allowing you to register up to three phone numbers at a time. If you have an e-mail address, you'll receive confirmation for each phone number via separate e-mails. You need to open each e-mail and click on the link it contains in order to activate the registration. You can also use the Web site to request verification that your number is registered; for example, if you have registered with your state and are not sure whether they sent your name on to the national registry.

Your phone number will remain on the registry for five years from the date you registered. If you move during that period and receive a new phone number you must reregister; if you disconnect and reconnect the same phone number (for example, during an extended vacation), you must reregister. Remember that each time that happens, the telemarketers gain another three months during which they can contact you.

If your parents live in a senior residence they may have trouble registering by phone, because if their phone calls go through a Private Branch Exchange (PBX) the Do Not Call system will not recognize their personal phone number. In that case, you would need to register your parents online and use your e-mail address to activate it.

Whatever way you choose to participate, it is extremely easy and well worth a minute of your time to keep your parents safe from potential scams and telemarketers. Just remember that nonprofit and political organizations along with telephone surveyors are still permitted to call, and so can those, such as credit card companies and banks, with whom you have a business relationship.

Q: How can my parents beat out-of-pocket medical expenses?

A: So many retirees complain that they feel like they are being "nickeled-and-dimed" everywhere they turn. According to a recent study by the Rutgers University Division on Aging, older Americans spend 19 percent of their total income on out-of-pocket medical expenses every year. Half of these dollars are spent on drugs and dental care. Older people who are in poorer health find that they spend nearly one-third of their income on health expenses.

Here are seven ways your parents can begin saving money:

1. **Find Doctors Who Take "Medicare Assignment."** Medicare "assigns" how much it will pay for services for a given condition or procedure. If a doctor takes as payment in full the amount that Medicare "assigns," then that means the doctor takes "assignment." In other words, the doctor won't be sending your parent a bill for the balance between what the doctor charges and what Medicare reimburses. If the doctor doesn't take assignment, then he or she is permitted to charge up to 15 percent more than what Medicare would have paid the doctor. Doctors in Pennsylvania must take assignment according to the law, but if your parent lives in another state, it's worth asking ahead of time whether or not the doctor takes "Medicare assignment."

2. **Secondhand Equipment.** Many senior centers have programs in which previously owned wheelchairs, quad canes, walkers, crutches, and other durable medical equipment can be leased for a small donation. Some even offer used hearing aids and glasses. If they don't offer this service, they frequently know of someone who does. A social worker at your local hospital may also know of organizations that offer secondhand equipment.

3. **Senior Discounts.** It's smart to ask whether or not a business offers a senior discount rather than assume that they don't—those 10 percents can add up. Ask every business that your parent frequents—restaurants, banks, dry cleaners, pet stores—if they offer a senior discount. Many grocery stores are now offering senior-discount days and free delivery to regular customers, which also saves on gas. During peak seasons of cold and hot weather, many utility companies will allow seniors on fixed incomes to pay their bills over longer periods of time.

4. **Free Health Care Screenings and Shots.** Flu shots can literally be a lifesaver for your parents, especially if they have lung problems. Most senior centers, state health centers and a good number of hospitals offer flu shots as a community service to seniors. Prior to flu season, call your local Area Agency on Aging to find out who is offering free flu shots in the area. You can call the Eldercare Locator to track down the agency closest to your parent at (800) 677-1116. Your mom and dad can also receive free screenings and health education programs at health fairs sponsored by local hospitals or local malls. Go to the information desk at the mall to get a copy of their Calendar of Events, and call the local hospital to get theirs. These free screenings, however, shouldn't be seen as a replacement for routine physicals with a physician.

5. Generic Drugs. Generics can cost about half as much as brand-name drugs, and they must be approved by the FDA as being therapeutically equivalent. So have your parents ask their doctor about getting a generic and tell the pharmacist they want it. Your parents can also ask the doctor for samples to make sure that they react well to the medication before buying a thirty-day supply. If samples aren't available, they can ask the pharmacist for a one-week supply.

6. Discount Drug Programs. The drug companies offer discounts for people who cannot afford certain medications. Go to www.benefitscheckup.org to find out what companies and state programs offer discounts. (See page 40 for more on lowering prescription drug costs.)

7. Volunteer Services. Your local Area Agency on Aging, senior center, United Way, church or synagogue will most likely be aware of volunteer programs and community-based services. Before your parents pay for companion services, cab rides, respite care, home-delivered meals, chore services or minor repairs, call one of these organizations.

Q: Should my dad drop his auto insurance while he recovers from a stroke?

A: If your dad does drop the coverage, he will likely trigger a series of actions that will fall under the category of "lapsed coverage." Insurance companies are very wary of drivers who have had a period of lapsed coverage. After all, it's in their best interest to insure drivers who regularly pay their bills and have had continuous coverage and good driving records.

An individual who does not have a record of continuous coverage raises red flags: Could they have had an accident while they were not covered? Could their lapse be due to a poor payment history? Were they dropped by another carrier for risky behavior? Continuous coverage provides insurers with a record they can verify rather than wondering whether or not "uninsured" periods were risk- and arrest-free.

Chances are your father has enjoyed a good history on all counts and he is in the "Preferred Driver" category, which yields him reasonable insurance rates. If he takes a break from paying auto insurance because he isn't driving during his recuperation, he will likely lose his preferred status and land in the "higher risk" category. This holds true even if he goes to a new insurance company, as most will request a Driver's History Record from your state Department of Transportation before they grant new applicants insurance.

The bottom line? The money saved by not paying the premium for several months of coverage is no match for the dramatically higher insurance rates he'll pay when he tries to reinstate his policy. By some estimates, his rate could quadruple when he involuntarily joins the higher risk crowd! If you want to save money, you could look into reducing his liability insurance to the minimum level required by law and removing his collision coverage while he is not driving the car.

Also note that your dad's insurance company is required by law to notify your state department of transportation when an insurance policy is canceled by the insured or the insurer. So, if you stop paying the bill, within sixty days his insurance company will notify the state, which will likely send your father a Letter of Inquiry to determine why the policy was canceled. If you don't respond to the letter, they may suspend his vehicle registration.

A greater concern is *whether he should resume driving.* After medical assessments, you and he should have candid discussions with his doctor, physical therapist and occupational therapist to determine whether or not he has recovered his functional abilities to drive safely. During his therapy he may find it motivational to have a goal in mind like driving; however, at the end of the day he must acknowledge his capabilities and limitations following his stroke. After personally experiencing the rigors of rehabilitation, surely he would not want to place other innocent people at risk for the same by getting behind the wheel when he's no longer a safe driver. Hopefully, things will go well for him and he'll soon be back in the driver's seat, getting his life back on track.

Q: **What is the difference between traditional Medicare and managed care Medicare?**

A: Medicare offers consumers an option as to how they'll receive their Medicare benefits. They can opt for the traditional plan or go with a Medicare + Choice plan, which offers either a managed care plan (e.g., HMO) or private fee-for-service plans.

"Original" Medicare is a traditional fee-for-service plan in which Medicare pays a set fee for covered medical services. Your parent pays a premium (deducted from his Social Security check) for Part A, which covers hospital costs (e.g., a room in a hospital, rehab, or skilled nursing facility) and Part B, which covers medical costs (e.g., doctors' visits, home health and outpatient services). You should also have a Medigap policy to pick up the 20 percent co-pay. You may go to any hospitals and physicians you want, where and when you want, and Medicare pays them directly.

With a Medicare managed care plan, you can save money. You won't need to pay for a Medigap policy; instead, you pay a lower monthly premium to the HMO. You also pay a modest co-pay (usually around $5 to $10) for doctor visits. Original Medicare doesn't cover annual checkups with your doctor or gynecologist, so this savings can really add up. Medicare gives the HMO a fixed amount of money for the year to take care of you. Whatever you don't cost them, they get to keep. Thus, their focus both philosophically and financially is to keep you well, so you'll get plenty of preventive care. The other benefits are: they usually handle all of the paperwork, and are very good about flu shots, mammograms, hearing and vision care. At a minimum they *must* offer everything that the original Medicare plan offers. Generally, people can join a Medicare managed care plan at any time; however, from November 15 through December 31 of each year the law requires that the plans *must* accept new members.

If you have complex needs and have been seeing specialists you really like, you might want to think twice about joining. Make sure your specialists are in the HMO network or that you can live with using the physicians, specialists and hospitals in the HMO network rather than freely finding your own.

Here are some questions your parent should consider when looking at a Medicare managed care plan:

- Are his current specialists and primary care doctor in the network?
- Is his favorite hospital in the network?
- Where does your parent go for emergencies? Is there a procedure he must follow?
- How easy will it be for him to see a specialist? Does he need a referral?
- Can he change doctors if he doesn't like the primary care doctor he is assigned to?
- If he lives a few months of the year at a second home or travels, how is he covered?
- What skilled nursing homes are in the network?
- What will his out-of-pocket expenses be (e.g., for prescriptions, doctor visits, hospital stays or outpatient surgery)?
- What are the monthly premiums and exactly what do they cover?

There's a terrific resource to help you decide whether or not you should switch from original Medicare to Medicare managed care, and it is available on Medicare's Web site at www.medicare.gov. Simply click on the "Medicare Personal Plan Finder" to compare Medicare health plans and develop a profile of your needs to cross-check against the plans. You'll receive comparisons of benefits, monthly premiums, co-payments, quality measures, and patient satisfaction surveys among managed care plans available in your particular region. There is also a guide to what to look for in a plan.

One final word of caution: HMOs can drop out of the Medicare program any time they want, so look for a plan with a solid financial history. On the other hand, you can leave a Medicare managed care plan at any time, for any reason. If you choose to go back to original Medicare, call (800) MEDICARE to reenroll. If you need more information, call your local Area Agency on Aging ([800] 677-1116) and ask to speak to the State Health Insurance Program representative. They'll let you know which senior centers provide volunteer counseling to help you sort through how different plans match up with your parents' particular needs.

Q: Who can help me figure out these confusing Medigap policies?

A: Trying to figure out which is the best Medigap policy for your parents or whether they should opt for a Medicare managed care plan is pretty daunting. Add the decision about buying long-term-care insurance to the mix and you can feel downright overwhelmed.

But thanks to a federal program known as the State Health Insurance Assistance Program (SHIP), every state in the country offers trained counselors to answer questions regarding health insurance in an objective and easy-to-understand manner. The counselors will also provide pamphlets and brochures that explain your parents' benefits and rights under various health insurance programs.

The best way to contact your local SHIP program is to call your local Area Agency on Aging at (800) 677-1116. There are eight essential ways that a SHIP volunteer provides guidance. They can help you:

1. Decide whether Medicare managed care is right for you by explaining the way it works compared to traditional Medicare.
2. Understand your Medicare benefits by explaining what services are covered under Medicare Parts A and B and the Medicare Summary Notice.
3. Select a Medigap insurance policy by explaining the benefits offered under each of the standardized insurance plans and provide a list of companies selling Medigap insurance policies in your state.
4. Obtain assistance to pay for your prescription drugs by telling you about the government and private programs that offer this service, the eligibility requirements and how to apply for them, including drug discount cards.
5. Find government programs that will pay for your Medicare deductibles, co-payments and Part B premiums, and assist you in filling out the paperwork.
6. Understand long-term care by explaining which government programs pay for long-term care and the eligibility requirements, and reviewing private long-term-care insurance and how to select the best policy.

7. Understand what Medicare + Choice means and all of the new options that will be available in the future.

8. Process and resolve disputes by being your parents' advocate if they have a problem with Medicare or their HMO.

All services are free and the information is kept confidential. They can really save you time and prevent a few headaches along the way.

Q: My mom moved in with us on the understanding that my siblings would share in the costs, but now they're not. What should we do?

A: Perhaps everyone's expectations were not "out on the table" and discussed before the big move. There must have been a number of factors that led your family to believe that your mother was no longer able to live alone. So let's go back to the place and time where you all agreed and work our way from there.

First, everyone should make a list of your mother's needs that they believe necessitated her moving in with you. For example, does she need someone to either remind her or give her daily medications? Does someone need to prepare meals? Does she suffer from any form of dementia that causes her to be confused and unable to be left alone for any period of time? Does she have a number of doctor's appointments that she must keep on a regular basis? Can she no longer handle her finances? Does someone have to help her with the tasks of daily living (grooming, getting dressed, bathing, using the toilet, eating)?

Once everyone has identified these needs, go over them and eliminate the duplicates to make a final list. Add two columns headed "Who and How Much Time" and "Costs." Enter who will perform each task and the number of hours per week you think it will take. Then enter an estimate of how much this service would cost. Even if you and your siblings will perform the task, assign a dollar value to it anyway. Most of the tasks you will perform are probably non-medical; as a guideline, most home care agencies charge $12 to $15 an hour for this type of service.

Since you're the one your mother lives with I suspect that many of these tasks will be performed by you. By adding up the amount of work and assigning a price to it, your family will be in a better position to objectively see the costs associated with your mother's care. In addition, your siblings will become much more appreciative of how much you do. However, I strongly encourage you—right from the start—to get your siblings involved in sharing some of these tasks.

Do not fall into the trap of a "solo act," because it will wear down you and your marriage faster than you can imagine.

The next step is to assign a dollar value to your mother's housing; for example, if one of your six rooms is now hers, you might "assign" one-sixth of your housing costs to her. In addition, any costs associated with modifying your home to meet your mother's needs (e.g., building a ramp) would be fair game for your siblings to share.

Since the move is about helping Mom, then you should certainly pay a share of her housing expenses. In other words, if you have three siblings then I'd take all of these costs and divide by four.

You also need to spell out what contributions you expect from your mother toward her housing and care. Will she pay a portion of the mortgage commensurate with her living space in the house? Will she pay for her share of the groceries? Will she pay for medications, health care supplies and her phone, cable and laundry bills? The more businesslike and objective you are in your approach the less chance of emotional conflicts between you and your siblings over what's fair and what's not. This same strategy applies to you and your mother.

If you think that your relationship is too strained to do this family exercise by yourselves, seek an outside facilitator, such as a geriatric care manager (you got it: split the cost by four) or clergyperson. You're obviously a family that cares deeply about what's best for your mother. You'll find your way by going back to what brought you here in the first place.

Q: Is a reverse mortgage a good idea for my mom?

A: A reverse mortgage is essentially a loan against your mom's home that she doesn't have to pay back for as long as she lives in it. Thus she can turn the value of her home into cash, giving her the ability to afford the remodeling she needs or maybe some long-term-care services that are not covered by Medicare. When she moves, sells the home or dies, the money is then paid back.

The loan can be paid to your mother in various ways: she could receive it as one lump sum, as a regular monthly cash advance like a paycheck, as a credit line that she draws against whenever she needs the funds, or a combination of any of these methods. One word of caution: If she receives public benefits such as SSI, make sure that her new income doesn't throw her over the eligibility limits. Check with your local Area Agency on Aging to make sure she'll still be eligible.

Reverse mortgages are available to people who are sixty-two years of age and older and own their home. The major benefit with this type of loan is that your mother doesn't have any monthly payments to make and she won't need a certain income to qualify.

Here are some of the basics of reverse mortgages: There will be financing fees such as closing costs and interest. Your mom will remain the owner of her home; thus she's responsible for property taxes, repairs and insurance just as she always has been. When the loan is finished, your mom or her heirs must pay back all of the cash advances plus interest. The lenders aren't interested in owning and selling her home; they just want their money back.

One of the most important features of a reverse mortgage is the "nonrecourse" limit. This means that the lender does not have any recourse to secure payment for the loan from any other source—your mother's heirs, assets or income. The only legal recourse they have is limited by the value of your mom's home. This is an important protection: your mom will never owe more than what her home is currently worth when the loan is to be repaid.

There are three major kinds of reverse mortgages. Some state and local governments offer *single purpose* loans, for example to pay property taxes or to make home repairs, but there are usually income caps to qualify. Multipurpose loans can either be in the form of federally insured *Home Equity Conversion Mortgages* (HECM) offered by banks and mortgage companies, or more expensive *proprietary* reverse mortgages, offered by private companies. These would enable your mother to use the money to, for example, both repair her home and receive a monthly income.

As with any decision of this magnitude, take the time to research all of your options. AARP has done an outstanding job of pulling the information together in a handbook, "Home Made Money"; you can receive a free copy by calling (800) 424-3410 or go to their Web site at www.aarp.org/revmort/ for the same information along with a host of links.

The National Reverse Mortgage Lenders Association has set best-practice benchmarks for their members, and you can find out who has met these guidelines by either calling them at (866) 264-4466 or visiting their Web site at www.reversemortgage.org. Not until you've done your research will you know whether or not it's the right choice for your mother.

Q: How do I talk to my parents about protecting their assets?

A: As many surveys have proven, most families tend to avoid the subject or wait until a health crisis hits to finally get their affairs in order. But when emotions are running high and you're fighting for your health, you couldn't pick a worse time to think through how to protect your assets and distribute them among family members.

Some parents may hesitate to talk about a will because it's a sign that their roles in the family are changing, or they may interpret the discussion as a signal that they are becoming more dependent. They may simply feel it's rude to talk about their personal finances. But wills are about a lot more than money: They are about values, meaning, relationships, and how family members see each other. It's no wonder so many people avoid the conversation. But *not* having a will can spell a lifetime of heartache for those left behind.

Here are tips to help you get the conversation started and what to discuss once you begin:

1. Start the conversation by telling your parents that you want to know what *they* want. Try something like "Mom and Dad, I really want to carry out *your* wishes, but I need to better understand them. What should I know? How can I help?"
2. Acknowledge that you realize that this is *their* money—not yours.
3. Let them know that advance planning through a will, living will and durable health care power of attorney will keep them in *control*. This is not about you taking over.
4. Stay focused on your parents' concerns, not what you want from them.
5. Approach the issue by sharing what you're doing about *your* will. Perhaps you've learned some strategies from your lawyer to better protect your assets, or you've read an article that you can share with them. They'll get the message that you practice what you preach.
6. Advise them to identify who gets what heirlooms through a "Letter of Instruction" to keep peace in the family. Many an estate lawyer will tell you that the bitterest family feuds are over seemingly insignificant items like a small piece of furniture, a set of dishes, or an inexpensive piece of jewelry. It is usually something family members feel attached to because it brings back fond memories of their loved one. If your parents have thoughtfully identified something that they want each family member to have to remember them by, it will help their children remain friends rather than arguing over who gets the ceramic frog collection.
7. Emphasize that they should use their assets to enjoy a good quality of life and to care for each other should either of them become sick. It is sad to see older people not spend their money to make the quality of their life better or for needed health care because they want to leave it all to their children.
8. If they are uncomfortable talking about this with you, share some names of elder law attorneys.

And finally, remember to keep in mind through all of your discussions with them on this topic that an inheritance is a *gift,* not a right.

INDEX